RACE TRAITOR:

The True Story of Canadian Intelligence's Greatest
Cover-Up

ELISA HATEGAN

INCOGNITO PRESS

www.incognitopress.com

For Martin Thériault
For Ruth M. and Annette H.
For Rodney Bobiwash
For Brian McInnis
For those who were harmed

For those who believed in me,
Whom I love deeply,
And for those who were there
And changed the course of things.

"We'll tear her to shreds."

CSIS Toronto Region Investigator speaking of eighteen-year old Elisse Hategan, whose affidavits implicated CSIS agent Grant Bristow in criminal activity. *CBC's The Fifth Estate, October 1994*

PREFACE

This story took place in Toronto, Canada between 1991-1994. In the twenty years since these events unfolded, new technologies have revolutionized the planet. But these advances in technology have also paralleled a confiscation of our civil liberties that has been so slow, so insidious, that we've hardly noticed it. In the name of "the war on terror", governments around the world have begun to erode away at our personal freedoms. New laws are being created that infringe further upon our human rights. And newly-reported cases of terrorism are hailed as proof of why this loss of privacy is a necessary evil in the fight for our freedom.

Sometimes the laws do work: we get the bad guys and everyone can breathe easier. But at other times, as shown in the events you will read about here, we lose the sight of who the bad guys really are.

So what really happened?

When I was sixteen years old I was recruited by a Canadian domestic terrorist group calling itself the Heritage Front, an extremist right-wing, white supremacist group with strong ties to Neo-Nazi Holocaust revisionists, the American Ku Klux Klan and even Muammar Khadafi. They became the family I never had. Two years later, after I witnessed the targeting of innocent people for harassment and violence, I realized I had to find a way to shut them down.

At first, I couldn't see a way out. After I found support from a few courageous anti-racist activists, I spied on the Heritage Front for four months. In March of 1994, exactly twenty years ago, I took the stand and testified against a handful of group leaders in a contempt of court case that led to convictions and jail sentences. Within months, it was revealed that one of the three founders of the group was a paid agent of CSIS, Canada's intelligence service. To put it bluntly, the Heritage Front had been created and partially-funded by Canada's own Security and Intelligence Service.

Despite the fact that I possessed a significant amount of information related to criminal activity within the Heritage Front, authorities showed no interest in taking any kind of action against the group. After repeated appeals to the OPP (Ontario Provincial Police) and the RCMP (Royal Canadian Mounted Police) were ignored, I was officially denied admission into the Witness Protection Program.

All my affidavits (detailing names and addresses of Heritage Front members who owned various weaponry and explosives, as well as detailed accounts of verifiable stalking, threats and harassment of community activists) were dismissed by police without as much as a single attempt to verify their authenticity.

I would later find out from an insider (as broadcast in a 1994 episode of CBC's *The Fifth Estate* that featured evidence obtained from anonymous, highly-placed police and intelligence sources) that a CSIS mandate had circulated advising police forces to deny me protection and ignore my information, even at the risk of Canadian taxpayers and the threat to my own life. Over a period of five years, CSIS had sunk a huge amount of money into Operation Governor, which involved the creation of a neo-Nazi organization in Canada and escalating its levels of violence and armament. They couldn't risk their house of cards to fall apart on the testimony of a teenage girl.

When details of CSIS' Operation Governor did come out in the press, after an exposé authored by Toronto Sun reporter Bill Dunphy in August 1994, the operation was terminated. The agent who had co-created the Heritage Front, Grant Bristow, was quickly whisked away into Witness Protection, given a payoff totalling hundreds of thousands of dollars, two new cars and a four-bedroom, three-car garage home in another Canadian province.

No testimony or information from Grant Bristow resulted in ANY arrests and convictions.

All things eventually come to pass. In the last twenty years I went to university, taught English in South Korea, became a writer. But no matter how far I ran from my past, it continued to haunt me. Each time I heard of a new arrest involving terrorist activity, I asked myself whether an agent provocateur was involved.

I unquestioningly believe that there are true cases of terrorism in the world. It would be foolish not to monitor dangerous, fringe extremists who recruit others to their cause. On the other hand, I also think that any of us – of any religion, race or nationality – can be accused of being terrorists by our own governments. It doesn't matter if you're Jewish or Muslim, if you're a woman or a man, a teenager or a senior citizen. With the rise of unprecedented powers given to intelligence agencies around the world, anybody can be detained without arrest or placed under surveillance under the guise of national security. The United States' PATRIOT Act, for example, has enabled the routine use of roving wiretaps and the surveillance of "lone wolves" (individuals who are merely *suspected* of terrorist-related activities, such as visiting a controversial website, but not actually linked to terrorist groups) without a court order.

The definition of what exactly is a terrorist, and what contributes to his/her violent escalation, is often left up to the determination of agencies that, at times, may resort to covert action to provoke criminal activity that justifies their surveillance operation.

Why do intelligence agencies do this? This kind of operation doesn't always start out with ill intentions. Most often, agents are ordinary people who believe they are fighting for a worthy cause, combatting terrorism, and infiltrating dangerous groups (even if, in their minds, this means attending local mosques). But as time goes by, some agents begin to cut corners. Maybe they're on a budget crunch and have to justify an ongoing operation; maybe they're tired of monitoring extremists who aren't actually contravening the law. Slowly, a "nudging" process begins: embedding suggestions of criminal acts, providing money and supplies for someone to make a bomb, planting the confidence needed for so-called terrorists to begin waging a proper attack.

And sometimes, as in the case of Operation Governor, it goes beyond nudging. The blueprint of criminal activity is handed out, as well as a list of targets. Illegal actions are planned, delegated and maintained by a puppet-master who himself is immune to prosecution. This is when the tables shift and the question rises as to who the real terrorist is.

Everything I wrote in this book is the truth to the best of my recollection. As is the case with any memoir, it is impossible for an author to transcribe conversations verbatim. However, I used every method I could access – my memory as well as journal entries I kept from that time, newspaper clippings, affidavits and existing video recordings, where possible – to enable what I feel is an accurate and authentic description of what took place in the 1990s.

Because so much of this book is a matter of public record, it would be pointless to alter most of the names of the individuals who appear herein. But wherever I could, I have changed or omitted the surnames of those who I felt might be harmed from the publishing of this book.

My journey to this point hasn't been easy. Three years ago, I decided to write this memoir and titled it *Race Traitor*. Most Canadian publishers had no interest in the subject. They thought it was a story about white supremacists, when in fact it's a tale of corruption: corruption of innocence, as well as government corruption. An editor at Douglas & McIntyre wrote, "The issue of white supremacy has had its day, and it would take something more current for a book on this to break out." Random House's non-fiction editor was even more dismissive, condescendingly pointing to the fact that as a working class, former high-school drop-out, I wasn't a good fit with their more illustrious roster of authors. "Elisa writes well, given her background, but not to my mind at a level that would allow the book's appeal to transcend what I'm concerned would be a limited audience."

Eventually Penguin Canada became interested in acquiring the manuscript, but after several meetings with the acquisitions editor, the reality of publishing this story sank in. With each day, I grew more scared of the potential exposure I would gain as a result of the book. Moreover, I was concerned that the most potentially-explosive parts of my memoir (involving rape and physical assault) were never going to see the light of day. With so many former victims of the Heritage Front having moved on with their lives, tracking every single person down to verify the most serious attacks (provided they were open to discussing their experience) would be nearly impossible. At the same time, the publisher was urging me to boost my 'platform' by engaging in public speaking tours where I would be forced to relive events I am still too traumatized to talk about.

So I walked away from a deal with Penguin. Yes, an unpublished writer walked away from a potential deal with one of the biggest book publishers on the planet. And to this day, I know in my heart it was the best thing I could have done. It just wasn't worth it: emotionally, financially, spiritually. In the end, I did what I felt was safe, and right, for my family.

In August 2011 I proceeded to write a novel that fictionalized many of my experiences. I wanted to create a fictional, modern-day scenario that would explore the question of *What if?* How far would a group like the Heritage Front, if it operated today, go in achieving its aims?

I named my new novel *Race Traitor* as well, and hoped that it would become a big hit. Of course, it didn't. Without a publisher, a marketing budget, media connections or a celebrity endorsement behind me, the odds against its success were astronomical and the novel rapidly sank into oblivion.

The years passed. I worked on other books. But no matter what I did, I couldn't ignore the obvious. People who read the novel saw the parallels to my story and demanded to know what really happened. I received several emails from readers who shared their own memories of that time and urged me to look to the riots in Europe and North Africa as an example for why a story like this is both timeless and relevant. The rise of nationalism and neo-fascism all over Europe, as well as the alarming increase in secretive measures carried out by police and international intelligence agencies against civilians, make this subject ripe for exploration.

"Just write it," they told me. "Just put it out there, and the audience will come."

A lingering voice at the back of my mind knew they were right – that no matter what my own fears were, I couldn't fail to leave a testament that challenges the official version of what happened. This certainty grew stronger after the Canadian government, as a "cost-cutting measure" undertaken in 2012, proceeded to cut the budget to CSIS's overseer, the Office of the Inspector General, effectively eliminating our country's most important watchdog agency from supervising the day-to-day actions of CSIS. The only ones left to oversee complaints would be SIRC, the Security and Intelligence Review Committee – the same group responsible for the methodical cover-up of the illegal activities of Operation Governor back in the 1990s.

But I was still scared.

And then a day came when I simply didn't give a shit anymore. I was a loser, an utter failure. I couldn't sell any books, I couldn't get a publisher, I couldn't get people to care that their own government had had a hand in creating a terrorist organization.

So I thought that I should just kill myself. I've battled depression since my late teens and have already made several attempts on my life. Even as I write this now, I don't see any hope that anything I do, or say, or write, will matter to anybody.

But a funny thing happens when you say to yourself, *Fuck it, I'm done. I don't give a damn anymore.* You begin to realize that, in the greater scheme of things, hardly anything at all matters. The latest fashion sported by a celebrity on a runway, the newest hockey cup winner, the cute baby video shared on Facebook, the spiteful comments made by anonymous bullies on the internet, the insipid memes we get about positive thinking....it's all meaningless. All of it.

Between the moment when we suck in our first breath and the day we exhale for the last time, only a few things really matter: Telling the truth. Standing up for something you believe in. Not allowing fear to stop you from achieving your potential. Contributing to the betterment of others so that the world becomes a better place. And most of all, allowing yourself the vulnerability to love.

I am only one person. But the things I saw as a teenager have shaped the individual I am today as surely as they shaped my view of the world. I believe in the power of truth as an instrument that can transform and inspire. Even though history has taught us, time and again, that truth is often swept aside in favour of an official story, I choose to take a stand. If I accomplish nothing more in my life, I want the history of what I witnessed in the 1990s to be preserved.

Elisa Hategan
Toronto, March, 2014

ONE

TRUTH AND CONSEQUENCES
Toronto, February 1993

I'm running to the edge of a mountain: wet tangles, stained sundress, soaked sandals. I run with all my might, eyes closed and breathing through my mouth, toward the hill that rises behind my grandmother's house, to the clearing where I can throw myself to the ground and face the sky. I spread my arms, feel the rush of grass overflow through my fingers, the fertile green cool like a river, smelling of morning rain. I am one with the earth. My hair is black like dirt and eternity stretches above me.

It is there, right at the border where earth and horizon intersect, that I open my eyes. But instead of glimpsing the infinite blueness of that Transylvanian sky, reality smashes into me and I see myself on a cement bench in an interrogation cell at 53 Division in downtown Toronto, knees drawn up to my chest, black bomber jacket strewn on the ground next to me. Not knowing what's about to happen next, feeling like I'm going to throw up.

I tapped my fingers against my shin, trying to distract myself from a headache that reverberated right through me, drenching the back of my shirt in cold sweat. Every crash that came from the world outside the whitewashed walls made me jump. My anxiety intermingled with a surreal sensation of displacement, a sense that, if I tried hard enough, I could will myself out of here. To shut out everything, I imagined that I was plunging into a cool, bottomless lake. The outside noises started to recede, diminishing into unidentifiable thuds, and all that was left was the echo of my own heart pumping furiously.

I wrapped my arms tighter around my legs. Huddled like that, chin braced against knee, I knew that nobody could force me to talk. If the cops thought I was stupid enough to sign the piece of paper they'd been waving in front of me for the last couple of hours, they had another thing coming. No way in hell was I going to let them put words in my mouth or make me confess to something I hadn't done.

My fingernails dug hard into the flesh of my palms, sowing a row of crescent moons. This was all my fault; I'd brought this whole thing on myself. If I hadn't given the flyer to those activists a week ago, it would never have been linked to me. The woman whose name was on the flyer wouldn't have freaked out and telephoned the police. The two police officers who showed up at my door wearing beige overcoats just like in the movies wouldn't have asked if they could come in. And if I hadn't been so taken by surprise, I wouldn't have opened the door to let them in without a warrant when they said, "We can do this the easy way or come back in twenty minutes and tear this place apart."

The thought of having to explain to my mother, who was due back from her late shift any minute, why the place was in shambles seemed more daunting than actually letting them into the apartment. That's where I made my biggest mistake. If I hadn't panicked, those cops wouldn't have looked over my shoulder and noticed my Smith Corona typewriter sitting on the kitchen table, the stacks of leaflets piled up next to it, or the dozens of books scattered across my bedroom floor. And then I wouldn't have been handcuffed in the doorway for all the neighbours to see. I wouldn't have been escorted out into the rainy evening, an evening so chilly that steam rose up from the laundry room vents and from the grills in the slick pavement and mingled with the drizzle, making my hair, damp as it was, stick to my neck. I wouldn't have been shoved into the back of a cruiser and most definitely I wouldn't have ended up here, in a video-monitored interrogation cell at 53 Division.

The door crashed open, startling me. A middle-aged man came to stand in front of me, his arms as crossed as his eyebrows. He was Detective Murphy, one of my two arresting officers and the one who had played the bad-cop role for the last couple of hours.

He hovered over me. His scowl deepened. "Don't you want to sleep in your own bed tonight? Just tell us where the flyers came from and you're free to go."

I shook my head silently. Ratting anybody out wasn't an option.

"But we *know* you distributed them," he said, pausing for emphasis. "We have some of your own comrades on record saying you were passing them out."

12

Impossible. It had to be a bluff. I continued to stare up at him, wide-eyed, but said nothing. The realization was rapidly sinking in: he was trying his best to intimidate me into snitching on the others. Isn't that what all cops did when they interrogated suspects? Said shit to mess with your head?

"Just give us a name. Who gave you those leaflets?"

It's not what you think, I wanted to tell him. I wasn't brainwashed. There was no way I could be expendable. And he was crazy if he thought I'd betray Wolfgang. Sure, I had messed up by feeling sorry for the target. But no tear could be severe enough to be irreparable. As soon as I got out, I'd see about mending it.

Murphy decided to pull out his trump card. "You've never been in trouble before. You haven't a clue what prison's like. Do you really want to spend the night in jail with big-ass dykes who'd love to get their hands on a girl like you?"

I looked at his blotchy face and started laughing. I laughed so hard my eyes got wet. He turned around and was going toward the door when I brazenly called out to him: "Hey, whatever happened to my phone call? Wasn't I supposed to get a call to legal aid?"

He slammed the door behind him and I started rocking back and forth, humming an old battle hymn, *Stand tall, stand strong, 'n the war against the world....* I had to transform into a rock. A rock you'd hurl through a window like a Molotov cocktail.

I stared at the bare walls and counted martyrs in my head. True heroes had suffered a lot more than one night in jail. They endured hunger strikes, electrical shocks and crippling beatings, and never once turned against their convictions. Wolfgang had warned me that everybody cracks at some point, but unless Murphy was prepared to break every bone in my body and pull out my fingernails to boot, I was going to volunteer nothing and that was that.

One more hour passed before Murphy finally brought me back out to the main precinct area and cuffed me to a chair next to a vacant desk. He reached for the phone, dialed the number of the legal counsel on duty and handed me the receiver. Ignoring his glare, I turned away from him and whispered what had happened to the man on the other line. *Say nothing to the police,* the counsel advised emphatically, *and most definitely don't sign anything.*

Just as I thought. I handed the phone back to Murphy when I was done. He slammed it down and huffed off to a typewriter in the corner of the room to put together my transfer papers – apparently I was to be sent across town to the female prisoners' holding tank. I looked toward a young cop, no doubt a rookie, who was shuffling papers at the adjoining desk. I cleared my throat and he looked up, questioningly.

"I didn't get through to my mom," I said, biting my lip. "Do you think I could call again, real quick?"

He noticed the pleading look on my face and his eyes become softer. "All right, but

make it quick," he said, reaching for the phone. "What's the number again?"

I got through to Gerry on the first try. "I'm at 53 Division," I announced. Before he could manage a response, I added, "Can you make sure someone shows up to the courthouse tomorrow to post bail?"

He sounded genuinely shocked. "Jeez, what happened? What'd they pick you up for?"

I darted a look around the room. "Can't talk too long, they're about to transfer me. Just make sure someone comes, ok?"

Gerry hesitated. When he spoke again, I could feel the tension rising in his voice. "You haven't been telling them stuff, have you?"

"Of course not."

"Good girl. Keep your mouth shut and don't sign anything. We'll be there tomorrow."

Detective Murphy led me to the back seat of his cruiser. After a mechanical "Watch your head," he slammed the door shut, got in the driver's seat and started the engine. The rain continued to fall, a relentless downpour, and the windows were hazy, streaked with water and fallen leaves that clung hard to the windshield and refused to let go. I listened to the sound of the windshield wipers as they swished back and forth and tried to make out where we were going by the city lights that blinked rapidly past us.

"You sure there's nothing else you want to tell me? Last chance," he said half-heartedly as he pulled in front of the detention centre. I looked at him through the dashboard mirror and shook my head. He exhaled in resignation. "Fine. Suit yourself. But don't say I didn't warn you."

I stepped out, feeling the drizzle against my skin. I tilted my face upwards, enjoying the coolness against my flushed cheeks. Murphy grasped my arm and pulled me forward. My hands were still cuffed in front of me as we entered the building. I took a seat on a plastic chair while he exchanged papers with the policewoman at the front desk. He signed a form, folded it into his pocket, and walked through the front doors without looking back.

A shorter, heavy-set policewoman in her forties came around the desk toward me. "Come now, let's get you processed," she said, whisking me through a door that buzzed as it opened and slid shut behind us. I went to stand in front of what I figured was a mug-shot wall.

"Hold still," she directed as she snapped a quick photo. "Turn left. And right."

Next up was the fingerprinting; she took an ink roller and smeared it over my fingertips, then pressed them firmly into the blank spaces indicated on the papers in front of us: one hand, then the other. She stood so close to me that I could smell the acrid odour of her deodorant wafting between our bodies. I felt like a child in kindergarten, when the teacher hovers over you, showing you how to finger-paint for the first time – an oddly intimate, awkward moment.

When we were done, she gave me a wet paper towel to wipe the ink off before gesturing for me to follow her down the corridor and into an adjoining room. Unlike the other rooms along that hallway, this one didn't have a window cut into the door. The reason became evident when she turned to me, slipped on a pair of latex gloves and waved her hand perfunctorily. "Remove your clothing and stack it over here." She gestured toward a low cabinet in the corner of the room. "If you have any valuables or sharp objects, keys or shoelaces, now's the time to hand them over."

I stepped out of my shoes gingerly. Started to lift up my sweater. Hesitated. "What do I have to take off?"

"Everything, of course."

It was at that point, with the policewoman standing there, staring at me quizzically, that my throat tightened and suddenly I couldn't contain my tears any longer. They burst through my eyelashes and ran down my face. I was mortified, unable to stop. "Do I have to?" I sniffed.

She nodded sympathetically, though I could tell she was getting impatient. It occurred to me that she didn't often run into people so embarrassed about being strip-searched. Most of the folks who came through this precinct were all too familiar with the process and certainly didn't make a scene about having to take their underwear off.

"Never had to go through this before?" she asked.

I shook my head, choking on a sob. In the starkness of this room I felt overexposed, bleached by the light and terrified at the prospect of being touched. The images of brave revolutionaries and martyrs who died for their cause instantly dissolved from my mind, replaced only by the intense fear of a cavity search.

We had reached an impasse. The cop sighed, looked behind her as if to make sure nobody else was coming in, and lowered her voice. "All right, just get down to your panties and hand me everything else."

She checked the pockets of my jeans, shook my clothes in the air to make sure they weren't concealing anything, and then she took a step toward me, coming so close that I could feel the heat of her breath against my shoulder. I cried harder, wrapping my arms around myself.

"Shh, it'll be all right," she said. "Just let me do a quick inspection. Only takes a second."

She ran her hands through my long hair, lifted my breasts. Then, before I could protest further, she pulled on the band of my underwear. Satisfied that I wasn't smuggling any drugs or weapons in there, she nodded. "Okay, you can get dressed now."

She leaned against the wall and watched me slip back into my clothes. I wondered whether she thought I was a big baby for bawling like that, but I didn't care.

"Try not to end up back in here again," she said. "You're only eighteen, right? Too young to waste your life in the system. You still have a chance."

The door of my cell slammed shut behind me, an automatic lock clicking in place. I was glad to finally be left alone, relieved that I didn't have to share my tiny cubicle with anybody else. How disappointed Detective Murphy would be, I thought, that I hadn't been attacked by raging lesbians or murderous inmates. I took in my new surroundings – the place was exactly as I had imagined a cell to be: it smelled like vomit and was equipped with a steel sink, an exposed steel toilet without a seat, and a wire cot with a stained mattress thrown on top. Trying not to think about the security cams that were overtly mounted to the ceiling outside the bars and pointed at the prisoners' cells, scrutinizing our every move, I walked over to the sink. The trickle of water that spurted out was just enough to let me remove the remaining ink smears that still coated my fingertips.

The bony frame of the metal cot beneath protruded through the threadbare mattress, as though it was made with the skeletal remains of its previous occupant. I lay on my side, facing the pockmarked cement wall and the milieu of scrawled obscenities that covered it, and tried my best to ignore the persistent light emitted by the neon beams that ran lengthwise across the corridor ceiling. My disheveled hair ran down my face and over my shoulders in furious red ringlets twisted like barbed wire. I rubbed my eyes, trying to ease their sting, but that only made them worse. They were itchy and swollen from all the tears, and my contact lenses stung like acid but I didn't dare take them out in case I lost one and ended up blind as a bat the next day.

No one had bothered to explain to me what was about to happen. I would find out soon enough. At eight o'clock in the morning, a paddy-wagon transported nine streetwalkers and myself, all of us chained together at wrists and ankles, to the College street courthouse. Then they uncuffed and directed us to wait in the lockup area, a large holding tank framed with steel bars that could have doubled as a cage at the zoo. I waited my turn until past lunchtime (ham and cheese slivers between stale pieces of bread), watching woman after woman get called up to see the judge. I remained behind, uncertain as to what the delay could be.

One of the prostitutes, a woman in her forties with her hair done up in cornrows, was sitting next to me. She leaned over. "What'd they charge you with?" she asked, a whiff of alcohol under her breath.

"Publishing defamatory libel," I answered.

She arched a bushy eyebrow. "Say wha'? What does that even mean?"

"They say I published something that I didn't."

"And they put you in jail for that?"

"Apparently."

"Well, honey, considering you ain't ever been charged with nothing before, I betcha they'll let you out on a five-hundred dollar bond."

The woman next to her clucked in agreement. I allowed myself to relax. If repeat offenders, drug-dealers and armed robbery suspects who'd shared the holding tank with me kept getting released on thousand-dollar bonds, how high could my bail really go? Maybe she was right. The fact that I'd never gotten in trouble before might account for something.

Just before I was to appear before the judge, I got whisked into a room where I sat across a Plexiglas window from the public defender who had been appointed to speak on my behalf in court.

"Is there anyone who can post bail for you?" he asked.

I shook my head. "Only people in the Front."

"That's no good. The cops are asking for bail conditions prohibiting you from associating with Heritage Front members."

"But I won't agree to that. They can't stop me from meeting my friends—"

"They can, and they will. You want to wait behind bars until your trial?" He glared at me, then looked back to the papers in front of him. He shuffled through them brusquely. "All right," he said, adjusting his wire-rimmed glasses. He peered down his nose at me like I was a speck of dirt on the bottom of his shoe. I was convinced he hated my guts.

Then he cleared his throat and spoke again. "So when they call you up, let me handle everything. But you have to agree to all their terms or you're not getting out." From the expression on his face, it was obvious that it wouldn't be any skin off his back if I went back into lock-up. I had no choice but to play along.

Finally, my case was called up to the docket. A bailiff came to escort me from the holding cell into the courtroom. He took me by the arm and nudged me into the front row of the prisoners' box. I stood there awkwardly, unprepared for the multitude of faces that gazed up at me. I snuck a peek at the spectators. Sitting right in the front row was Marc Lemire, with Ken Barker behind him. Making eye contact with them, albeit briefly, made me feel better.

Just as I was starting to think everything was going to be all right, the duty counsel walked over to me, holding a list of conditions I had to abide by. I peered at it and couldn't believe what I was seeing. "Are you serious? They want to stop me from meeting everybody? What's that got to do with publishing libel?"

"Listen here, young lady. I'm not going to fight the prosecution," he whispered under his breath. "You've got to get yourself a lawyer for that. You agree to everything or you go right back to jail. Your choice."

He pointed out the lines where I was to sign. I scribbled my name with mixed emotions; in rapid procession, anger, sadness and despair inundated my consciousness. The Heritage Front was my entire world. I depended on them. Severing ties with them so abruptly would be like cutting my arm off.

In the aftershock of this realization, I barely registered the bailiff leading me back into the holding tank. I collapsed on the bench and closed my eyes. As I tried to keep myself from shaking, a familiar voice interrupted my thoughts.

"Heya girly, you still in here? What'd they give you?"

"Five thousand," I said.

The streetwalker gasped. "No way! Your bail's higher than some people I've seen in here time and again. You must've pissed 'em off something awful. Whatcha gonna do?"

I shrugged. "They're letting me out on my own recognizance. Some charity signed for me. I never want to be in here again."

She laughed harshly. There was something about that laugh that made me look straight at her. An unpleasant expression was taking hold of her features.

"Don't know nothing, eh? Once you're in here one time, you'll always be back. Sure, everybody cries at first – *I ain't comin' back, no siree, not me!* – but you wait and see how fast you end up back in the slammer. Once you go lock-up, you never go back."

She put her head back and started to cackle hysterically at her own joke. I shrunk against the cell bars, which continued to reverberate with the sound of her laughter.

Sometime after two in the afternoon, I was released. My head spinning, I made my way out slowly and almost didn't notice that Ken Barker walked by just as I entered the elevator. Spotting him, I reached for the doors but someone else darted inside and grabbed my shoulder, pulling me back in. It was Marc Lemire. "Act cool," he whispered fiercely.

We got out on the main floor and he tried to steer me right. I wavered. "I…I can't do this. My bail conditions…"

"I know. We were there, remember? Let's just get the hell outta here quickly."

I couldn't move. It was as if my feet were glued to the ground. My mind raced. I was about to break the rules and we hadn't even left the building.

Marc scowled. His tall, ungainly frame towered over me, and for a moment there I thought he might just sweep down and throw me over his shoulder. Even though we were around the same age, he was as built as a fully-grown man. Unfortunately for him, it seemed, in my mind anyway, that his physical prowess had surpassed his cognitive development.

"Look," he said, "I was told to come and get you. If anyone asks, tell them I'm your boyfriend. They can't expect us to break up just like that, at a moment's notice. Let's just focus on getting out of here. We're gonna go meet some people."

"Who? Where?"

Marc sighed in exasperation. He looked to the left and right. Then he stepped forward and made a thrusting motion with a newspaper he had folded under his arm. I blinked in disbelief. Was he trying to threaten me? I didn't believe for a second that he had a gun inside that newspaper. He wouldn't be stupid enough to walk into a courthouse with a concealed weapon.

"We can do this the easy way or the hard way," he said. "You have two options. Plan A is you walk out of here with me, we take the streetcar to a certain stop and you meet these people who wanna talk to you. Plan B is we follow you out, our car swings by while you're walking down the street and we pick you up, like it or not. Either way you're gonna have to come with us. So what's it going to be?"

"Who wants to meet me and why?"

"They wanna ask you some questions, is all," Marc continued, refusing to answer me directly. "Get the details of what happened. Wouldn't you agree it'd be so much easier to come outside with me than let this thing escalate? Just leave it up to us, we know what we're doing."

I narrowed my eyes, looked at him sideways. Why was he being so cocky, referring to himself in plural? He was acting like he was on a secret mission and wasn't about to fail his first assignment. Since it was in my best interest, I decided to go with Plan A.

"Walk out the front doors as fast as you can. But don't run," he instructed, grabbing my hand and slipping something inside. "Here's a TTC ticket."

He shoved me onto the first streetcar heading east. I went all the way to the back and looked through the rear windows to see if we were being followed. The coast was clear. I sat down next to an elderly Chinese woman holding large grocery bags full of vegetables between her knees, averted Marc's eyes and tried to think of a good story. I couldn't let them know the truth.

Marc nudged me to get off at Riverdale station. No sooner had we stepped off the platform than a car materialized out of nowhere and came to a screeching stop in front of us. In the driver's seat, Ken Barker thrust his thumb at me and pointed to the back door. "Get in. Now."

I obeyed while Marc jumped in the front seat. Ken drove erratically through back streets and alleyways to lose anyone who might have been following us. It worked; I lost my own sense of direction. Halfway through the ride, Ken stopped to let Marc get off. He'd done his part.

Fifteen minutes later, Ken pulled up on the curb of an unfamiliar street. He got out only to walk me into a dark, empty Italian restaurant I'd never stepped foot in before. It reeked of cigarette smoke and the floor was sticky from spilled beer. Uneasily, I followed Ken to the back, to the only occupied table in the place. I didn't know what to expect – a Mafia boss, perhaps? And then I spotted him. There, next to a cup of steaming coffee and an open notebook, sat none other than Grant Bristow.

The boss nodded and Ken disappeared.

"How ya doing?" asked Grant, waving me to sit down. Not waiting for me to answer, he continued. "Wait, don't tell me what happened yet, we're waiting for Wolf."

I sat uncomfortably across from Grant, staring at my shoes, trying not to meet his gaze. I could tell he was dissecting me with his eyes. The glow of his scrutiny brought the blood rushing to my face. Thankfully I didn't have to wait too long, as Wolfgang arrived just as the waitress was topping up Grant's coffee. He eased into a chair and looked straight at me, his icy blue gaze unwavering.

"Tell me everything that's gone down in the last twenty-four hours," he said calmly.

I took a deep breath and began to recount what happened. As I talked, Grant took copious notes. He wanted to know the arresting officers' names and every detail that had transpired.

"Are you hungry?" Wolfgang interrupted after a while.

"I don't have any money on me," I said.

"I'll pay," he offered.

Feeling queasy, I accepted his offer and he ordered me a sandwich.

"You understand why this debriefing is necessary, right?" Wolfgang asked.

I nodded. Yes, they had every right to get full disclosure. Yes, it was perfectly normal for two forty-year-old men to order that I be picked up on the street, by force if necessary, and brought here for a spontaneous questioning session.

It went on from there. What did the police ask? What did I say? Did I give any names? No? Good girl. Let's see those bail conditions. Pity to give up the firearms acquisition certificate.

"The worst part's the ban on any type of political activity," Wolfgang said. "No association with any Front people. But hey, you know what? At one point, I was stuck with similar conditions, PLUS a curfew, and I still went out every night."

"Really?"

Grant joined in. "You think they've got enough manpower and money to place everybody out on bail under surveillance? Don't be ridiculous."

"Just act cool. Wear a disguise if you come to a rally," said Wolfgang. "Rules are meant to be broken, don't you know that?"

"I've got to get rid of all my literature. I don't want to risk it if they come back with a search warrant."

"I'll take it off your hands," Grant volunteered.

"So what am I supposed to do now?"

Grant explained how the legal aid process ran: I have to apply for it first, and the system pays an attorney to represent me. As he talked, Wolfgang pulled a business card out of his jeans pocket and slid it across the table.

"Here's your lawyer. He comes highly recommended by Ken – apparently the guy got Ken off on an assault charge, so he ain't bad. We've already called him. He wanted to be at the courthouse this morning but couldn't get away from another case in time."

I sat back, stunned.

Wolfgang grinned. "Didn't think we'd take care of our own like that, did you?"

Relief spread through me. I was thankful not to have to worry about anything anymore. The job was done for me, a sympathetic lawyer found, and all I had to do was listen to everything they said and not let it slip how the flyer was tracked to me.

Almost as though he read my mind, Wolfgang frowned. "There's just one thing I'm curious about, though," he said, scratching the side of his goatee. "How did they pin that flyer on you? Did someone see you pass it out?"

I decided to go with that theory. I didn't want to imagine their reaction if I told them that I'd given the leaflet to those anti-racist activists on purpose. I couldn't handle the sight of betrayal on Wolfgang's face or incur Grant's anger, which seemed to always seethe beneath the surface. "I was distributing it at Brock High School where I was taking my night class. Someone must have seen me."

When they were fully satisfied that the situation was under control, Grant drove me home. "Remember, get all your propaganda packed up and out of the house as soon as possible," he reminded me as I stepped out on the curb.

I walked unsteadily past the bulletproof Plexiglas entry doors of my low-income housing complex, crammed into a tiny spray-painted elevator that reeked of curry and piss, and took it up to the sixth floor. My hand shook slightly as I unlocked the door to my apartment. As soon as I stepped in and found the place empty, I breathed easier. With any luck, my mother wouldn't be back until nightfall. She was fond of working overtime and taking a cab home on the company's dime, so I had enough time to clean up, dispose of all the pamphlets and brace myself for the inevitable battle that would come.

I got out of my clothes and slipped into the shower, letting the scorching hot water rinse away the aches and grime of last night's detention cell. My hair plastered over my face in long, soaked strands, and it was then I finally allowed myself to break down.

Tears spilled out, turned into sobs, and then it felt like my throat was jammed with rocks and I was choking. I'd have done anything to rewind time back to a week ago and undo the damage I caused by giving that flyer to the enemy. I should never have permitted myself to have a conscience. Look where it led me.

TWO

"History is written by the victors. It doesn't necessarily make it the truth."

Wolfgang told me this when I met him for the first time outside the Eaton Centre Cineplex in Toronto on a Tuesday evening he called "nigger night" because of the large group of black youth who converged there for half-price movies. That night I stayed up until dawn learning that Anne Frank's diary was a hoax and that the white race was on its way to becoming extinct.

When Wolfgang had walked up to me, the intensity behind his expression lit up his eyes like embers glowing in the night. He had put his hand on my shoulder and asked, "Elisse, did you know only two percent of the babies born on our planet are white? Our race is going to die off in two generations."

"I didn't know that," I said.

He shook his head in pity. I had so much to learn. "How old are you?"

"Sixteen," I said.

"Are you in school?"

I looked down. "No, I left six months ago."

"And you don't want to go back?"

"No way. I hated it. I wasn't learning anything I can't pick up just by reading on my own."

"That's true," he agreed. "Schools are just playgrounds for indoctrinating kids into the status quo. For brainwashing youngsters into believing whatever the government wants them to think. So what was the final straw for you? What made you quit?"

"My last school was actually okay. It was in a town just outside Toronto and the kids were friendly enough, but my foster family was in the business of taking in kids because they got 20 bucks a day per head from Social Services. The wife just had a baby and all they wanted us to do was clean their stupid house and do their laundry. So I ran away from there and went back to live with my mother and by then I didn't feel like going to another high school for the third time in a year."

He nodded. "So how long have you been back with your mother?"

"Just under six months. I quit school and moved back all in one day."

"Are you having problems with her again?"

"Nothing I can't handle," I said sourly. I wasn't meeting him for therapy.

"Well, good for you," he said with a smile. "You seem to have a good head on your shoulders, or you wouldn't have gotten in touch with us."

A day earlier, I had telephoned the 24-hour Heritage Front hotline and listened to a recorded message praising me for having the strength to be proud of my race. Emboldened, I had left a quick voice mail with my telephone number, and before I could come to regret what I had done, Wolfgang had already called me back and arranged to meet up. "In a public setting, of course," he assured me, almost as though he sensed my apprehension.

I was terrified to meet him. What sixteen year old girl wouldn't be, when faced with the prospect of an encounter with a much older man who seemed nice on the phone but was the leader of what might turn out to be a white supremacist organization? But the alternative – continuing on alone, friendless and angry, with nobody to talk about the fears that rumbled around in my head unimpeded – seemed even worse.

Every time I walked by the black panhandler at the intersection of Shuter and Parliament, I couldn't shut out the memory of being picked on at the Browning Street group home. For a good portion of the year and a half I spent at Browning, I had been the only white girl there. What made things worse was that I'd been in Canada for only two years and didn't even know what rap music was. The other kids made fun of my accent and the way I braided my hair, and told me that I dressed weird. Every day after school I would run to hide in my room so I wouldn't get singled out again, only to have staff knock on the door and insist that I head downstairs again since apparently one of the house rules was that you weren't supposed to hang out in your room except after dinner.

Eventually I became friends with my roommate, a heavy-set Jamaican girl named Karen who had picked on me at first; as time went on, we got to know each other by trying to top one another's scars. She won that contest – one of her parents had thrown scalding water on her and she had third-degree burns all over the lower half of her body.

The few marks I had on my skin were absolutely nothing in comparison. She'd had several plastic surgeries over the years and would continue to get them as she got older. Karen was a tough girl, streetwise and smart, and I was a fish out of water. We made an odd pair, but somehow it worked. She stuck up for me and the others left me alone. She also grew so tired of hearing me cry at night that she proposed we pull our beds together and cuddle ourselves to sleep.

We were inseparable for more than eight months. Karen taught me a lot about the latest fashion trends and popular music, and also how to suck my teeth and swear like a full-blooded Jamaican. We hung out at the mall, poked our noses in the thrift markets along Danforth Avenue in Greektown, and once she took me along to her boyfriend's place, where I watched a movie on his huge-screen TV while they snuck in the bedroom and had sex. But then she was sent off to a foster family in Richmond Hill and once again I was alone and getting picked on by the black kids.

It was like somebody had walked up behind me and stuck a Kick Me sign on my back. Whether I liked it or not, I wasn't one of them and that's just the way it was. I didn't bother trying to make friends anymore. Hardly a day went by without me wondering why it was supposed to be cool to walk around with your pants hanging so low they might have fallen off at any minute, not that it mattered since half your butt was already showing. Back in communist Romania all kids had had to wear uniforms. If we didn't look tidy enough in class, our homeroom teacher rapped us against the knuckles or made us face the wall for punishment. But in this screwed-up country everything was upside-down – you got rewarded for being bad. For refusing to do chores. You were cool if you acted tough, smoked pot and talked back to staff. And if you got too chummy with a staff member, you were called a brownnoser and other nasty things behind your back.

If they could be bad, so could I. And I'd beat them at their own game. Stealing books came naturally to me. I wasn't really interested in anything else. Every three months we got a clothing allowance from Children's Aid and I still hadn't grasped the concept of why brand-name running shoes were better than their Wal-Mart counterparts. But the five dollars I received for completing my weekly chores didn't even begin to cover all the magazines and books I wanted to read, and the local library didn't carry many of the newer books I had my heart set on. To make up for the injustice, I started stealing from the gigantic World's Biggest Bookstore at Yonge and Dundas. I'd hide in the isles and rip the barcodes off back covers, then walk calmly past the magnetic detectors into the street. Back at the group home I hid my loot under the bed, secure in the knowledge that staff would never question me showing up with something that didn't have the perceived value of a new pair of Nikes.

But the fear of being detected always gnawed at my mind. What if this time I made the detector beep? After a while, my nerves got to me and I decided to go for smaller, discount shops that lacked security cameras and monitoring equipment. It was safer. One afternoon I glided into such a store, one that carried cheap books along with assorted dollar-store-type junk, and went through my usual routine: I walked to the back, glancing around at stuff on the racks. When I was sure nobody was watching me, I slipped a handful of paperbacks into a tote bag hanging off my right shoulder.

A customer was standing at the counter when I turned around. That was good; I could slip out before anyone noticed. I glanced toward the entrance to make sure the coast was clear, only to crash into a pair of angry black eyes. The owner, a little Chinese man with a pinched look on his face, was glaring at me from behind the cash register. A cold realization struck me – he knew what I was up to. But it was too late to turn back now. I'd shoved the books so deep in my satchel and it would have been too obvious if I tried to get them out. I made a beeline for the door but a short, middle-aged woman I guessed was the owner's wife jumped out from nowhere and blocked my path. Holding her arms out like a quarterback, she prodded me back toward the cash register. She wrenched the satchel from my hand and plopped it on the counter, spilling the contents.

The little Chinese man picked up the telephone receiver, holding it up to his ear. "I call police, now," he cried. "You hooligans think you come to my store and rip me off, I show you."

The customer at the counter, a guy in a ripped-up tee-shirt who was about to pay for a pack of smokes, looked at him and shrugged, "Aw, give the kid a break, man."

The store owner and his wife ignored him and proceeded to argue furiously in Chinese, their voices rising louder and louder while I stood there stupefied, wishing I had the nerve to push past that woman and run. Red with fury, the owner finally glared back at me and spat out a question. "You, how old are you?" he shouted, index finger pointed at my face.

"Fifteen," I said.

I heard an audible sigh from the guy in line. He shook his head. "Man, police don't do nothing to juvenile delinquents. More trouble than it's worth to involve them, if you ask me."

Through my blurry vision, I gawked at the owner and his frazzled wife. I wanted to sink right into the ground. To shove past her and take off. Anything but just stand there, awaiting my verdict at the hands of two people who couldn't even speak English properly. It wasn't like I took anything valuable. All they did was sell cheap Made in Taiwan shit and rip off people anyway.

The owner narrowed his eyes. "If I see you back here again, I call the police," he said. He put down the receiver painfully, looking at me as though I'd kicked him in the face.

It took me about ten seconds to realize that they were going to let me go. Without another word, I snatched my empty bag off the counter, dashed out the door and didn't look back until I'd gotten around the bend from the Moss Park Armory and Queen Street had shrunken into a streak of dirt and streetcar lines behind me.

That was the last time I ever took something without paying for it. Months had passed since I'd left Browning Street and ran away from my foster home but my wounds never scabbed over. I was still angry – pissed off at those black kids, at the Chinese shop owner who'd looked at me like I was dirt, at the drabness of everything that surrounded me.

And now there was Wolfgang standing in front of me, like a magical feel-good fairy, telling me that I *should* be angry. That my anger was justified, it was a natural defense reaction that had kept me going for this long. This new perspective thrilled me to bits – it absolved me of any embarrassment over what I'd done. I was enveloped in a mirage of blamelessness through which I saw myself as innocent as a newborn lamb. I could do no wrong.

Wolfgang's intensity was striking; when he spoke, you knew there was a fire burning inside him. He truly believed that he could make the world a better place. From his heavy German accent over the phone, I expected to come across a six-foot something, SS-uniformed soldier out of a history textbook. But Wolfgang was none of these things - a short, stocky, dark-haired man sporting a black goatee, he could have blended into a crowd of middle-Easterners on the street. But when he fixed his attention on you, he conveyed a tacit acceptance that just put you at ease. That's where he really shined. As a listener, he was so attentive it was as if a hundred pairs of eyes were trained on you, and you could almost feel the hush of a crowded room fall silent.

In the years to follow, I often wondered how I came across to him that night. I imagine he saw a diminutive, lonely kid he could befriend, a fatherless thing with a bratty streak and a mouth to match. But there was something in that young girl with reddish-brown hair and dark eyes, a naïveté that betrayed her streetwise attitude and which intrigued him enough to want to enlist her into his own army of misfits. An army he hoped would one day take over the world.

From the moment Wolfgang opened his mouth, all my fears vanished. It didn't matter anymore that I was a sixteen-year-old meeting a much older stranger under the cover of night. We were two people united by a greater cause. He praised me generously for having made that first phone call, and I relished in the warm glow of approval that emanated from him. He wanted to know everything about me. He was attentive and engrossed in my story, interrupting only to ask more questions. When I posed the same questions back at him, he told me that he'd grown up in a small town in northern Bavaria, and that he'd lived in the United States for many years before moving down to Toronto.

We got into his small navy sedan and headed down to a tavern he described as a local hang-out for Front supporters. We could talk freely there, he said. And what a coincidence that it was only a ten-minute walk from my home. "You're lucky you live so close," he added. "I hope you don't mind I took the liberty to ask my friend Gerry to meet us there. He's one of the co-founders of the Heritage Front and the editor of our upcoming magazine. We're hoping to put out the first edition sometime next month."

The Parkway was a cozy little place in the heart of Cabbagetown, right at the corner of Carleton and Parliament street. It was an old-style pub with lots of beveled mirrors, carved wood tables and chairs, and had apparently become the unofficial meeting place of the Front. We'd barely sat at a table in the back room when we were joined by a stoop-shouldered middle-aged man wearing a thick pair of bifocals who introduced himself as Gerry Lincoln. He was behind the articles and press releases that came out bearing the group's logo.

"You should get her to meet Grant," Gerry said, gesturing to the waiter to bring him a beer. "I thought he might be coming by tonight but he hasn't shown up yet."

"The Heritage Front was founded by three people," Wolfgang explained. "Me, Gerry, and there is another fellow you've yet to meet, Grant Bristow. The three of us sat down together a couple of years ago, formulated an idea, designed a plan, and ultimately came up with what became known as the Heritage Front – an umbrella lobby group that incorporates different networks of like-minded people, but has its own distinct personality."

I did my best to follow the Front's complicated history; I didn't know much about politics or revolutionary movements, but the way Wolfgang was dropping names, it all sounded impressive. He smiled at me indulgently, as though he knew I could barely keep up but didn't mind teaching me the ropes. My eyes grew wider as he told me that one day the Heritage Front would rival the Conservative Party of Canada, and then take over the country. Maybe someday he would even be Prime-Minister.

Gerry adjusted his bifocals on the bridge of his nose. "Wolf here is the official leader, I'm secretary behind the scenes and run Up Front magazine, and Grant is in charge of security since he's a licensed private eye. We've put together a nifty organization if I may say so myself."

"Hey, you want something to eat?" Wolfgang offered.

I had no money on me. "Um, no, that's okay, I'm not hungry."

"Let me buy you a coke then, all right? I'll get one too."

Wolfgang didn't like to touch alcohol, he explained, since he used to have a drinking problem back in the day. "I've been sober for several years now," he said with a smile.

The conversation drifted to their publication-in-the-making. "If you're really enthusiastic about helping out," Gerry said, "you could write the Letters to the Editor section of *Up Front*. I'm just putting together the first issue but David Duke himself has already committed to a regular column. You can pretend to be anyone: an old woman reminiscing about the good, old days when there weren't any immigrants, or maybe a teenager struggling for equality in a school overtaken by non-whites."

"Sure, I can do that," I said. I'd never been published in a real magazine before. It sounded so cool. "I've always been good at writing stuff. It was my best subject in school."

"Would you also consider recording messages on our hotline? There's a shortage of people composing messages and it would be good to have a female voice on there once in a while."

"But what would I say?"

"Anything you want," said Gerry. "Watch what's going on in the news. If there's some police shooting, talk about how criminals are taking over now that immigration rules are letting more people in…talk about anything you want. Sky's the limit."

I hesitated. The suggestions they were throwing at me seemed a bit overwhelming, but it felt rude to refuse them outright.

"Look, why don't we do it this way. You write out a message that's about a minute or two in length, then call me up and read it to me. If I think it's okay, you go ahead and record it. How's that sound?"

Perhaps I could manage it under Gerry's supervision, but everything seemed to be going so fast, I needed time to think. "Could I sleep on it?" I asked.

"Sure, of course," Gerry smiled. "Take all the time you need to think about it. But let me write my number down for you, just in case."

After he finished his beer, Gerry got up and excused himself. I looked at my watch: it was half past midnight. "You have a curfew?" Wolfgang asked. "I can drop you off."

Unlike the group home, where I had to be back by nine o'clock sharp, living with my mother didn't entail any curfews. I could come and go as I pleased, but this was a redundant issue since I didn't have any friends and therefore no reason to come in late. Midnight *would* have qualified as a reason for my mother to have a conniption fit, but as she'd decided to spend her week off from work at her friends' house in Mississauga, I was on my own. I could stay out all night and she'd never find out.

Wolfgang and I walked out into the slick midnight air toward his car. "It's just up the road," I said, buckling into the seat. "The Shuter Street complex."

He whistled appreciatively. "Jesus. If being surrounded by all those drug-dealing gangbangers doesn't turn you into a racialist, nothing will." As he started the engine, he cleared his throat. "You should know I've done some time behind bars. As a matter of fact, I was released just a couple of years ago."

I swallowed. The warm and fuzzy feeling I'd had all night evaporated in an instant. *WTF. I'm trapped in a car with an ex-con.* I looked sideways at him and he glanced back with a twinkle in his blue eyes, as though anticipating my anxiety.

"See, that's why I'm telling you now," he joked. "So you don't hear it from somebody else later and think I wasn't honest with you. There were only about a dozen of us mercenaries, but we had a near-foolproof plan and got within a hair's breadth of overthrowing the government of Dominica. I did three years in the federal pen for it," he said, darting a glance to his dashboard mirror.

The dark sedan whose lights had flickered behind us took a sharp turn into an underground lot, and Wolfgang looked relieved. He turned his attention back to me.

"But I'm not *really* racist," I said awkwardly. "I mean, the black kids at my group home gave me a hard time because I was the only white girl there, but I don't have a problem with anyone else. I don't have anything against Jews. I support native rights and I marched with the Mohawks during the Oka crisis. Do you hate aboriginals?"

He was slow to answer. He gripped the steering wheel and kept both eyes fixed ahead of him. I chewed my lower lip; had I said something wrong?

"The way I see it," he started hesitantly, "we've won this land fair and square, through battle. Know what I mean?"

I blinked. Yes, but...

"And when it comes to Indian reservations," he said again, this time more firmly, "the mere concept makes my blood boil. That is precisely what I have been fighting for all along – to get a separate area for us white people, where we can maintain and develop our traditions without any outside interference. But they call *us* racists..." his voice trailed off.

After allowing me to contemplate, he spoke again. His voice was low and gruff, and there was a certainty to it that made my blood run cold.

"You know, Elisse, a race war is going to take place in our lifetime. Governments will collapse and it's gonna be every man for himself. The shit's really gonna hit the fan. When there's violence and total anarchy, it's going to come down to the survival of the fittest – us or them. Which side of the fence do *you* want to fall on?"

A huge part of me wanted to scream at him to stop the car. I'd jump out and run away as fast as I could. I'd try my best to forget everything he told me and pretend tonight had never happened, that people like this didn't exist.

"Black folks blame us for their failures in life," he continued. "It's easier to scapegoat us as perpetual oppressors than look at their own shortcomings and improve themselves. I'm not surprised those kids in your group home picked on you. You have no idea what is going on in the world."

We had pulled over in front of my building and I was turning to get out when Wolfgang stalled me. "Hang on a second. There's something I want you to have."

He reached over to the back seat and started rifling through what seemed like one big mess of papers, envelopes and empty coffee cups. Once he extracted a random sampling, he thrust the stack at me. "Something to keep your hamster busy until we meet again."

I stayed up half the night going through it all. I'd never seen anything like that before: Ku Klux Klan zines, British ultra-nationalist clippings, photocopies of an American underground publication titled White Aryan Resistance. It astonished me to think there were people out there who broke the rules, who could publish such hateful propaganda and get away with it.

It was like watching a horror movie – you want to look away from the gruesome scenes, but you're afraid that if you do you'll miss the best part. This couldn't be for real. People weren't actually serious about *believing* this stuff?

THREE

THE FAMILY

By the next morning I'd written off my encounter with the Heritage Front as a surreal experience I wasn't sure I wanted to repeat. After the shock value of Wolfgang's papers wore off, I took them across the hall to the garbage chute, sent them hurling down the shaft and thought nothing more of the whole encounter. Until Wolfgang called again that evening.

"Are you busy tonight?" he asked breezily, knowing that I wasn't. "Wanna come over to the Parkway? I know all that stuff I gave you yesterday was pretty hardcore, but we're not all that radical. There's some people I'd like to introduce you to. Good friends of mine, a couple of ladies who are leaders in the movement. They're members of the Reform Party, actually. And they would *love* to meet you."

Two women huddled at a table next to the frosted mirrors that lined the far wall of the tavern, their heads close together as though they were whispering. One was a tanned brunette wearing dark red lipstick, the other a huge, big-boned woman in her fifties with a shock of bright red hair and several rings circling sausage fingers. As we walked in, the brunette's gaze lifted toward Wolfgang. While her face gave no sign of recognition, her hand raised and fluttered slightly, a nearly imperceptible wave.

I stood in front of them, tongue-tied, until the brunette finally flashed a smile. "So Wolfgang, aren't you going to introduce us to this lovely young lady?"

A look of faint amusement played on her face as she stretched, then slowly rose to her feet. She looked to be in her late-thirties and wore a sleek blouse tucked into a charcoal skirt and a pair of dark pumps. She was attractive in spite of the thick layer of foundation that powdered her olive-complexioned face, an attempt to cover what looked like pockmark scars. The dense waft of perfume, a mix of sandalwood or patchouli and something spicy and likely very expensive, reached my nose at the same time her arm reached around my shoulders.

"So nice to see a fellow woman at these things," she mouthed in my ear. "It gets to be such a bore having all these macho men around."

"Nicola, this is Elisse, the girl I was telling you about," said Wolfgang. "I've been trying to explain to her the movement we are creating here."

Nicola's teeth flashed in a dim lights. "All this political gobbledygook can overwhelm a newbie, don't you think? Why don't you come and sit with us for a minute."

Without waiting for a response, she pressed me to sit in the chair she had just vacated. I barely had time to register that Wolfgang had walked away from us when Nicola pointed to the red-headed woman. "This is Donna," she said. "Her husband is an old friend of Wolfgang's. They all live in the same apartment building. Their place is right below his apartment, actually. As for me, I've been in the movement for years."

Nicola dragged a nearby chair to our table and nestled it opposite from me and Donna, who beamed at me and reached to refill her glass from the pitcher of white wine on the table. Her face was canvas for a million tiny freckles that extended past her cheekbones and as far away as her earlobes. "You want something to drink, sweetie?" she asked.

"A coke would be fine," I answered, and she promptly waved to the waitress.

Nicola's hand landed on my arm, demanding attention. "These days I like to keep myself in the background," she said, addressing me with the kind of familiar, conspiratorial tone one reserves for an old friend. "I don't have the time to be an activist and frankly, I don't want to be on the news every night. I have three children to worry about. But I always make a point to come out to the Parkway. That's how I get to meet bright young people like yourself."

She must have seen the incredulous look on my face because she nodded and went on. "Trust me, you're very special. Girls are rare in the movement, especially pretty ones. So many girls your age are race-mixing and getting knocked up. But I can tell you're smarter than that."

I bit my lip. "Actually, I didn't even know about the Heritage Front until this week. I only came because Wolfgang said you guys wanted to meet me –"

Nicola put up her hand to shush me. She leaned in closer to me, eyes sparkling. "Do you believe in coincidences? That's there's more to *this*, the world we live in, than meets the eye? Because – and I'm telling you this because I believe in it absolutely – I've seen this a thousand times in my life: there are things that happen to us, unexplainable events that propel us in the path of something we are supposed to do, take us someplace where we're supposed to be. Did you know that statistically more people sleep in and miss their flights when that plane ends up in a crash? It's like something held them back, saved them so they could fulfill another purpose. Know what I mean?"

I just stared at her, saying nothing. Her irises were light chocolate, speckled with gold, fringed with wet eyelashes visible even in the dim lights emanating from the frosted glass sconces that dotted the far wall. She squeezed my hand, and for a moment it seemed that the heat emanating from her would singe right through my skin.

"I believe you're here for a reason, Elisse. That we were supposed to meet and have this conversation tonight."

I took a deep breath, stared at her evenly and blurted out, "I know the Heritage Front is supposed to be all about having pride in your race, but isn't this some sort of hate group?"

Nicola looked down and said nothing. I wondered if she felt insulted, but then her head snapped up and her eyes burned brighter than ever. Her expression was ardent, unwavering.

"Do I look like a skinhead to you? I don't hate anybody. In fact, I'm convinced we can all live just fine without having to interact with one another. No, I'm doing this because of *love*. Love for my own people, who have been made to feel ashamed and inferior for the deeds of their ancestors. It's my belief that we are all a family."

She squeezed my hand again and repeated that word, *Family*, and in that moment I knew she was telling me the truth. At least, I believed that *she* believed the stuff. And she definitely didn't come across like the goose-stepping neo-Nazi types they warn you about in after-school specials.

Almost as if she'd read my mind, Nicola cocked her head sideways, inquiringly. "Ever asked yourself why we have to celebrate

Black History Month, but it's taboo to celebrate White Heritage month? Doesn't it seem unfair?"

"I've never thought of it that way," I said.

Nicola's pearly whites flashed again. "That's right, Elisse. And were you aware that at the UN they're refusing to penalize nations who condone honor-killings and genital mutilation because they don't want to be seen as 'insensitive'?"

I scowled, thinking of all the stories in the media where women were murdered for nothing more than being seen with a man their family didn't approve of. "Cultural sensitivity has nothing to do with stoning women to death for being raped."

Nicola leaned back triumphantly. "Well, honey, that's all I'm saying. Am I a neo-Nazi for calling such practices barbaric? Have I suddenly turned into a racist if I openly declare that I'm proud to be European? How does that statement offend anybody? It's no worse than somebody stating they're proud to be African."

"You tell her." My head snapped around to see Wolfgang behind me, grinning from ear to ear. "Political-correctness will be the death of us."

I liked Nicola, the passion evident in her voice when she spoke about her Ukrainian heritage. The pride she had of the medieval battles waged by our East European ancestors to fight back the Ottoman invasions told me she was sincere. Better yet, she had me convinced that she was someone who genuinely wanted *me*, a sixteen year old drop-out with no friends and future prospects, to be her closest confidante. So when she phoned me at home a week later, I was happy to hear from her.

"Can you babysit for me for a couple of hours?" she asked, sounding desperate. Before I could tell her that I'd never babysat before she offered me ten bucks, a deal I couldn't refuse. "And I'll give you the subway fare but just please get over here before six, all right?"

When I finally got to her house, a red-bricked semi in the east end, Nicola was in a huff. "My meeting got cancelled," she said, gesturing for me to follow her into the kitchen. "I had no way to reach you. Why don't you stay for dinner? There's some leftover lasagna."

"That would be great, thanks," I nodded, waving hi to Nicola's three kids who were watching cartoons in the living room.

Nicola took a tinfoil-covered pan out of the fridge, cut a piece of lasagna and placed the plate in the microwave. "I divorced their father a couple of years back," she said. "Don was like a lot of the men in the movement, arrogant and full of himself. A real dictator who always had to have things his way. Typical Hitler complex. It's no wonder the Nationalist Party fell apart. Once Wolfgang and Grant put their heads together, the concept of the Heritage Front made a lot of sense. It's a real collaboration, not a one-man operation."

She sighed. "Not that I regret my marriage, of course. I wouldn't trade my kids for the world." She glanced me up and down. "And you? Got anyone special in your life?"

I shook my head and smiled awkwardly. "Nah, not really…"

The microwave beeped and Nicola took out my lasagna, grabbed a fork from a drawer and sat me down at her dining table, sitting across from me with a glass of white wine in her hand. "That's a surprise. You're a beautiful girl," she started to say, embarrassing me. I looked down and blushed fiercely.

"No, it's true," she continued. "Why don't you sleep over tonight? I'll do your hair. You think your mom would mind?"

I shook my head. "She's pretty much out of it."

Nicola said nothing more, but when I'd finished eating she took me upstairs and sat me down in front of her bedroom dresser. She picked up a hairbrush, stood behind me and met my eyes in the mirror. With a gentle hand, she began to run the brush through my tangles, wincing sympathetically each time I jumped. "You're lucky to have such natural ringlets. My hair's so thin I've had to perm it since I was a teenager. Wait, don't tell me – you've always wanted it straight, right?"

I nodded. She smiled, put the brush down and started to plait my hair into a long braid. "We always want what we can't have," she sighed.

My silence seemed to make her think I agreed with her, because when she spoke again she placed her hands resolutely on my shoulders. "What do you think you'd want? I mean, if you could have anything in the world, anything at all?"

I shook my head. "I can't tell you. It's silly."

"No, come on," she insisted, her eyes growing bigger in the mirror. "It's just us girls in here. You can tell me anything."

"It's right out of Pinocchio. You know, when he tells his fairy godmother that he wants to be a boy, a *real* boy, not a puppet made out of wood."

"So your secret wish is not to be a puppet?" Nicola joked.

I bit my lip. "I wish I had a real family. I used to be so jealous of all the kids around me who wore clean clothes to school and had packed lunches while I was always that dirty, hungry kid nobody wanted to play with. Even in care, the kids at my group home bullied me constantly."

Nicola placed the hairbrush back on the dresser, leaned over and wrapped her arms around me. "They picked on you because you were white, didn't they?"

Suffocated against her breasts, I squinted hard, refusing to allow any tears through. I pushed away from her; I wasn't going to be weak. But Nicola's arms locked tighter, refusing escape. "At least you have the Front now. And you can come over to my place anytime there's trouble at home, day or night. You have a right to be angry, Elisse. You have every right to hate those who have hurt you."

FOUR

RULES OF ENGAGEMENT

Whereas Nicola brimmed with maternal warmth, Wolfgang was the father figure missing from my life. Whenever he spoke, a fire raged inside him. He called himself an underground revolutionary and a bailiff by day, which was a misnomer since he slept through daylight hours and went out after darkness fell. He said that he preferred to repo cars at night because the owners were already asleep and wouldn't cause trouble. So he roamed the city like the lone wolf he identified with and sported on his favourite shirt, eavesdropping on news that sputtered out of his police scanner, keeping on top of all the action.

Whenever he passed by Regent Park, he got in the habit of pulling up to my building and hitting the downstairs buzzer. His voice crackled over the intercom: "Wanna come out with me tonight?" He got off on the ability to snap his fingers and have me come running: no matter how late it was, I'd throw on my jeans and tee-shirt and be downstairs in five minutes. "Did I get you out of bed?" he grinned as I buckled my seatbelt, daring me to admit it. I never did.

From the appreciative way he checked me out every time I got into his car, I knew he wanted to take things further. I blushed, looked away and persistently ignored it. I needed a father, not a boyfriend. And he was too smart to push the envelope with an underage girl. Years of working with the Ku Klux Klan and David Duke, spending time in prison for his failed attempt to overthrow a foreign government, and then again for selling cocaine, had taught him the importance of keeping his nose clean. I had more value to him as a recruit than as a lover. He wanted to use me as the face of a new, softer and more appealing Heritage Front, and wasn't going to do anything to screw that up.

Under his tutelage a new world unfolded before my very eyes, complete with its own heroes, its own secret language, its own set of moral codes. My mind absorbed Wolfgang's doctrine like a proverbial sponge. I was embarrassed that I knew so little.

"Have you ever dated someone of a different race?" Wolfgang asked while we were driving to Gerry Lincoln's place.

I was too shy to admit that I hadn't dated anybody, period. I'd been too busy moving through group homes, foster care and different schools to develop much in the way of attachments. "No," I said.

He seemed relieved. "Race-mixing is against the laws of nature."

As he parallel-parked in front of Gerry's building, Wolfgang made a point to swear me to secrecy. "It's very important that nobody knows where we're located."

By then I knew better than to ask why.

Gerry Lincoln lived like a mole in a subterranean one-bedroom basement apartment a block north of The Parkway. The hall that led to his front door was dimly-lit and smelled like old cat urine, with the apartment itself being so smoke-congested it made me wonder if I shouldn't be hooked up to an oxygen machine just to breathe.

It was very much a man-cave: overstuffed black leather sofa flanked by a pair of chairs that looked like they'd been rescued from a dumpster. Toward the back of the liver-shaped living room was a tight space that seemed designated as an office nook. It was crammed with ashtrays full of smoldering cigarette butts that were in turn piled shakily atop yellowing newspapers with frayed, curled-up edges. The remaining space was taken up with precariously-stacked towers of videocassettes. Gerry made extra cash selling bootleg copies of movies that still aired in theatres for about five bucks apiece.

"Got an extra copy of *Betrayed* laying around?" Wolfgang asked Gerry after they proudly admired the freshly-printed stack of inaugural *Up Front* magazines Wolfgang had brought over. "I really want Elisse to see it." He turned to me. "This movie's based on a real-life white separatist group in the United States called The Order. I was part of it," he bragged. "The FBI might have killed Matthews, but they never shut us down. Not in *here*," he said, pointing to his chest. "Not ever."

Gerry fished around in a stack of identical tapes and pulled out a video that he passed to me. "Overrated. In the end, he was brought down by a woman."

My eyes drifted to the time on the VCR player. "Shit, is it one already? My mother's going to kill me."

"Want me to drop you off?" Wolfgang volunteered coyly, knowing well that I did. This wasn't a neighbourhood where anybody was particularly safe walking in the daytime, much less after darkness reigned, when gangs took over the streets and shots began to ring out in the alleyways between the buildings.

I thrust out my chin defiantly. "I can walk from here."

He laughed and reached over to scoop his car keys off Gerry's coffee table. He waved them at me. "Come on then," he teased. "Let's get you back in one piece."

My mother was still up and watching television when I slipped into the apartment. She was curled up on the sofa, wearing her cotton nightgown, a cream-coloured granny dress with little pink rose buds all over it. Her usually-coiffed blonde hair was disheveled. Her red-rimmed eyes fixed on me in accusation. "This is when you decide to come in? I was going to call the police."

"I'm home, aren't I? What more do you want?" Given that I'd ran away before, no cop would bother filing a missing person alert for at least twenty-four hours. Add to it the fact that she could barely speak English, I doubted she'd make good on her threat. "I'm going to bed now," I added.

I started to head for my room but she was up in a flash. She raced after me, grabbed me by the shoulder and spun me around. "You think you can just come and go as you please? Think I won't call Children's Aid?"

I turned and stared directly into her beet-red face. I was already an inch taller but that wouldn't matter if she got angry. I tried not to wince at the thought of the smack I anticipated would come at any moment. With my mother you never knew which way the wind was going to blow. I chose my next words carefully. "I could phone Mrs. Persad myself, anytime I want. I still have her number. I'll tell her you're never home and that I want to go back to the kids' home. You'd never see me again."

That shut her up real fast. She knew I was crazy enough to do it. If there was one thing I'd inherited from my parents, it was their temper. If I made up my mind to up and leave she'd have nobody to yell at, nobody to pounce upon whenever she was in a bad mood. But without my head as a target, at least the dishes in the cupboards would remain intact.

I surprised myself at how well the threat worked. She looked startled, like a toddler who falls accidentally and hasn't quite decided whether he wants to laugh or bawl. I decided that the trick was to get to her before she decided on a particular reaction. "I had fun," I said. "I was out with my friends. Don't you want me to have any friends?"

Her anger diffused, she grumbled something like *Try not to stay out so late again.* "Fine," I said and slinked past her, not giving her any time to change her mind.

I leaned against my bedroom door, desperately wishing it had a lock. My mother didn't believe in locks; no good could come of them. She had such a fear of being accidentally locked inside someplace that she'd even asked the superintendent to change the bathroom knob to one that didn't have a locking mechanism.

But there were other reasons she didn't want locks anywhere, and most of them had to do with me. I was never quite certain when a door was going to be flung open and I'd be exposed to my mother's rage, swirling between us like a destructive tornado, sweeping up everything in its path – shoes, plates, schoolbooks – but maintaining only one trajectory: my head. So, as I did every night, I listened for the familiar creak of her mattress in the next room and the rumble of her snoring before I relaxed enough to change into my nightshirt and slip into bed.

That Friday, two exciting things happened: my mother passed out early in front of the television and Wolfgang invited me to my first official Heritage Front get-together at the Parkway. After throwing a glance to my mother, slumped as she was on the sofa, puddles of drool soaking through the sleeve of her housedress, I figured she'd be none the wiser.

The elevator was broken as usual so I raced down the fire-escape stairs breathlessly to the curb where Wolfgang was waiting for me. He flashed a generous smile after I slid into the passenger seat. "Excited to meet people closer to your age? I should caution you though, some of the regulars can be a little weird. Don't let that intimidate you though, they're harmless. I can vouch for all of them."

Operated by sympathetic managers who turned a blind eye to the nature of our meetings, I could understand why the Parkway had become a second home for the Heritage Front. When you walked through that frosted glass doorway and got hit with the smell of fried fish and chips, you forgot about the sleazy stripper joint next door – you became engulfed in a world of beveled mirrors and oak furniture, burgundy runners and painted plates hanging from hooks in the walls.

The Parkway's owner, a balding, pudgy little man with a European accent rushed to greet Wolfgang at the door, shook his hand and smacked him on the back. "Good to see you again," he gushed. "Everybody's here already, waiting for you."

When I saw the crowd gathered in the back room, I froze in place. Truthfully, I would have turned around and walked out if Wolfgang hadn't placed his hand firmly on the small of my back and pushed me forward. "Can't say I didn't warn you," he chuckled under his breath.

All the tables had been pulled together and roughly twenty young men were sitting there, drinking beer and talking politics. Nearly all wore shiny black Doc Martens boots and army fatigues. Black bomber jackets hang off the backs of their chairs. Most of them had shaved heads and colourful patches sown onto their clothes. Some even wore swastikas.

Maybe I shouldn't have come after all. These were the sort of scary-looking people you crossed the street to avoid. Even though I was used to Wolfgang's radical politics by now, it freaked me out to be surrounded by bona-fide neo-Nazis. Nicola and Donna were nowhere in sight. I was younger than everyone else and the only girl; worse yet, I wore a skirt while the rest of that bunch were dressed for combat.

"Hey, Wolf's here!" someone called out. That announcement prompted several guys to scramble to their feet and make room for us at the table. But Wolfgang didn't rush to sit down. Instead, he held me by the shoulders like a proud papa and made an announcement that made my ears burn red. "This is Elisse, our newest supporter, who is already very interested in helping out the cause. And she is *only* sixteen years old! Please make her feel welcome."

I squeezed into a chair between two tough-looking characters. Wolfgang was out of my reach, probably on purpose. A clean-cut blond guy to my right introduced himself as Alaric and said his dad owned the Doc Martens shop downtown. "It's great of you to join the Front," he said. "We need more kick-ass girls in the movement."

As the evening progressed, I realized the guys weren't as tough as they looked. Some were even polite, appointing themselves my educators and taking time to correct my terminology. *We aren't racists, but racialists.* Cross-burnings were known as cross-*lightings*, ancient traditions passed down from the pre-Christian Scottish rite of lighting crosses on hills to call attention to the spirits. I heard the word "*muds*" thrown around quite a bit.

"What does *mud* mean?" I asked, confused.

"It refers to any species that isn't readily identifiable. Also includes all spawns of cross-breeding," Wolfgang said. "We also don't use the word supremacist – it's gotten a bad rap. Nowadays we are white separatists. And we call the Holocaust the *Holohoax*, because that's what it is."

"What do the colours of your bootlaces mean?"

Alaric volunteered to explain. "Red is for National Socialist, White is for Aryan Separatist. You wear yellow if you really hate or have killed a cop. If someone wears any other colours, like green or purple, they're anarchist punks. Rainbow belongs to the queers. The colour rule applies to suspenders too. If they're down, no problem. But if a skinhead puts them up, he's getting ready for a fight."

"Just one more question, I promise," I interjected. "Why do skinheads shave their heads anyway?"

"So that when we get into a fight, nobody can grab us by the hair," he answered, not batting an eye.

Before I could keep track of everyone around me, people started to leave. I looked to my watch and realized that three hours had evaporated since I'd sat down. Wolfgang's voice boomed from behind me. "No worries, there'll be plenty more get-togethers in the future."

I glanced up and saw him grinning, and for a split second I was irritated at his smug self-assurance, that flippant way in which he always seemed to read my mind.

After that night, everything started to fast-forward. Each day took on the quality of an old silent film reel, where moments skip ahead by several beats and everybody lurches and teeters around like a marionette dangling from wire strings. Overnight, I grew intensely proud of my skin colour, and faster than I could have imagined that pride evolved into hate. The prouder I became of my race, the greater my contempt for those who did not share it.

46

I didn't supress the hatred that began to burn inside my heart; I gave myself to it. My comrades said it was a raw energy meant to be cultivated like a rare, delicate pearl. Hate was a natural human instinct tied in with self-preservation and a tribal, primeval desire for supremacy. It was exhilarating to hate. I was empowered, awakened from a great big sleep. We weren't bleeding-hearted hippies motivated by love. Love was a weakness of the spirit. For the fittest to emerge victorious, emotions had to be shed like old layers of snake skin to give way to our rawest senses. Only our Cause was the priority.

I once saw a movie called *They Live*. In it, an average Joe finds a pair of sunglasses. When he tries them on, a disparate world reveals itself, a world invaded by aliens and controlled from the highest sectors. Those magic glasses allow Joe to see the hideous monsters concealed beneath the skin of seemingly normal people. Magazine covers, billboards, radio, TV, the airwaves – all distorted, carrying subliminal messages only the sunglasses could decipher, messages programmed to brainwash the remaining Earthlings into a state of submission.

I now walked the downtown streets in wonder. I had found those sunglasses, I could see it all so clearly. The advertising signs at bus stops, urging people to stop racism. Posters that portrayed different races together, always together – drinking milk, chewing gum, wearing Benetton clothes. Movies and TV commercials that all accumulated into the subliminal brainwashing of Aryans into servility, into accepting affirmative action without fighting back.

I was disgusted with myself for ever hanging out with the Native street kids at the Evergreen. For participating in the Oka protest camp-out at Queens Park. All Indians were boozers and beggars, Wolfgang told me. I didn't know if he was making it up, but by then it didn't matter.

"Just look at those red niggers," he said, "sprawled out on the street begging for spare change. You really have to hold yourself back from digging your boot into their ribs."

FIVE

RECRUITMENT DRIVE

According to Wolfgang, it had taken a good year of planning to launch the Heritage Front. The final concept was hatched while Grant, Wolfgang and several of their Nationalist Front buddies were invited on an all-expenses paid delegation to Libya. They were taking part in a worldwide convention hosted by despot Moammar Khadafy, who'd managed to round up leaders of every guerrilla group he could think of and get them all in one setting – a tenuous situation at best, considering many of the terrorist factions invited were rubbing shoulders with sworn enemies – to discuss training strategies for global domination.

I'm being flippant about it now, but even at sixteen I thought it all sounded awfully like an evil-scientist-world-takeover movie. Yet it was for real – I'd watched the recorded video footage of their sun-scorched trip, shot by Gerry on a shaky camcorder, when I was at his place. Even Nicola Polinuk had gone. All the delegates had been on their best behaviour – not a surprise, given that they wanted to impress Khadafy into funding their actions. Unfortunately for the Nationalist Party, they hadn't received as much cash as they would have liked. But the visit had made a lasting impression on Wolfgang. He had crossed paths with the big boys. He knew the value of strategic international alliances.

Now, after registering the Front as an official business in the province of Ontario, the only way to go was up. What exactly my role was remained a mystery, but he was keen to get me up to speed as quickly as possible.

"You must fight fire with fire," he told me while we were having dinner together at the Parkway. "If you want to defeat an enemy, you must first understand him – his philosophy, his arguments, what makes him tick. If I had a dollar every time someone asked me, *Why don't you just go back to Europe if you want to be around white people so much?*, I'd be a rich man. But I tell them that Europe is no longer white; it's been invaded by hordes of illegal refugees. Might as well call it Eurabia because in twenty years it's gonna be a Muslim-dominated continent. Our brave Crusader ancestors must be rolling in their graves, knowing we gave it all away to the Ottomans."

He shook his head bitterly. "Not that anybody's really indigenous to North America, you know. Indians themselves crossed over from Asia ten thousand years ago. Now, I've never blamed anybody for wanting to come here and build a better life for themselves and their children. So what's wrong with me for wishing to carve out a piece of this country for my own kind?"

I jotted down everything he said in a little red spiral-bound notebook I got from the dollar-store. Wolfgang encouraged me to take copious notes. He wanted to prepare me to recruit others. That's where it got tricky. "Start by asking, *Are you proud of your heritage?* That's a no-brainer, everybody's gonna say yes to that. After that, ask them about their background. Get them talking. When they say they're proud of their ancestry, come back at them with, *We should all be proud of who we are. Is it really fair for affirmative action policies to single out particular races for special favours and discriminate against whites?* Make sense?"

It seemed surprisingly easy. "Does it work?"

Wolfgang grinned. "It gets people talking, and that's what you want. All right, next question. What do you say when people ask if you're against blacks or Jews or whatever?"

I raked my brain for the answer. Wolfgang helped me out. "*I'm only against those who are against white racialist groups.* Now you say it."

I repeated after him, mimicking his tone of voice. "*I have a right to freedom of speech, politically-incorrect or not. And I have a right to be proud of being White, just like all the Blacks, Hispanics and Asians out there.*"

Wolfgang seemed amused. "Remember, we don't hate anyone," he said. "We just love our own race and want to keep it from dying out. It's a biological instinct, this drive for self-preservation." He cocked his head and smiled like he knew something I didn't. "So you came here when you were eleven. Old enough to form an opinion. What did you think of Canada?"

I really had to think about that one. To me, Canada meant living in Regent Park, and Regent Park was a place where poverty bred violence, and violence bred crime, and it seemed to me that every drug-dealer or pimp hanging around the corner had dark skin. It was perfectly rational, a form of self-preservation in fact, to cross the street when a black guy walked toward me. My mother had warned me from the very first day we moved there to "Stay away from those negroes, they're trouble!" and she continued to flip out each time one of my classmates came over at lunchtime. "I don't want any of those kinds of people in my house," she'd insist, giving me a dirty look. "Can't you find some nice white kids to play with?"

Other people also had the habit of crossing the road when they saw a black man coming toward them, and they weren't all white. The elderly Asian man who lived above the corner store did the same thing, as did an Indian mother pushing a baby stroller up Shuter Street. Not all racists were white; divisions and hate spilled across all nationalities.

"It's funny, I never noticed differences until I came to Canada," I finally said. "Here, it's all about celebrating differences. They push diversity so much I wonder what the hell we have in common with anyone else."

"It's the end of patriotism as we know it, Elisse. This brainwashing is part of a conspiracy to devalue all our accomplishments."

"A conspiracy? By who?"

Wolfgang's small teeth flashed in the dim pub light. "The media, of course. And guess who's behind the media? Who all the outlets?"

I shook my head. I had no idea.

He leaned closer. "The Jews. The Rothschild bankers, the Illuminati. They're behind it."

I thought of the stereotype of the crazy old man who lives in an attic somewhere and rants on about The Jews and secret societies that control the world. Was Wolfgang like that? Sensing that I was uncomfortable, he laughed.

"You think it's a joke, don't you? That it can't possibly be true? Who do you think owns all the networks? The newspapers? Look up the names, educate yourself. I'm not sitting here trying to convince you of anything. Do your own homework. The facts cannot be ignored."

50

What if what he was saying *was* true? Would the fact that a tiny number of über-wealthy families owned most of the media corporations lead to potential biases? Wolfgang seemed utterly convinced. "You should read Manufacturing Consent. Written by a Jew himself I might add. He says that whoever owns the media outlets owns the public mind. Because you can shape how people feel about something via the news and newspapers, you can manufacture public opinion, just like that."

He snapped his fingers. "The first thing you should learn is that people are sheep. Sad, but true. There's only a small number of us out there who know what's really going on. It's not just the right-wing that's educating itself. The Arabs are doing it. The Black separatists. The Christian Fundamentalists. It's for our own protection. Of course, the powers that be don't want us to know about it."

It was mind-blowing. Wolfgang paused to let me take it all in.

"You must open your eyes, Elisse. This is the first step in your inoculation."

It can take weeks, endless hours of conversation over coffee, before you can be deprogrammed. Before you can recruit others to The Cause. You have to learn how to turn a person's arguments against them, how to plant that first tiny seed of doubt in their mind and hope that it grows to create enough damage to their feeble, milk-toothed ideology. Average length of time a teenager will wait before resuming contact: one week.

"Everybody's got a weak spot," Wolfgang said. You've got to hone your instincts to find it. Maybe Johnny had a girlfriend who dumped him for a black guy. Maybe little Jane was snubbed at school by a JAP clique, or didn't get that scholarship because she came in second to an oriental. Whatever. You just find that soft spot and dig your claws in as hard as you can."

We were silent for a long time. Wolfgang's blue eyes were piercing, making me uncomfortable. I quickly averted my gaze. He exhaled deeply.

"No one likes to think they're a failure. We're a cheap breed of shrinks who boost egos and tell them it's not their fault they didn't get that promotion. We're right there next to them through thick and thin, providing the answers. Whatever they want to hear, you give it to them. And that is how you deprogram them from society. That, my dear, is how you recruit them."

And recruited, they were. In larger numbers than ever. The P.O. box was starting to overflow with requests for information. It got to the point that if Wolfgang forgot to check it for a few days, the post office guy called to remind him to come and collect his sackful of mail, which was pretty much split in half – 50% hate mail from anti-racists, with the other 50% messages praising our work with generic quips like '*Right on, man. White Power!*'

Wolfgang was keen that I complete my ideological training that month and get on with the bigger job at hand – recruiting other youngsters, picking them up at runaway drop-ins like the Evergreen or outside high schools where I'd blend in easily and hand them a flyer. I secretly wondered if, like Fagin in Oliver Twist, he'd also get me to teach the others how to pickpocket or beg for change in a cockney accent.

I watched the other young people who ran with the Heritage Front with curiosity. They all seemed so *normal*. There was this misconception out there that everybody who joined a group like ours had to come from a single-parent abusive family or be a runaway. In fact, I was the exception rather than the rule. The majority were bored white youth from suburban areas, the type who were bussed to school, who came from middle or working-class families where the parents were frazzled and overworked, overextended on their credit cards and mortgage, and the kids were able to sneak out and run amok in the afternoons.

Often, all you'd have to do is ask them one simple question: "Wanna come to a concert? We're putting on a show on Saturday night." At the concert you'd smuggle them a beer, put your arm around them and whisper in their ear, "Isn't this fun? Aren't you glad to be white?"

It didn't matter what their hair or eye colour was. All youth who looked white enough were targets of recruitment. You asked them redundant questions you knew they'd say yes to, like *Are you proud of your heritage? Your ancestry?* Then you followed with the clincher: *Do you see me wearing a white robe or swastika? No? Well, then? Not all white supremacists are violent. We're not really as threatening as they (the System/the Government/ZOG) would want to have you believe.*

But above all, we were the rebel fighters of an underground cause. That made us sexy, dangerous – revolutionaries fighting a courageous war of ideals. By joining us, you got to shock your parents at the same time as befriending others who shared your angst. Together, we'd march toward a collective, utopian world.

Our recruiting tactics were no different than those of a Marxist underground movement or a religious cult. The strategies of emboldening a kid's fragile ego have always been the same: you pumped them up first, then tore their previous ideas down. You took apart everything they'd learned in school only to rebuild them into a stronger warrior who you could send out into battle. Someone committed to laying their life on the line for you.

Before long, the kid got too entangled to leave. He was used to the euphoria of brotherhood, addicted to the sense of patriotism and loyalty to a Cause. It became easier to be vicious, to abandon all preconceived social responsibilities. *I have a new home now where I can go after a fight with my parents*, the kid began to think. My new family understands me – I don't need a parent or guidance counselor to boss me around. For the first time in my life, people are telling me that everything I do is right. I am the cream of the crop, the one-percent breed who will rule the world. I am a member of the Aryan elite. So what do I need school for? To brainwash me further with Jewish propaganda?

I have better things to do with my time, the kid thought: flyering the town with Heritage Front pamphlets, going to rallies, sieg-heiling at white-power concerts, going out with my friends looking for someone to beat up. People give me respect now. They cross the street when they lay eyes on me. They recognize my fierceness, which comes from the assurance that a whole army of comrades is ready to back me up anytime. In this war of attrition, my bomber jacket is my uniform. My boots are my weapon. My mind is the only propaganda I need.

At the Parkway, more and more tables were pulled together in the evenings. Soon the entire restaurant was overrun with neo-fascists. Sometimes they brought along their girlfriends, mousy-looking girls who hung off the arm of beefy bald guys like live accessories. Most were Chelseas, the female version of a skinhead. You could tell them apart from other girls by the fact that they also shaved their heads, leaving intact only bangs and wisps of hair that framed their faces. What was left ended up bleached to a platinum blond, which never looked good against their darker eyebrows.

A girl embraced the Chelsea style to show off as a bad-ass, hard-core member of the movement, but the look itself was an acquired taste and had the unfortunate side effect of making its wearer look cheap and sad, much like an aging prostitute at the corner of Dundas and Parliament on a weeknight.

They sipped their draft beers and talked about rock concerts and how awesome their boyfriends were and looked at me expecting that I should add to that discussion. I didn't know what to say; I was much more comfortable talking about politics and organizing for change than planning on getting pregnant.

"But we need more white babies in the world, our race is dying out," they'd say with this glossy look in their eyes, making me choke on my soda. "We as Aryan women need to start young so we can have as many babies as possible. Hitler awarded mothers a Cross of Honour if they had more than five children, you know."

I wanted to shake them and say, Why don't *you* go have your babies then, but don't force them down my throat. You can change all the diapers you want while I hang out with the guys and strategize about the future. Besides, in Children's Aid I knew plenty of teenage mothers who'd had a rough time and either had to give up their kids for adoption or went on welfare to support them. No way was I going to end up like that. No freaking way.

And even *if* I lost my marbles and wanted to commence breeding en masse, there was one insurmountable obstacle standing between me and well-decorated Aryan womanhood – the lack of a male to help bring my progenies into being. But it wasn't like I couldn't have landed a willing sperm donor at any point: given that males outnumbered females ten to one in the movement, there were plenty of boys who came to the Parkway in the hopes of hooking up and getting laid. I called them boys because that's exactly what they were, little boys dressed up in adults' clothing, acting tough even as their voices broke when they tried to sound gruff.

I knew that Wolfgang expected me to pick out someone for myself. "There's so few women around, you could have any of the

54

guys," he told me once while we were in his car, in a teasing way that made me turn red. "But there's no rush," he added quickly, a small consolation for having just offered to help me out. Even Gerry had started to taunt me. *Anybody tickle your fancy?* he'd ask, and then proceed to rattle off some sleazy quip or another. '*If you don't use it, you lose it,*' was a perennial favourite.

I didn't know how to respond. How could I, when I too had a hard time trying to make sense of it? The simple answer was, none of the dozens of skinheads around interested me. *Maybe there's something wrong with me*, I mused, annoyed that it had become such a refrain, the constant state of wondering if there was something broken, something defective in me. But how else could I explain why I was reluctant to turn my face toward the young man sitting to my right, who was so painfully trying to get my attention with tales of street brawls and subversive actions?

I asked myself, *Why don't I want to be kissed? Why does the image of his hands all over me make me cringe, rather than swoon?* It would be so easy to pretend to go along – I could allow my fingers to wander up his leg slowly, to feel that coarse denim against my palm and see the effects of my touch in the flush of his skin. I could let him caress my hair like a doll's, unbutton my blouse the way he's been doing all night with his eyes. How simple it would be to arouse him. Some things come so easily for girls; we don't have to do anything, we can just sit back and let someone else lead the way.

But even the idea of doing nothing paralyzed me. Time after time, nothing made my heart thaw out, nothing made me melt in that magical way romance books described. Nothing stirred in me the sort of breathlessness that's supposed to heat you up inside and make your body ache to be touched.

It just wasn't happening.

At the end of November, the Heritage Front hosted a rally to celebrate Memorial Day. Wolfgang booked the Latvian Hall on College Street in a traditionally left-wing part of Toronto on account that it was: a) cheap, and b) it could easily accommodate several hundred supporters. Three hundred people showed up and paid five dollars each to get in, which didn't include the cost of the booze women were selling at the back of the room. Most were in their early twenties, young skinheads sporting freshly shaved heads, shiny black bomber jackets and ankle-high Doc Martens tied up with either white or red laces.

I spotted Wolfgang as soon as I crossed the threshold into the wood-paneled auditorium. His face was electric, glowing with unbridled excitement. As though he sensed my eyes trained on him, his neck turned. He waved me over. "Come, I wanna introduce you to Grant, the other leader of the Front. I don't think you've met him yet."

He pointed to a tall, broad-shouldered man hovering over the back tables, leather briefcase under his arm. I could only see his back, and that he was wearing a corduroy suit jacket and a pair of blue jeans. Wolfgang tapped him on the arm, making him spin around to face us. He appeared in his late thirties and around six feet tall. He had wispy chestnut hair that fell into his eyes and sported a short-cropped dark beard. A knowing smile broke on his face, revealing a set of small, widely-spaced teeth. He extended his hand and I shook it.

"Finally I have the pleasure of meeting the notorious Elisse," he said in a booming voice. "I hear you're making a speech tonight?"

I nodded, self-conscious under his scrutiny. In one sweeping glance, he seemed to take in all of me: my pleated skirt and short-sleeved blouse, the scuffed shoes on my feet, my awkward stance. "Wolfgang talked me into it. I told him I'd probably freak out standing in front of all these people, but he didn't give me a choice."

Grant didn't appear as laid-back as Wolfgang. He was more put-together and had an air of confidence that commanded respect. I wanted badly for him to like me, but something about him intimidated the heck out of me.

"Well, good for you," he said. "Don't be shy, we're all family here," he added as an afterthought, watching my face. "You'll do just fine."

My speech came after the yawn-inducing talk of a young man from Windsor. He droned on about immigration and how our forefathers wouldn't have stood by and allowed it to happen. They'd have fought against the dilution of their culture, he insisted. People applauded him lukewarmly and then Wolfgang went up to the mike. "And now, I'd like you all to welcome a newcomer to the movement. She's only sixteen years old, but in the three months I've known her she has proven to be someone who can always be counted on. Come join me up here, Elisse!"

My stomach lurched as I made my way onto the stage and peered over the podium at all the expectant faces gazing up at me. I struggled to stop my hands from shaking as I smoothed the three pages of my speech in front of me and adjusted the microphone, bringing it down a notch. Nausea rose up in my chest and I swallowed hard.

"H-Hello everyone," I said nervously, my voice on the verge of breaking. Public speaking was clearly not my forte. "Thank you for coming down tonight."

As my speech progressed, I grew more at ease. It helped that I'd memorized half of it so I could look up every now and again to make eye contact with the audience. Encouraged by their smiles, I told them how special they were for having shown up tonight. "We are here to show that we remember the thousands of Germans who lost their lives on the battlefront and in Eisenhower's death camps. But now they live forever in our hearts. Wherever brave men fight for liberty, our heroes march alongside. We're here to pay them tribute."

When I fell silent, ovations rocked the house. Skinheads and senior citizens, all nodding up at me, united in unequivocal applause. Their captivated faces sent my heart pounding. Always the shy, unkempt kid in the corner of the room, I was now welcomed and accepted into the fold of this subterranean world, where I belonged in a way I'd never belonged anywhere else.

Wolfgang looked terribly proud of me as I stepped off the stage. He smacked my back and leaned into my ear, whispering, *See, I told you you'd do fine!* before going up to announce the next presenter.

I spent the rest of the evening manning the display table where we were selling magazines, baseball hats and black tee-shirts with the HF logo embroidered in white. When the speeches wrapped up, people started filing past my display area. Many stopped to talk to me. "I wanted to shake your hand. Yours was the best speech of the night," one skinhead beamed. "Everybody was up there speaking about The Order, but you were the only one to mention all those soldiers martyred in the war. I thought it was very moving. Bravo."

Wolfgang came to stand next to me and put his arm around my shoulders possessively. "Lots of people have been coming up to me and asking about you," he winked. "They're asking, 'Where'd you find that girl? She's a real spitfire."

An elderly man approached and shook his index finger at me. "We need more of you," he said. "More intelligent and articulate young people with leadership potential. You should be very pleased with yourself."

I looked to Wolfgang. All this time it was him I had wanted to make proud, and the expression on his face told me that I'd succeeded. "I want you to speak at the next rally," he said. "It was so good to have a female up there, a different face for a change. We need more women in the media. Not just a hard-core skinhead stereotype, but the face of a young girl like you. Someone innocent."

Grant himself walked past the display table. "Nice job," he said. He gave me a thumbs-up and kept on moving through the crowd. I didn't doubt that the comment was just an automatic, impersonal gesture. Even so, that generic indication of approval infused me with a warm, fuzzy glow. I wanted to make a good impression. Someday he would notice my loyalty to the movement.

Someday, he'd trust me as much as Wolfgang did.

SIX

LAND OF MILK AND HONEY

In my darkest dreams I am back there again, an eleven-year-old in the middle of Toronto's Pearson airport, a place more foreign and scary than I could ever imagine. Flashes of light are going off all around me, crowds of people pushing with elbows, with luggage carts, shoving me forward. I am disoriented and nervous, when a voice calls out for my attention. A strange woman, fat and blonde, is reaching for me. My brain struggles to pinpoint who she is, and all of a sudden everything comes rushing back and we are running toward each other, crying. My mother. I hadn't seen her since she defected from Romania when I was nine.

My first memory of Toronto consists of an indigo skyline made up of modern skyscrapers with shimmering, mirror-like facades. The mushrooming lights were beyond dazzling, reflecting electrical blues and pulsating reds against the car windows and my wondrous eyes. We pulled into the city late in the evening, sometime after ten o'clock. Back in Bucharest the lights would have been dimmed by now, but here everything glowed bright and beautiful, like an image out of a holiday card.

We left the parking lot and dragged our luggage toward the entrance doors of a massive building. I was jet-lagged, oozy, floating on air. When we went through those doors toward the elevator area, I was astonished again at how bright the hallway really was, and how there was not one, but three elevators in place. *Everybody here must be so rich*, I thought, watching with curiosity as a dark-skinned man wearing a turban, accompanied by a woman in a wispy green sari and a thick braid that reached past her bottom exited the elevator.

We got off on the second floor and I marvelled at the carpeted corridors. The carpet felt nice under my feet, minimizing the echoes of our footsteps as we shuffled toward an apartment door. My mother fished around in her purse until she found the keys, and then the door opened, the entrance light clicked on, and we were here at last – our new home in Canada.

There was the brown sofa I recognized from the photos my mother had sent. Next to it, a small television set propped up on a tiny stand. A *colour* TV, my mother bragged. In the far corner of the open space that constituted the common area of the apartment, a Formica table was flanked by two leatherette chairs on steel frames. The fake leather had a scratch through it and you could see all the yellow stuffing coming out of it.

"Come, let me show you the place," my mother said. She waved me over to the bathroom. "Look, a tub if you want to take a bath."

Next to the tub was a basket of shiny red candies. I reached for one and nearly put it in my mouth when she stopped me. "Oh no, we don't eat those, they're made of soap. They call them bath beads. I'll get you something to eat if you're hungry. But first let me show you where you'll sleep."

Left of the bathroom was the apartment's only bedroom. Two twin beds covered with pink floral coverlets were pushed against each wall, leaving open a small path toward the large window. Next to it was a small nightstand, and perched on top was a framed photograph of my mother with a man I'd never seen before.

"Do you like your room?" she asked. I glanced around and didn't say anything. She took that as a yes and went back into the living room. I dragged in my bag and sat on one of the beds. I could hear her bustling in the kitchen, pulling plates out of the cupboard, but I didn't feel like eating. I looked to the floor. What a funny parquet, I thought, shiny and made up of small, mustard-coloured squares of wood placed in alternating rows.

The sleeping arrangements had already been decided: my father was going to sleep on the pullout sofa in the living room and my mother was going to take the bed opposite from mine in the bedroom. While she was still making up the sofa-bed and chatting with him, I changed into my nightgown and snuck under the covers. Sleep overtook me before I could say good night.

I woke up in the middle of the night, disoriented. Where was I? I wanted my best friend Pereta, I wanted the comfort of the bed I'd shared with her over the past month. But wait, was I back in our old apartment? My eyes and brain got their messages crossed. The walls shifted toward me, then seemed to cave in. I started to howl like an infant. I sat up, drew my knees up to my chest and shook hard. Slowly, my perception began to reintegrate and everything came back: the scary airplane ride, the sparsely-furnished apartment and the woman who was my mother and yet I hardly recognized.

For breakfast my mother directed my father and I to sit at the table while she brought out two plates of boiled eggs, sliced tomatoes, burned toast and a bunch of skinny boiled sausages. "They're called hot dogs," she said.

I looked at them in disgust. "Are they made with dog meat?"

"No, no, I think there's beef and chicken in them."

"So why do they call them that?"

"How should I know? It's a Canadian thing. Just eat it!"

I poked it with my fork. It made a bursting, wet noise as the metal pierced the sausage skin. *Put some mustard on it*, my father gestured. He was old school, he believed anything could be improved with a squirt of Dijon. Doubtfully, I raised it to my mouth. Took a nibble and was suitably impressed. It didn't taste bad at all.

I started sixth grade one week later. Not long after that, my parents got involved in their first violent argument on Canadian soil. It happened days before my twelfth birthday. Just like in the old days, my father flew at my mother with his fists, landing blow after blow. She screamed at him, completely hysterical, and I stood in the doorway and stared at them mutely. My thoughts turned to the time in ESL class when our teacher Mrs. Friedman said that if anybody hit us, we should call 9-1-1. That was what people did in this country, she'd said; beating a kid or a spouse was illegal here.

I went to the telephone and dialed the number. In broken English, I did my best to explain what was going on. Half an hour later, a policeman was pounding at our door. He took my father to the side and explained to him that he could not conduct himself like that, and if it happened again he'd be taken to jail and charged with assault. My father nodded that he understood and threw an ugly glance at me. After the cop left, my mother looked at me and shouted, "Is this what you want? To get your father arrested? You should be ashamed of yourself, you little bitch. We wouldn't be fighting like this if it wasn't for you."

By next summer they had separated. My father, who was twenty-seven years older than my mother, went to live in a seniors' residence too far across town for me to visit. He had been diagnosed with prostate cancer and already had surgery to remove the tumour. I dropped by to see him in the hospital once. He was miserable, forlorn, unable to learn the language. He longed badly to return to Romania. "I wrote to the embassy to tell them I didn't want to stay here anymore," he said to me. "I'm going back. I'll die on Romanian land."

"Take me with you," I said. "I never wanted to come here."

"You're crazy," he said. "Your life is here now. Your mother would never consent."

I was sure he wanted to go back just so he could see his mistress again. He knew that he had terminal cancer and wanted to spend his remaining days back in Bucharest with her. He'd saddled me with a stranger who called herself my mother, who I hadn't seen in more than two years, and now he was going to leave me here forever.

Two weeks after he left Toronto, a postcard from Romania arrived in the mail. My mother was at work and I found it slipped through our door's mail slot. Maybe it was from my father. I curled up in an armchair by the window and turned it over. It was from the Dalius, our old neighbors from across the hall.

"*My dears, we regret to inform you that Mr. Hategan has passed away,*" the postcard said. "*Three days after he arrived in Bucharest, he collapsed and was taken by ambulance to the hospital where he died some days later. We are very sorry.*"

That was it. No information as to whether there had been a funeral, no idea of what had happened to his belongings, nothing. The Dalius had kept the message short and to the point, impersonal. Silent, burning tears ran angrily down my cheeks. I wished that I had been there with my father, to hold his hand. As badly as he had hurt me in my short life, I wished so desperately that he hadn't died alone.

The second time police knocked on our door was during seventh grade. I was thirteen and my father had been dead for three months. We had moved from Don Mills to a rent-controlled apartment in the inner city, in a building complex nestled within an area known for drugs, gang violence and frequent shootings. But the school I attended, Park Public, was wonderful. I had the best teacher in the whole world, Mr. Godlewski. He was the kind of teacher they made movies about, the type who took his students to baseball games and barbecues in his own backyard, who dropped by your house when you didn't show up for school and wasn't afraid to be called a pedophile if you needed a hug or shoulder to cry on.

Even with the language barrier, I tried to fit in the best I could. In seventh grade, I brought home a black classmate during lunch period, one of my best friends from Mr. Godlewski's homeroom. We were going to finish our homework early and then she promised she'd paint my nails the way she'd done hers, with tiny sparkles on top, a perspective that thrilled me to bits. My mother made us sandwiches and I thought everything was okay, but after Vanessa left, she flipped out.

"Didn't I tell you to stay away from them niggers?" she screamed, whacking me with the sharp edge of a high-heeled shoe. The angular scar I carry on my forearm would immortalize that particular fight and my conviction to never introduce her with any friends, black *or* white.

One day I made the mistake of going home during lunchtime. I'd hoped my mother had already left for work, but no, she was still getting dressed when I went into my room. A wave of shock washed over me when I saw my bedroom closet door open.

A quick inspection confirmed my worst fears – the two dresses I'd brought over from Romania were missing, the one I wore on the plane and the pink one that Gina, my best friend's grandmother, had made for me just before I left.

I burst in on my mother as she was curling her hair. "Where's my stuff?"

"What do you mean?"

"The clothes I brought from Romania. Where are they?"

She shrugged. "Those old things? You're growing out of them so I gave them to Adina, the Runcanus' daughter. Such a nice girl."

"You don't have the right to do that. Get them back!"

"Don't speak to me like that," she said nonchalantly. "I'll do no such thing."

Lately she had gotten in the habit of getting rid of my things, probably as a way to separate me from my Romanian past. First up, she disposed of the only gift my father ever bought me, a little watch with a radiantly blue dial and a silver band. After he'd died, every time I thought about that little watch I dissolved into crying fits. My father bought it for me the week before we left Romania and I'd worn it non-stop, taking it off only to wash my hair, until my mother insisted that I'd scratch it and I should keep it safe in my room.

The next time I looked for it, it was gone.

And now she'd given away Gina's lovely pink dress, the one she had labored for days to sew for me and was the only thing I had left of the Gancius, the people who had looked after me after my mother left the country on vacation two years ago and never came back.

"How can you do that?" I yelled. "They weren't yours to give away!"

In response, she came after me, screeching at the top of her lungs. I lunged for the front door but she cut me off in the hallway.

"You're not leaving until I say you are," she screamed again, spit flying out of her mouth. Her hand came up swinging. Before I could duck, her fist smashed right into the side of my face, sending my head into the wall.

Blood started to gush out of my nose. I ran to the bathroom and tried to rinse it off in the sink. My cheek was beginning to swell and turn purple. Outside, I could hear her shouting and banging against the bathroom door. I had to get the hell out of there. I took a deep breath, opened the door and shoved her out of my way, losing a clump of hair in the process.

I ran the whole way back to school and hid in the empty classroom. My body still shook when Mr. Godlewski came back from lunch early. "What happened to you?" He crouched down next to my desk. "What happened to your face?"

I just looked at him, tears running down my face. He touched the collar of my blouse, which I didn't realize had ripped. "Did you get in a fight? Do you want to go home?"

I shook my head vehemently. "No, I never want to go back there."

"Did your mother do that to you?" he asked.

I opened my mouth but was too choked up to speak. All I could do was nod. He looked concerned, stroking my hair lightly. "I have no choice but to report this to the principal, and he has to call the police. Will you be all right with that?"

I blinked my approval. He handed me a handkerchief out of his pocket and I blew my nose. A little blood made its way out onto the white cotton. Mr. Godlewski straightened and left the classroom.

The bell rang and everybody came back to their seats. I waited at my desk, head buried between my hands. Ten minutes later, Mr. Godlewski came back in the classroom and motioned to me to come to the doorway. "Go to the principal's office. Don't worry, everything will be all right," he said, squeezing my shoulder. "I'll check in on you after class."

This was the first of several police reports that would be filed with the police, charging my mother with child abuse and neglect. As though to compensate for what was going on, a teacher gave me a winter coat her daughter had outgrown. Another one put together a parcel that they placed on our doorstep – along with a Christmas turkey, it was filled with goodies like gloves, hats and scarves for me. I was touched that they'd thought of me, and wondered how they'd noticed that I didn't have any of those things when my own mother hadn't.

The kindness I experienced at Park Public (now renamed Nelson Mandela P.S.) got me through that year. But it wouldn't last. Midway through seventh grade, thinking it was in my best interest, Mr. Godlewski said I was ahead of my class and called in a lady from the Board of Education. After she administered several tests, she recommended me for enrollment in a gifted, advanced-level studies program that was being offered in only two schools in all of Toronto, and both were located an hour's travel outside of Regent Park.

The Gifted Program I ended up in was run out of a junior high school located in an upper middle-class neighbourhood full of leafy boulevards and snotty kids. The program itself was okay; there were twelve of us and we were all quirky in our different ways – there were math geniuses who only played chess, girls who were exceptional in the sciences, nerds who could build elaborate science projects with little more than string and a cardboard box. I was the designated storyteller. My talent lay in writing stories that my teacher and principal said were good enough to be published, even at my age. The gifted students were all nice enough. But then again, there were only a dozen of us.

Since there were only seven girls in my homeroom, we had to join a regular class for Physical Education. It was filled with blonde girls who went by names like Michelle and Tammy and made my life an unadulterated hell. I'd get tense just walking by the lockers, praying I wouldn't run into them. But a loud slam of a locker door and a giggle told me they were always there, watching, whispering. "What planet do you think she's from?" their ringleader, a queen bitch named Michelle, asked within earshot. "Ooh, look how gross she is, she doesn't shave her legs." "Peasant," giggled another of the girls. "She's not wearing a bra either."

As I walked past them, one purposefully thrust out her shoulder and bumped into my arm. I kept my eyes down and started running. The sound of their laughter echoed through the corridor and bounced off the gym floors like a basketball.

I used every excuse to sit out the class. The solitude of sitting on those dusty bleachers that smelled like cedar and antiseptic marked most of my grade eight experience.

As for the leg-shaving, that was a whole other story. We'd sit on the floor doing our stretches and I'd feel the other girls' eyes boring into me. I scoped out their eight-grader legs: hairless as a boiled chicken's skin. Same thing with their armpits: everything plucked, waxed and suntanned to perfection. Whenever I watched them lather on lip gloss as gooey as lard, I felt like a retarded kid from the backwoods of Eastern Europe.

Before the year ended, I hated school with a passion. The teasing was endless – it followed me from the time I stepped off the streetcar, through recess, through my walk back to the TTC stop. I kept fantasizing that a gas pipeline or water-main underneath the building would explode or something, just so I didn't have to go back there anymore. But as much of a nightmare as Fairmont Park was, life at home was a bigger can of worms.

Like other latchkey kids, I flipped on the TV as soon as I came home, indulging in an endless stream of after-school specials, comedy sitcoms or trashy talk shows about cheating spouses or baby mama dramas that usually ended in fists and chairs flying. By the time my mother returned from work, she wasn't particularly choosy about what she watched so long as the TV was on. By Friday she settled on the couch where she'd spend the rest of the weekend.

One evening I was boring into a book on my lap when a sudden flash of darkness against the pink carpet made me gasp. I jerked my knees up to my chest. The reflexive motion made my mother turn her attention away from the TV and follow the path of my gaze down to the floor. Unlike me, her instinct wasn't to shrink away. She jumped to her feet.

The mouse traps had not been enough. Nor the rat poison she'd so carefully dribbled in the corner between the kitchen and the living room, forming white, flour-like mounds. None of it had made the scurrying noises in the cabinets go away, or the little shit pellets left on the counter during the night. Whether she liked it or not, there was the embodiment of her failure, right by the balcony door: a charcoal-coloured ball of fur.

The mouse pretended it hadn't heard us, or otherwise didn't seem bothered that we were watching it. It had no fear. It clasped its strangely human-like paws together and ran them over its head, over and over: it was washing its ears. For a creature supposed to be filthy, its grooming habit rendered it oddly endearing.

At the sight of that indifferent mouse, my mother froze. She stared at it for a split-second, as if daring it to move, then made for the toilet. For a minute there I thought she was going to throw up. But then she emerged again, face contorted with rage, her hair wild, as though tousled by an uncontrollable wind. Her expression was at once both horrified and triumphant. She held her fist up and I had to blink twice to register what it was that she was holding. When I saw the toilet plunger, I knew what she was about to do. I was already fast-forwarding to the part where she would pick up the bloody, crushed pulp of what had once been a mouse and toss it over the balcony onto the patio below.

My mother leaped forward, the plunger's suction cup sealing the fate of that mouse inside its rubber dome. She locked eyes with me, then sucked in her breath and pressed down with all her might. I don't remember if I screamed. Either way, the squeaking noises that emerged from underneath that toilet plunger were ear-splitting enough to drown me out. My hands flew over my ears in a failed attempt to shield myself from the crunch of bones, from the pain that vibrated in the air.

The tiny creature's suffering was palpable, wrenching. A kaleidoscope of colours exploded across my brain and I flashed back to a memory of my five-year old self, crumpled in the dirt at the foot of a bridge in my grandmother's Transylvanian village. My mother walking away from me, her sandals scraping up the dust in the road. I am sobbing frantically, gasping for air, the images of tiny kittens fighting for their lives underneath the rippling waves seared into my toddler brain. Moments earlier, my mother emptying a sack of striped furballs into the river, me screaming for their lives, grasping to catch them while she elbowed me in the ribs, lifting me over the stone railing, forcing me to watch.

I was thirteen years old when I first ran away from home. It was on a school field trip to Washington, DC, and when I finally turned myself in to police after a week of being declared missing, I refused to go back to my mother's apartment. "If you send me back there, I'll kill myself," I declared to the Children's Aid authorities who picked me up Pearson airport. The threat worked. After being locked up for two months in a secure facility for suicidal youth, I was sent off to a group home on the Danforth, in Toronto's Greek village. It was far enough away from my mother and it gave me a chance to learn how to be a kid. We got three nutritionally-balanced meals a day, one outing per week and friendly staff, and for the first time in so long, I felt content.

At my new high school, Jarvis Collegiate, I slumped in my seat and kept my eyes down throughout the day. I wore bangs to hide the expression of utter boredom in my eyes. I was the sort of kid you meet in high school who keeps to herself, who's completely unaffected by the elements, the one who even the bullies leave alone because they can't predict whether she's a crazy genius, a transient weirdo or the type who might just blow her top one day and take them all out with a butcher knife.

I liked the solitude and anonymity of being an outsider in a school of more than three hundred students. After the nightmare of junior high, I'd learned that my best defense against more teasing was to alienate myself rather than try to befriend anyone. Nobody could upset me if I didn't allow them into the secret world inside my head. And indeed, nobody at Jarvis took the time to either befriend or try to bother me. Not talking to people does that; when they can't figure out who they're dealing with, when they can't put you inside a predictable category, they stay away.

One day, my social worker called: they had found me a permanent foster home in an affluent suburb of Pickering. From now on it was going to be rolling hills and being bussed to school – no more long subway rides, no more graffiti in the alleyways, no more waking up to the sound of jackhammers, bullets and sirens. I was giving Toronto the middle finger and had no intention of every going back. The farther from the city, the better.

The first night I arrived, just hours after I had unpacked my two garbage bags of belongings in the upstairs bedroom I would share with another CAS girl, my foster dad Randy burst into the room. He screamed in my face until he was beet-red, accusing me of polishing off a six-pack of Krispy Kreme donuts he said he'd left on the kitchen table that afternoon. I started crying, shocked at his rage. "I didn't eat them, I swear I didn't!"

"Yes, you did, you little pig!" he shouted hoarsely, punching his fist inside his other hand. "I'll get to the bottom of this or nobody's going to bed tonight!"

I clutched my knees to my chest and sat on my new bed, shaking. I could hear screaming drift up from downstairs. About half past midnight, Randy rapped on the door and let himself into my room. He cleared his throat. "Um, just wanted to let you know that Adam finally admitted he ate them. He figured he could get away with it because the new kid was gonna get blamed. Anyway, he has been dealt with. You may get ready for bed."

I sniffed. He stomped his foot and made me glance up. "Are we cool?"

"Mh-mm." I managed a smile. "Good night."

I lasted six days there before I ran away again. The nightly ritual of Randy and his wife violently arguing made me shove the pillow over my head and wish for suffocation. I felt like I'd jumped from the pot into the fire and there was no way out. They'd taken me in, one extra kid in an already crowded household, because Darlene was on maternity leave with their first baby and they needed the extra income. What with the daily per-head fee they received from CAS, running a foster home was a profitable business for them. And of course, me and the other two girls were expected to provide all the babysitting they needed.

The last day I was there, Randy screamed at me again because I wasn't friendly enough. "Why can't you try harder to fit in?" he scolded me. "All you do is disappear after school, and then I find you up in your room with a book. That's not the way we operate in this house. You need to be more respectful, and you show that by hanging out downstairs with the rest of the family!"

Apparently he also thought I was lazy because I'd missed a spot when we were washing the walls on Sunday. We were expected to clean the house top to bottom, make everything sparkling, and that included scrubbing the oven, the fridge, and dusting the draperies. The job took until eight o'clock at night, when I crawled into bed, angry and exhausted, wishing Randy would just drop dead.

On Monday afternoon I was supposed to go into town for my weekly appointment with a counselor. Darlene gave me the train fare and forbid me to spend a moment longer downtown than I had to. I took the money and the train, but never made it to the appointment. As soon as I got into Toronto, I rode the subway up to Queen station and started the long walk eastward toward the housing projects.

I phoned my social worker, Mrs. Persad, from my mother's apartment later that afternoon. She was hysterical. "We were just going to call the police," she said.

"No need."

"Are you sure you want to stay back there? I could put you into an emergency group home tonight, get you on a fast-track list for another family. You don't have to go back to Pickering, you know."

"I know. But I'm done with all that."

"But your mother….are you absolutely sure you want to do this?"

I was done with group homes, with queen-bee bullies, with foster parents who felt no inhibition when mistreating their charges. It was over. I'd rather have one person treat me like shit than a dozen. It was simple math.

"What about school? Want me to transfer you back to Jarvis?"

"I don't think so. I don't want to go through all that again."

"But you have to go to school…"

"No, I don't."

"You're fifteen years old, young lady. Legally you have to stay in school for another year. We can bring charges against your mother if you refuse –"

"I'm turning sixteen in a couple of months. By the time you get the paperwork going, it'll be too late."

"But what are you going to do?"

"Nothing. Nothing at all."

Sometimes it seemed like I'd never left my mother's place, like the last couple of years had folded into themselves like the edges of an envelope and sealed in past and present face-to-face. Every day I got up around eleven and flicked on the television while I ate a microwaved meal. By mid-afternoon I'd spend hours roaming the downtown core. I could do pretty much anything I wanted, provided that I didn't get in my mother's way. Her form of discipline was pretty straight-forward: she smacked me when she was irritable, she threw plates at my head when she wanted my attention, and when she was enraged she came running at me with her sharpened fingernails, trying to dig them into my flesh as deeply as she could.

Her intention was always to wound and scar: my face, my hands, any part of me. Most of the time I was able to catch her by the wrists before she could draw blood. She flailed around like a rabid animal then, panting, her face tomato-red, spittle flying from her open mouth. She kicked me in the shins so I'd let go, so she could grab a fistful of my hair or try to rip my shirt, and that's when I'd shove her back as hard as I could and run to my room and bolt my shoulder against the door. She followed, fists pounding the door so hard I could hear the wood start to split against the frame.

"Ha, you bitch, you can't get me," I'd laugh maniacally. It was better to mock her than allow myself to fall for the temptation of smashing her head in.

Propped against that door, I waited for a long time, because I could never tell when she might back off only to fling the door open a short while later and come at my head with the thick handle of a broomstick or her high-heeled shoes. I'd wait twenty minutes, sometimes more, until I heard her exit the apartment. As I waited, I wiped the oozing gashes on my arms with spit. My skin stung like acid. Furious crimson welts popped up, as red as her face had been when she'd inflicted the damage.

I couldn't imagine what the neighbours must have thought of the reverberation of fighting that came from our apartment. Then again, screaming matches between husbands and wives, parents and kids, were as rampant as loud music, the scent of pot in the alleyway or spray paint in the stairwells, and nobody would ever consider calling the cops on their neighbours for fear of retribution.

Every day I told myself I'd made the right choice by refusing Mrs. Persad's offer. Who knew which group home I'd end up in? Some of the girls at Browning complained that there were far worse places out there. What if she dispatched me to the same kind of foster home I'd just run away from? No, it was better to be on my own. All I had to do was steer clear of the bitch and I could come and go as I pleased. Not that I had anywhere in particular to go, but I liked having the option open, just in case. And now that I had the Heritage Front, this freedom came in handy.

The next few months were mundane; I slept in and watched TV all day long. It was one of those shows, specifically a Geraldo Rivera segment featuring white supremacists, that gave me the idea to reach out to others who shared the anger brewing within me. One of the men on Geraldo was being interviewed via satellite from Toronto. He was a "reverend" in an organization that called itself the Church of the Creator and had its headquarters in North Carolina. COTC had been created by Ben Klassen, a one-time Ontario resident who penned a manifesto he called The White Man's Bible, which the young Torontonian was holding.

"All we want is the freedom to celebrate our European heritage," said the guy who was introduced as Rev. Eric Hawthorne but whose real name I later found out was George Burdi. He was the lead singer of a racist rock band called RaHoWa, which stood for Racial Holy War. "Just like every other minority who gets their own special month to celebrate their ethnicity. We just want the same equal rights for whites."

The screen flashed to a piece of their propaganda flyers for a few seconds, enough time for me to scrawl down the address of the organization's post office box. At the end of the show, I impulsively jotted a quick note requesting more information, stuffed it into an envelope and walked it to the mailbox before I could lose my nerve.

Over the next couple of weeks I waited with trepidation, regretting my rash decision to write those people. I thought about all the movies I'd seen with Ku Klux Klan and neo-Nazi characters, dreading the possibility that some goose-stepping skinhead would show up at my door. What if they were really radical? What if they didn't want to let girls into their group? By the time a week went by, I was mad at myself for having written them. I decided to forget about the whole thing.

And then the reply came.

The tone of the letter was warm and friendly. It praised me for my desire to know more. Enclosed were the address and telephone number of a Canadian organization that would provide me with information, an organization with the conservative, unassuming name of Heritage Front. After a couple of days I gathered the nerve to dial their hotline. A middle-aged man's voice boomed out, "Thank you for calling the Heritage Front, Canada's premier organization for the advancement of European people. Please leave a message after the tone and we will contact you shortly."

It took me another week to decide if I should leave a message. But now, after having met Wolfgang and seen how nice he was to me, I was glad I did.

SEVEN

FORESHADOWS

By the end of 1993, Friday evenings at the Parkway were official Heritage Front nights. The entire back room of the restaurant was taken with skinheads and neo-fascists, all competing to out-do each other in machismo and fervour for the movement. The Parkway had morphed into Berlin in the 1930s, with everyone thinking himself invincible. But when you have an unstable foundation, it's only a matter of time before cracks appear and the façade crumbles, letting a sliver of light to shine through.

On one particular evening I ended up sitting across the table from an intense Serb with a scowl tattooed onto his face. The other guys called him Zvonimir. The conversation drifted from talking about the escalating war in the former Yugoslav republic, back to the excitement of planning for the next rally. As people got drunker, the numbers dwindled. Soon there was nobody next to us. That's when Zvonimir leaned over to me, his black eyes burning like coals:

"Don't listen to them," he rasped. "It's all the same bullshit. I know exactly where you are. I was there once. You think it's all so great, that you're fighting a real war. But guess what? It's all crap, what these guys are saying." His arm swept outwards to include everyone in the room. "They've been talking the same shit for the last twenty years. That the time to act is NOW or else."

The alcohol must have turned him into a bitter drunk. He snorted and took a long drag of his cigarette, sucking the nicotine into his lungs (it would be another decade before smoking was banned in indoor establishments). I decided to interject just as he cut me off again.

"Let me tell you something. I was just like you, real eager to prove myself. I'm only telling you this 'cause you remind me of myself back then – all that energy, wanting so badly to make a difference." He pulled his chair closer and lowered his voice. "I'd decided that I'd had just about enough of all that talk – because that's all there is, you know, just talk and no action. I thought that if I did more, if I *acted*, people would respect me. So one night me and a few friends got some spray-paint and went to do over a couple of synagogues. We got into a car and went from place to place, using the same spray-can all over town. We sprayed swastikas and things like *White Power* and *Smash ZOG*. We were totally wasted, falling over ourselves drunk and making a lot of noise but we didn't care, we were invincible. Then the cops came after us."

He stared off into space. His eyes became glossy. "My friends ran, and I got caught. I spent a year in jail over that. I was just about your age. Stupid as fuck. I had no clue what it would be like to do time. And you wanna know what happened?"

I didn't, but he would not wait for an invitation.

"Nobody cared. Everybody I thought was my friend just disappeared. Didn't give a shit about me. The rest of the outside world forgot I existed. All those comrades, and not one of them wrote me a letter. Here's an idea – go ask your pal Wolfgang how many of his friends came to visit him in prison. The lines they're feeding you, kid, are all bullshit. Once you get in trouble for them, they drop you. They don't care about you."

"Wolfgang's not like that," I said, trying to remain calm. It pissed me off that a guy like him would show up at our meeting only to share his sour grapes views. "The Heritage Front is all about making progressive changes…."

Zvonimir snorted as he put out his cigarette. "Heritage Front, Nationalist Party, they're all the same. Bear that in mind. They all say how noble it is to sacrifice yourself for the Cause. They cheer at rallies and praise Bob Matthews, the Order and the POWs rotting in jail now, and maybe if we're lucky they'll throw in a buck into a donation jar for their defense fund…and then what do they do? They go back home, get drunk and forget. Until the next rally. You go ask any 'POW' how many letters of support they really get. And let's not forget Matthews – all that wooing and ahhing over him – what of him now? He's dead. Where's the glory in that?"

"Why are you here tonight then?" I asked him in annoyance. "If, according to you, everybody's just bullshitting anyway?"

He refused to answer, the dark look on his face a clear indication that our conversation was over.

As usual, Wolfgang drove me home later that night. "Something bothering you?" he asked as he pulled over outside my building. I told him what Zvonimir said and he looked irritated. "That guy was never '*in*' the first place. He was on the fringe of the movement, him and his skinhead buddies doing their own thing. Since he didn't have that many friends to begin with, no wonder nobody visited him in the slammer. Who'd want to be associated with a criminal element? Zvonimir knew what he was doing but he was stupid and got caught. Now he's just bitter."

Wolfgang threw his head back and laughed. "I mean, who goes around spray-painting a freaking synagogue anyway? All it does is give the Jews sympathy and detract from our cause. Makes us look like loony-bins. But if you're hell-bent on doing something like that, don't get caught. Shit, what with having to serve that much time, he could've done something a lot better...."

EIGHT

DER BUNKER

I watched the Parkway from the distance, scanning the cars parked along the curb to make sure none of the regulars had arrived early. Satisfied at last, I pulled my hoodie over my head and bolted across the road. I swung open the pub door, walked in and made my way briskly toward the washroom at the back.

I leaned over the sink and splashed cold water on my face. My reflection in the mirror caught me off-guard: heavy circles around my eyes, so dark they looked as though someone had punched me, an effect not to be confused with the welt that still lingered high on my left cheekbone, a parting gift from my mother. A rat's nest of dishevelled hair framed my face, completing the wretched tableau. I looked like a meth-head. That was what sleeping on a bench in Allen Gardens did to you. To top it off, a chill now steeped in my chest, threatening to turn into a cough.

Loud voices pierced through the wall, announcing the arrival of the Front members milling in for the regular Friday meeting. I smoothed down my hair with water, took a deep breath and exited the washroom, taking my place along the row of tables. I could only hope that my clothes didn't reek.

Wolfgang was already at the head table, but when he saw me he got up and walked around to my end. He touched the shoulder of the girl sitting next to me. "Mind if we trade seats?" She scuttled away and he sank into her chair, turning to me.

"What's going on?"

"Nothing."

"Bull. Is something wrong?"

I shook my head. "Not unless you count living on the street as wrong."

"Fuck." He frowned at me. "Why didn't you call me?"

"And say what? I'm not your problem."

"We take care of our own," he said matter-of-factly, in a heavy voice that prompted instant guilt. "Let me think," he mused, scratching his goatee. "I'm gonna introduce you to Ernst Zundel. He's only ten minutes from your place. I can't promise that he'll let you stay there but I imagine he'll put you to good use."

I hesitated. "Who's that?"

Long pause. Wolfgang cleared his throat. "You haven't heard of Ernst Zundel?"

Clearly this was a major faux-pas. "Uh, maybe I just forgot," I scrambled.

"Ernst is a worldwide celebrity, a crusading champion of our time. He's a famous publisher of right-wing information, originally from Bavaria."

Wolfgang's conciliatory tone made me feel so stupid I wanted to sink through the ground. "Back in Germany he suffered a great deal of persecution from Jewish lobbying groups who tried to shut him down. He's been in Canada for the last twenty years." Wolfgang shook his head in disgust. "Did you know that in Germany it's illegal to question the Holocaust? Can you *imagine*?"

If it came down to a choice between sleeping on a wet park bench for another night, trying to dodge the pimps who always roamed around looking for fresh runaway meat, or crash in Hitler's own bunker, there was no question that I'd opt for the latter.

"I'll let him know to expect you," Wolfgang said.

The tall, three-story century-old brick townhouse at 206 Carlton Street had wrought-iron grills covering all its high-arching windows. I stepped through a black iron gate and proceeded up a short, narrow path to ring the doorbell, all too conscious of the unblinking eye of a video monitor mounted on the roof right above the front entrance.

The intercom let out some unintelligible static. I waved to the rolling camera I saw propped inside the lobby door. "I'm Elisse," I said. "Wolfgang sent me."

A sandy-haired middle-aged man sporting a matching moustache buzzed me in and introduced himself as Jürgen. *Wait in the lobby*, he said, pressing another intercom button to let Ernst I'd arrived.

Reminiscent of an office, the reception area was plastered with all kinds of posters, most of them printed in German. Beyond the front desk I saw five black-and-white monitors that reflected five different shots of the building entrance, side and back alleys. I'd never seen this sort of security set-up. *To think all this is going on in someone's townhouse.*

Heavy footsteps descending the stairs made me look up.

"So *you're* Elisse," a balding, portly man beamed at me. "Wolfgang has told me lots of good things about you."

He was well into his fifties, with thinning hair, and wore a knitted sweater and fuzzy slippers. With a ruddy, rotund face and lively blue eyes, Ernst Zundel was far from the frail senior citizen I'd pictured. He looked about as Germanic as I pictured a German to be, complete with gold-rimmed glasses and the belly of an Oktoberfest gnome. He stared at me expectantly, a friendly smile playing on his face. I couldn't help but smile in return.

"Hi, Mr. Zundel," I said, my discomfort over the cameras starting to rescind.

He waved a hand in the air. "Call me Ernst. No need for formalities, we're all *kameraden* here. So I hear you were born in Europe?"

Ernst kept up the quizzing even as he directed me into a pair of house slippers. I slid my feet into them and tried to answer his questions as rapidly as they were being fired – how old was I, what my political allegiances were, how did I come into the movement. I didn't know what he was looking for, but it was becoming clearer by the second that my answers would determine my fate. Although I'd already made up my mind to go back to my mother's apartment, having Ernst so close by would give me a place to escape to when things got ugly.

Ernst finally flashed a smile and proclaimed, "Today's a remarkable day – I have a new addition to my Bunker brood. A bona-fide little legionnaire."

The blank look on my face made him catch on that I was clueless. "You don't know about Romanian Legionnaires? About Codreanu? *Mein Gott*, what a shame."

My ignorance seemed to astonish him. I had to be educated at once; naturally, this monumental task could befall only someone as astute as himself. "Romanians made a huge contribution to our cause," he said. "Did you know that the oil that fuelled German tanks came from your homeland? My dear girl, it is gravely important that you learn Romania was one of our allies until 1944!"

He parked me at the long table that ran down the centre of his front library room. "And here we are," he said, pointing to several stacks of old newspapers piled along the table. "This is what I need you to do for me today – sift through these papers, clip out relevant articles, and organize them by categories. Save anything related to crimes committed by non-whites, refugees and anything to do with Jews. And of course, anything that mentions yours truly."

It was a pretty easy job. Ernst shuffled away and I furiously set upon decimating the stacks. After that, I stamped the return address on outgoing envelopes. By the time I'd clipped the articles and stamped over two hundred letters, my fingers were black with printer ink, my muscles were sore and a pounding headache was starting to build behind my eyes. A quick glance at my watch told me I had been at it for over four hours. I pushed back from the table.

Ernst's voice rang out behind me. "Let me give you a tour of the place."

He started to tell me that the room where I'd been working contained much more than just out-of-print books and Hitler-era propaganda. It was one of the few libraries on earth to document revisionist material from across the globe. Bookshelves lined the walls, stacked floor to ceiling with volumes and thick file folders. Some of the more intriguing brochures involved the hypothesis that Hitler had survived the war and was in an underground bunker somewhere at the North Pole, emerging only to fly around in UFO crafts invented by elusive Nazi scientists.

Pinned over the entrance, a black and white poster declared, *Arbeit Macht Frei.*

Ernst got a kick out of it. "It's German for Work Shall Set You Free –like the slogan they hung over the gates of Auschwitz. Did I work you hard today or what?"

He seemed very pleased with himself over that joke and I got the feeling many a visitor before me had heard it. He pointed to another sign hung next to the lobby that warned everyone not to discuss the work done inside the house. "It's a precaution," Ernst said. "I've been legally muzzled, ordered to cease all publishing and mailings. This is why everyone who comes here has to use extreme caution. Thousands of people from all over the world count on me to send them my newsletter. So keep your lips sealed about what we do here, *ja*?"

He pulled an invisible zipper across his lips to emphasize his point and watched me until I nodded that I understood. Then he crossed in front of me, leading the way upstairs. On the wall to the right of the stairwell another couple of posters screamed out, GERMANS! STOP APOLOGIZING FOR THE THINGS YOU DID NOT DO! and *Achtung! The Thought Police is Coming*! I didn't understand the latter one yet, but I wouldn't read Orwell for another month.

The home's only kitchen was on the second level, starting at the top of the stairs. Branching to the left was a generously-sized dining room where I could take my breaks and have dark rye bread and knackwurst if I was hungry. Ernst's own quarters, as well as a spare bedroom dedicated to his attorney Doug Christie were on the third floor but he didn't want to show me around up there just yet. "Let's have a sandwich in the kitchen," he suggested.

We chatted over sauerkraut and goose-liver pâté sandwiches, and when we were done he insisted on taking me to the tiny basement alcove that held the metal-framed cot where I would sleep if I needed to rest. "It's the least I can do for all your hard work," he said.

He stood in the doorway, continuing to watch me as I looked around curiously. "I hope you'll be happy in the Bunker. That's what everybody calls my cozy old fortress – the Bunker. You'll always have a home here, with your own people."

"I'm sure I will," I beamed.

He started to turn away. Then, almost as an afterthought, he swept me up into a grandfatherly embrace. "We need more young people like you. You're our brightest hope for the future."

Later that day Ernst introduced me to Hans, a tall, aquiline-nosed blond German printer in his late twenties who hardly spoke English. He hailed from South America – Argentina, Uruguay or Brazil, I couldn't remember which. We communicated through an odd mixture of sign language and grunts, and because of the language barrier I never did find out precisely why he was always on the move. He was too young to be a war criminal.

Hans was a little strange but amicable enough. He had the palest blue eyes I'd ever seen, icy-cold as the sharp edge of a knife. When he caught me staring, I felt I owed him an explanation. "They'd have picked you for a poster boy," I said. "Back in the day."

His lips curled up, exposing a set of teeth as white as a snow-capped alpine range. He'd heard that one before. "*Danke*."

Hans was implacably patient whenever he was demonstrating what he wanted me to do. Most of the time he had me labouring alongside him in the basement. Hitler peered at us from framed portraits on the walls as we folded pamphlets, chapbooks and booklets that would be distributed to every continent. It was hard work, but Ernst was right: it strengthened my muscles and taught me about underground printing presses.

I liked to stand behind Hans and watch as he rolled up his sleeves to his elbows and single-handedly produced leaflets using manual-cranking machinery that looked as though it dated back to the 1940s. I leaned against the Bunker wall, crossed my arms and reflected on how similar we were to all those groups of socialist youth rebels who had conspired against Hitler's regime.

They too, had huddled around secret printing presses in dimly-lit basements, churning out leaflets that were intended to educate the masses, to change the world. They too, knew the risks they were taking when they embarked on producing propaganda and documents for those escaping wartime Germany. They too, had been fuelled by the vision of a utopian, working-class world that could only be achieved through bloodshed, struggle and sacrifice.

What was the difference between them and myself, other than an ideological line drawn in the sand? Like them, I was a child of revolution, nurtured on ideas and political discourse. Like them, we were now being persecuted by a government that refused to allow us freedom of thought. We had no choice but to fight back. Goethe's words repeated in my mind, *None are more hopelessly enslaved than those who falsely believe they are free.*

As Hans went about his business, it felt like time had folded itself into quarters, like the pages of the freshly-printed propaganda churned out of that basement on Carlton Street. Hans first set about the metal letters of the typeface, which would imprint the words onto the paper. After that, he added the thick black ink to the typeface and pressed the blank sheet into place, fastened underneath the belts at the top and bottom of the cylinder. He turned the crank carrying the cylinder, pressed his foot firmly upon the lower lever, turned the crank in the reverse direction, rotating the cylinder, and then somehow, magically, removed the freshly-printed sheet and laid it to dry on one of the adjoining tables.

Within a week I had the run of the house and met the rest of Ernst's brood, the core group of helpers who considered *Der Bunker* their second home. When you came in the door, you had to get past Jürgen Newmann first. He manned the video monitors and spliced wartime film reels, transferring the ancient footage to videotape formats that would broadcast censored material all over the world. He was forever busy, pen behind ear, unlit cigarette dangling from the corner of his mouth (Ernst had prohibited all unhealthy behaviour such as smoking or drinking spirits inside his house).

Put aside his beliefs and Alfred was an ordinary, white-haired little man in his early eighties, complete with a shaky walk and a comb-over. He wore old-man trousers and a knitted vest and liked to poke about from one room to another, busy with some never-ending task. I always watched Alfred with a faint sense of panic, thinking he might keel over at any minute, but no – he always, miraculously, kept on ticking.

He liked to invent new, mostly-useless contraptions like the magnetic broom he was now working on to pick up loose staples on the floor. He was absolutely loyal to Ernst and would have laid what little remained of his life on the line for him, no questions asked. Ernst knew this and let Alfred stay there permanently. I had a feeling he had his own tiny, mouse-trap room somewhere, not that he ever slept.

Alfred was obsessed with the horoscope to the point of madness. In fact, the second question he'd asked me after we first met (the first being my name) was *When were you born?* "December 17th," I'd answered. He responded with a short grunt. "Rasputin's murder. Stalin's birthday." He tilted his head to the side and looked me up and down suspiciously, as though trying to decide if I was related to either of the men. I shifted from foot to foot, cringing under his gaze.

Other regulars included recurring guests like Munich neo-Nazi Ewald Althans and Ernst's snobbish girlfriend Anne, whom we all called Eva Braun behind her back. Famous for having made a half-hour speech extolling the virtue of coffee enemas, she had a habit of enunciating in a crusty English accent exactly what she thought was wrong with everybody. Jürgen hated her. There was also fiftyish, cow-eyed Joyceline, who wore the same smelly dress for the entire two years I knew her, and Frau Klannert, an elderly German widow who drove in from out of town to bring Ernst preserves and envelopes of cash, incurring Anne's furious glances.

Ernst's most surprising visitor was a giggly Orthodox Jewish boy around my age who dropped in every couple of weeks in full Hasidic garb, only to be taken upstairs for private meetings with Ernst. "You see my little Jewish friend here," Ernst boasted, wrapping his arm around his skinny shoulders. "He's one of the few good Jews out there. David *knows* what happened in the war, and now I have it on tape. Now I have proof that Jews know it was all a hoax."

The Bunker was bigger than it seemed from the outside, filled with nooks and crannies where you could easily get lost. I had no doubt that if I took a wrong turn at the top of the stairs, I might accidentally trigger a secret trap door. Alternately, if I shifted a statue or book imperceptibly out of place I might prompt a false wall or bookcase to slide open and disclose a hidden room with all the world's greatest secrets locked within, where everything from Illuminati to Nostradamus prophecies were splayed out beneath thick panes of glass.

As if to complete the fantasy, Ernst never stayed in the townhouse alone. If Jürgen was away over the weekend, he'd call Alfred or even Hans upstairs. Somebody always had to sleep on the same floor as him. If for whatever reason he was forced to run an errand, we had to stay behind and keep watch. The Bunker was never to remain empty. Ernst had good reason to guard it like a hawk: all his life's labour was inside those four walls, decades' worth of valuable papers and rare books produced by the Third Reich. In that sense, I realized that the Bunker was an extended part of himself.

By the second week, I'd become Ernst's errand girl. It began one afternoon with an instant craving for corned beef that he just couldn't put out of his mind. "Be a dear, run to the corner store and pick me up a tin of the stuff," he said, pressing a five-dollar bill in my hand. "That should cover it, and keep the change."

After that, I started going to the post office to do the mail-outs. He liked that I was responsible with money and remembered to ask for receipts, and that I tolerated his rambling at lunchtime, when he chattered about his boyhood in the heart of the Black Forest. "Just around the corner from where our Adolf was born," he reminded me.

A giggle escaped my lips. I instantly covered my mouth, but it was too late.

"And what's so funny, *fraulein*?" he asked indignantly.

"You tell me that every day," I said, trying to keep from laughing.

"Enough out of you, smartass, " he snapped, pushing the Dimpflmeier rye at me. "Have another slice, you'll need your strength. You're on yard work duty this afternoon."

He spread his favourite goose liver pâté and topped it with a spoonful of homemade cherry jam. "Frau Klannert brought me an extra jar on Sunday. You've got to try it before Hans or Drew polish it off."

That month, thanks to Hans' hard work, Ernst's *Power* newsletter was ready to go. Everybody was in a mad rush to collate and stuff it into a mountain of envelopes. The newsletter was Ernst's baby, a monthly summary of the latest neo-fascist activities, and it went out all over the world. There were two lists of mailing addresses – A for German and B for English, the two languages *Power* was printed in. The newsletter only consisted of a couple double-sided pages of fairly small print (to keep the postage costs down). Most of the news was made up of Ernst's latest court proceedings and his urgent need for donations; however, it managed to roll in enough cash to keep Samisdat publications running comfortably for months.

"We need money to arm ourselves," Ernst said during one of our lunch breaks. "To pay Doug Christie's fees when he represents me in court. The Jews are getting aggressive. But I tell you, the only way I'm leaving this country is feet first."

Although a permanent resident, Ernst had never been granted Canadian citizenship, something he was constantly reminded of by scores of lobbying groups made up of concentration camp survivors and their adult children who frequently called for his deportation back to Germany, where he could be put on trial for denying the Holocaust. "That goddamn Canadian Jewish Congress are the scum of the earth," Ernst said, shaking his head in disgust. "Nothing better to do than spew their venom against me, trying to get me kicked out of Canada."

He paused, glanced over to me, and his anger seemed to diffuse. "You know, Elisse, it's not that I don't want to see my homeland again," he explained. "It's a beautiful country filled with lost, confused people who'd rather put me in jail than give me my right to freedom of speech. But there's plenty I miss of it."

"You know what *I* miss?" I asked, out of the blue. "Snowdrops. In Romania we had real spring – blooming trees and everything – but here the seasons shift so quickly from winter to summer that there's never enough time for snowdrops to grow."

He smiled, full of nostalgia. "*Ja*, in Bavaria snowdrops filled the forests by end of February. They broke right through the ice. I used to pick them for my mother on my way back from school. Ah, those were the days. You could walk around and never be afraid of being snatched by a child molester."

"And I miss…I miss my old schoolbooks. Writing with a fountain pen. Reading all the classics by the time I was ten because there weren't any other books around."

Ernst leaned forward, a conspiratorial glint in his eye. "The best book of all was Winnetou – ever heard of it?"

"No way," I exclaimed. "That was your favourite? Mine too!"

A grin broke on his face. "You see, they're not politically-correct enough nowadays. It ruffles Indian feathers so they will deprive this generation of Karl May's works; hell, even Tom Sawyer's been pulled from school libraries. But you and me," he reached over to grasp my elbow, "we know better, don't we? We can appreciate the adventures of the Wild West. If you think about it, it's not that different from the age we're living in today – you hunt or get hunted. It's as simple as that."

NINE

"Of course people died," Ernst was saying. "It *was* war, after all – people die in wars, don't kid yourself. Supplies were scarce and many people starved to death. Young German soldiers died too. The *real* holocaust is what happened to all those poor boys, the mass raping of German women by the Soviet army. Of course, *that* stays covered up."

I took a nibble of my rye toast while Ernst spread a thick layer of pate over his bread and topped it with a slice of bratwurst. "Was your father drafted in World War Two, Elisse?"

I shook my head. "No, he couldn't be conscripted on account that he was deaf. But a lot of men in his village had to. Very few of them made it back. I remember my grandmother telling me about a neighbour whose son was so afraid he'd get killed in battle that he went out back to the wood-chopping block, put his left hand on it, and cut it off with an axe."

Ernst nodded as though the story was intimately familiar. "You see how many cowards are out there? Men pretended they were crippled or mentally diseased to get out of service. And the funny thing is, it's always the cowards who make it back alive, after their entire battalions get killed and there's nobody left to tell that they ran off in the heat of battle."

When I pushed away from the table and stood up, ready to go back downstairs to help Hans at the printing press, but Ernst put his hand on my arm. "Not yet. Today I have something important I need your assistance with."

Intrigued, I followed him down the stairs to the library. He gestured for me to take a seat while he sifted through the bookshelves, inspecting spines, and plucked out several dusty volumes. He deposited them in front of me and leafed through one of the books. When he found what he was looking for, he plopped it open.

Scores of grainy black and white images filled the pages, photographs of muddy trenches and haystacks. Upon closer scrutiny, I realized they were bodies: lots of pale, naked bodies, dumped on top of each other. I caught my breath.

"Look at this stuff," Ernst said, shaking his head. "They accuse the German people of mass-murdering six million Jews, but where are they?"

He leaned over my shoulder and pointed at every photograph. "Look closely and count these bodies. Where's the blood if they were beaten? Do you see any gunshot wounds? These people clearly starved to death. *Why*? The allies kept dropping bombs on the food convoys - that's what killed these prisoners."

He pushed a notepad and pencil at me. "I want you to go through these books and count every dead prisoner you find. Write down the book, page number and how many bodies you counted. Make sure to count them twice, in case you get it wrong the first time."

Why did he make me do this, I wondered after he ambled off. He was the worldwide expert on the Holocaust hoax, wasn't he? This chore didn't make me feel as productive as cutting up press clippings or folding pamphlets; rather, it was exhausting and monotonous. Depressing, even.

After several minutes of trying to make out individual dead bodies from the masses of inert limbs stacked atop one another, my eyes began to blur. I rubbed them, trying to shake off the double vision. A curious numbness set over me. I was no longer counting bodies, but sticks of straw that made up one haystack after another. The dizziness inside my head was replaced by the constant hum of turning pages. I saw only the black and white dot matrix inside those pages – nothing above or below the task at hand, nothing remaining of the left or the right.

I covered my face and felt Ernst's heavy paw came to rest on my shoulder. "And how are we doing here?"

"Four hundred sixty-five so far," I answered flatly.

"Where are the thousands? The *millions*? You're telling me there's only an average of a hundred in each picture? I was right, a million people would be impossible. Good girl, keep counting them. Don't take a break until you are done."

He must have heard me sigh under my breath, because when he looked down at my face he added softly, "It's sad, isn't it? How so many people starved to death because the Russians cut off supplies to the camps? So many died, including our young German boys. What could anybody do? Dig graves individually? No, it would have taken too much time. Disease spread extremely fast through the work-camps. They had to bury them like this."

"What happened to their clothing?" I asked.

Ernst clucked in sympathy. "They didn't need them anymore, did they? Whenever a soldier died, if they had strong boots or a thick coat, those things were recycled. That's wartime for you, young lady. Whatever things the dead leave behind, someone else will make use of them. Come, I have something else for you."

We descended the creaky steps to the basement, where he set me up at Jürgen's workstation, next to a stack of videocassettes. "It's part of your education, *fraulein*," he said. People would go to theatres and see these films produced by the Department of Culture."

The first was called *Hitler Youth Quex* and told the story of a young boy who was stabbed to death by a violent group of resistance fighters who had cowardly ambushed him because of his uniform. As he lay bleeding to death on the pavement, he bravely saluted the Fuhrer and started singing the Hitler Youth anthem (which Frau Klannert later taught me to play on Ernst' basement piano, along with the National Socialist battle hymn).

I knew a propaganda film when I saw one, and Ernst didn't make any attempts to hide what I was watching. Propaganda is simply information, he said, that can be used or twisted depending on who is in power. All you can do is try to think for yourself – but in order to separate the truth from the lies, you have to watch these videos.

The series of films were from the late 1930s, stamped with the seal of the German Reich. They depicted Jews as hook-nosed rich jewellers and usurping money-lenders who didn't give any breaks to the starving German working class. Images of Jews were juxtaposed against footage of rats scurrying in city sewers, breeding en masse and always looking for ways to infest their way into poor people's homes. And then there were the pro-eugenics images of disturbed and deformed people languishing in hospitals for the criminally insane.

Ernst came back downstairs an hour later. "Now, what you need to watch is Leni Riefenstahl's *Triumph of the Will*," he said. "*There's* an example of the extraordinary height humanity can reach when mind and body are brought into alignment," he said. "When we celebrate perseverance, rather than fuel a culture of inferiority. Look at how beautiful those young people in the crowd are! How happy they are when they see their Fuhrer!"

TEN

THE REVOLUTION IS COMING

I was helping Hans change the ink plates when Alfred poked his head in the printing room. "Someone's here to see you," he grunted before toddling off with his latest invention.

Standing in the lobby of the Bunker, arms clasped behind his back as he studied the German posters, was Wolfgang. He heard me bouncing up the stairs and turned to me with a grin. "Got a minute? I was on my way to my bailiff office when I thought you might want to come along. Got something to show ya."

I threw a glance toward Jürgen, who never took his eyes off the computer station but with a slight nod of his head indicated I was free to go. Wolfgang handed me my wool coat and held the door open as we slipped into the starless, icy evening, crunching along the front pathway toward his parked car.

As we were getting in, I turned to Wolfgang curiously. "What's going on?"

His teeth flashed in the headlights. "Ever heard of The Turner Diaries?"

I shook my head no, and he grew serious. "It's only the most important book for our movement. More than the Protocols of the Elders of Zion, no matter what Ernst tells you."

My interest was piqued. "What's it about?"

"The Turner Diaries was written by a guy who's been assassinated by secret agents of the state," Wolfgang replied. "It inspired the group I was involved with. We called ourselves The Order, or the Silent Brotherhood – we took the name right out of the novel. It's a blueprint of what's to come." He looked sideways at me, a grave expression shadowing his face. "The race war that will soon engulf the world. Some of the Order guys went so far as to follow the book to a tee – they started doing armored truck robberies, even blew up a black church down south in Alabama. It all went wrong when we started improvising by trying to overthrow Dominica."

"Do you have a copy?"

"It's banned in Canada. How committed are you to the movement?"

"Come on, let me see it," I pestered him. I wanted to read it all the more *because* it was banned. He wouldn't have brought it up only to tease me about it. It wasn't like him.

Finally he relented, as I suspected he would. We were on the expressway when he pulled a slim book out of his inside jacket pocket and prefaced it by saying, "If you want to get anywhere in the racialist movement, you have to know it by heart. The Revolution is real, Elisse. It is coming, and we all have to be prepared."

According to him, the inconspicuous novel whose badly-drawn cover depicted two paramilitaries, a man and a woman, was a prophetic manuscript that contained a code to the Seven Signs leading to the Race War Apocalypse. It would start when the Jew-controlled System, or ZOG (Zionist Occupation Government), pushed us over the edge. Race riots were going to break out in all major cities. A state of utter chaos would descend, precipitated by increased racial tension from forced affirmative action, discrimination against whites and systemized race-mixing.

Society as we knew it would collapse. People would kill each other for food as supplies dwindled. A small group of racialist revolutionaries who had split into independent cells and stocked up armaments in preparation of this event would take over the country. The non-Whites would be disposed of: a small number were to be enslaved for free labour, the rest shipped overseas or eliminated, whichever option was more cost-effective.

"With the Apocalypse will come the glorious moment every racialist in the world has waited for: the Day of the Rope. That's when every traitor, rat and race-mixer will swing from the neck off of every tree and lamppost in the country. This day marks the climax of our Noble Race's struggle against the forces of darkness."

"Is that really going to happen?"

Wolfgang changed lanes, turning south toward the Beaches. His hands were firm on the wheel. "You bet your ass it will. As we speak, people are stockpiling munitions. There's a whole reality you're not aware of, brewing beneath the surface. Your everyday sheep, the nine-to-fivers, have no clue what's really going on in this country. Why do you think we were invited over to Libya? Khadafy *knows* that something major is coming, and he wants to be on the right side of the bed when that happens."

I fell silent. Images of corpses swinging from trees and lampposts floated in my head. As though he could read my mind, Wolfgang added, "And don't think for a minute that other paramilitaries don't know the Big One is coming. Islamic fundamentalists and black separatists are training and getting guns, just like our side. They share the same objectives – get rid of this Zionist Occupation Government. The question is, who will be victorious in the end? Do *you* want to be on the end of that rope?"

"We don't really have a choice, do we?" I said, watching the multihued array of Toronto's downtown lights flicker past us. "We either have to kill or be killed."

"You got it. But even though your eyes have opened, be careful who you share this with. Watch what you say in public. The official Heritage Front line is we're fighting for White Separation. We just want a separate enclave where we can live homogeneously. And by infiltrating the Reform Party, we're about to take that to the ballot box."

If my nights were spent driving around with Wolfgang, listening to his wild predictions of the Revolution to come, my days – with their orderly, monotonous routine – belonged to Ernst. And inserted in between were the surreal evenings when Ernst's elderly supporters descended *en masse* to the Bunker to hear him give his impassioned speeches.

Several hours before their arrival, I helped to arrange rows of chairs in the basement's great room. The guests had a habit of arriving early, hoping for a chance to chat with Ernst before the meetings got underway. These were among Ernst's most prized donors, some having flown in all the way from Germany to see their hero in person. Their comfort was of utmost importance. I wore my best clothes, tied my hair back with a black ribbon and ushered in each person with a smile. I helped the ladies with their coats, fetched beverages and subsequently faded into the corner, emerging only when someone needed directions to the toilet.

For no apparent reason, some guests liked to break off from the crowd and stand next to me, telling me in conspiratorial whispers that I reminded them of themselves when they were my age. On my first get-together, a white-haired woman with too much eyeliner smiled at me nostalgically. "I pity you, my dear girl. If only you could have been there, in the old days..." Her eyes travelled to the wall, where they lingered on Hitler's framed portrait. "We had such wonderful parades back then...."

A mild irritation came over me. Why did old people always have to see the past, with all its horror and destruction, as some sort of sepia-tinted golden era of order and stability? I bit back a sarcastic remark when a touch fluttered on my shoulder. I turned my head and found myself staring right into Frau Klannert's rheumatic, watery blue eyes. "Elisse, won't you be a dear and play *Horst Wessel Lied* like I taught you?"

I took my place at the piano, took a deep breath and began to pound out the chords to the official Nazi Republic anthem I'd practiced all week.

Gasps of pleasure rose from the crowd. Out of the corner of my eye I glimpsed Frau Klannert take a seat among the chairs in the front row. She clutched the necklace around her neck, not so much to make sure it were still there as to gesture how deeply moved she was. She closed her eyes and tilted her head back, a morbid smile stretching her papery-thin cheeks into a skeleton smile. Her mouth moved silently, and it took me a moment to realize she was singing – yes, singing along with the piano, the words of the national socialist melody imprinted in her memory. Then the man beside her bellowed out the German words and soon most of the guests were singing along.

I had to blink multiple times to shake off the sensation that the room was morphing into something else: a living graveyard, a hideous spectacle of people mourning a lost, untenable youth. As mouths moved mechanically in tune with old Third Reich anthems like soldiers marching in a wartime procession, shrivelled women with too much rouge on their cheeks were once again tight-bodied maidens, their blonde braids twisted into pretzel shapes and tied with cornflower-blue ribbons. Giddy white-haired men in brown coats with leather patches sown on the elbows were transformed into the ruddy-cheeked Hitler Youth they once were.

I had to get some air.

I gestured to Anneliese, Jürgen's girlfriend, to come replace me at the piano, and slipped out of the room unnoticed. I ran up the stairs and burst out into the darkness of the cement walkway. The chilly night wind made me shiver uncontrollably. I crossed my bare arms against my chest, bracing myself against a shaft of cold air. A powerful, unexpected sadness slammed into me and I found myself gulping in air as if I were drowning.

My hand reached up to the wall for support. I glanced upwards, trying to make out some sort of illumination in the night sky, but only the North star remained unshielded by the black clouds that covered the heavens, and it shone cadaver-white, like bone.

The door behind me swung back, and my head snapped to attention.

An elderly man was gawking at me. His wizened face broke into a grin. "*Alo!*" he greeted me in Romanian, startling me. "Nice night, isn't it?"

"Cold, though," I replied.

"So Ernst tells me you're from the old country. Where do you hail from?"

"I was born in Bucharest but I have relatives all over Transylvania."

"Me, I emigrated after the war. Before that, I was in the Iron Guard and served under Codreanu. Highlight of my life. There are Iron Guardsmen all over the world, you know. We keep in touch to this day. There's even a solid network in this country but it's top secret. A secret society," he winked.

The way he was talking, I wondered if they had secret handshakes too, or if they wore dark robes with gold and purple stripes and worshipped obscure Egyptian deities. "Let's go back inside," I said, shivering again. I didn't want him to catch his death out here, not that he showed any indication of being cold himself.

He insisted on holding the door open for me as we stepped back into the foyer. "You're fortunate to be so close to Ernst," the old man added. "Did you know he supplies all of Europe with his publications? Twenty-five years he's been fighting the Jews. A hero to National Socialists worldwide, that's what he is."

I nodded.

"Me, I do what I can. I own a paper factory and bring supplies whenever he needs them. But what we *really* need are young people.

Strong, solid Romanians who'll carry on after we're gone. My own son has taken up the flame. All the former Guards are sending their children into the old country to help with the underground. Soon we'll seize back power. By no means should you think the Iron Guard dead. *Never*! We'll have to meet again. It would be a pity to lose track of each other. Remember, every single man and woman counts." He patted me on the cheek just like Ernst liked to do, then shuffled off to rejoin the party. I snuck into the spare bedroom, sat on the edge of the cot and put my face in my hands. I couldn't pinpoint exactly the source of the weight in my chest, but it was cavernous, draining.

The image of my grandmother flashed before my eyes. I was nine years old and had just witnessed her arguing with my father. She vehemently opposed his decision to emigrate to Canada, wanting him to remain in Bucharest and keep his apartment. He, on the other hand, refused to listen to her pleas and stormed out of the room even as she clutched desperately at his shirt, stumbling over herself, a feeble, eighty-five year old woman whose only boy was about to leave her.

I'd ran to her as the door slammed behind my father. I grasped her elbow and steadied her into a chair, aching at the sight of her tear-stricken face. A litany of curse words came out of her mouth, half in Romanian, half in Hungarian, the language she had been educated in as a girl. I'd never heard her swear before, and that rocked me back on my feet.

"No-good loser, just like his father," she sputtered. "Lousy yid."

"Baba, what's a yid?" I asked. When she didn't answer I tugged on her sleeve again. "What's a yid? What's a yid? What's a —"

Her damp eyes, flashing with rage, turned to me. "Shut up, Eliza." Her shoulders quivered uncontrollably. Her hand shook as she reached up to smooth the white hair that had fallen out of her bun. "Bastards, the both of them. I wasted my youth working the fields all by myself to put that child through school in Bucharest so he could have the future his father cheated him out of. And for what? To throw me away just like *they* did, because Papa wouldn't give me my dowry. I wasn't good enough for them, those goddamned Debrecen yids."

"Why not?" I asked, my brain trying to process her story. "What happened?"

"Enough of this. *Enough*," my grandmother said, pushing me away as she stood, reached for her cane and hobbled toward the door.

Once her hand was on the doorknob, she turned to me. "Don't ever ask me about this again. *Ever*."

Nearly a decade later, the memory of her expression was still powerful enough to knock the wind out of me. I slumped down on the bed and buried my face in the pillow so nobody in the room next door, where the party was still in full bloom, could hear me weeping.

ELEVEN

INITIATION

One day Hans was there and then he was gone, back to whatever Nazi war criminal outpost in South America he hailed from. Besides the fact that there was a lot more work to do, his sudden exit haunted me for days on end. "It's bugging me that he took off without saying goodbye," I complained to Wolfgang after he came to pick me up in the afternoon for my driver's lesson, which seldom went beyond driving around the block or doing figure eights in a desolated parking lot. "Do you think he got into trouble?"

Wolfgang threw his head back and laughed. "What gives you that impression? You know he was a peculiar fellow. He could just as easily have decided he'd had enough of Ernst's *Arbeit Macht Frei* and flown the coop."

I shrugged, coming to an abrupt stop at the lights. "I guess."

Wolfgang's hand flew forward, bracing himself against the dashboard. "Jesus, Elisse, turn in here," he pointed to the nearest lot, annoyed. "I think that's enough for today. Isn't it time you told me where you want to go this weekend?"

Wolfgang had found out about my birthday completely by accident. We'd been talking about me applying for a firearms license and I'd said, 'Oh well, after next week I only have one more year to wait!', to which his face took on a stunned expression. "You're turning seventeen? Why didn't you say something?"

"I'm telling you now," I said. "It's no big deal."

He scoffed. "Well, we can't have that. I'll get a bunch of people together and we'll all go out and celebrate. Where would you like to go?"

"I don't know. I never go to restaurants."

"How about East European? In honour of your Romanian heritage."

As promised, he picked me up Saturday night and drove to a Hungarian restaurant in the west end. "Pick anything you want," he instructed me, perusing the menu.

I went with the schnitzel, and sat awkwardly while taking in the linen tablecloth and intimate setting. It made me feel like we were on a date. Maybe Wolfgang saw more potential in me than I could deliver on, I thought. I didn't want to turn into one big disappointment.

"I thought Nicola was coming," I said, glancing toward the door. Her absence, coupled with tonight's fancy setting, was starting to make me antsy.

"Her boyfriend has the car," he replied. "When he's done running errands he'll pick her up and meet us here. She's really looking forward to the paprikash."

Our schnitzel platters arrived. He picked up the sliver of lemon on the side of his plate and squeezed it, shaking lemon juice all over his cutlet. He licked his fingers clean one by one, deliberately, then picked up the knife and fork and met my eyes.

"You shouldn't let yourself be easily impressed, Elisse. Everybody wants to be Fuhrer. In any revolution throughout history, Marxist or Fascist, the freedom-fighters liberate the people and right away start bickering among themselves over who's going to take power. Before you know it you've got a whole new dictatorship going on, with one party ruling with an iron fist and a new batch of freedom-fighters plotting how they're going to take over. Funny, isn't it?"

"That's what they did in Romania," I said, stuffing a piece of schnitzel in my mouth. "The communists sent the king into exile, took over and started a dictatorship. So then they had to be disposed of, and everybody's turned ultra-religious again and wants the monarchy back. It's like a yoyo."

"So you're picking up what I'm laying down." He nudged me. "You think you're gonna usurp me someday?"

I scoffed. "I hate being in the public eye."

"Public speaking skills can be learned," he said, reaching for his drink. "But that fire you've got in you, that defiance – nobody can create it if it's not inside you already. That's the spark that fuels revolutions."

"Do you think they're ready for a woman to lead the far right?"

He put the glass back down, pursing his lips. "Perhaps not now. But you're still a teenager. When you're thirty, they *will* be ready. And we'll need *educated* women to lead, not ones who dropped out of eighth grade and had half a dozen babies. But if you want to be a role model you need to do both, don't you?"

The look I gave him prompted him to laugh. "Tough cookie, aren't ya? Listen to me, I'm telling you like it is – Machiavelli had it right. Keep your friends close and your enemies closer. In any movement, everybody pretends to be your friend until they have enough dirt on you to take over. Stupid cliques sprout up at the drop of a hat, complete with post-office boxes. But guess what? Behind all the smoke and mirrors there's just a fat guy in his parents' basement. Never allow yourself to be impressed by bullshitters, not until you see for yourself what someone's made of."

As our eyes met over the flickering orange flame of the candle, it struck me that I was seeing the real Wolfgang for the first time. More than a mentor determined to shape my political education, he was a user. A pragmatist who could, in one glance, calculate the value of any human being in terms of what they had to offer him.

How strange, I thought, that no matter how charming he was at Heritage Front meetings, he always saw skinheads as the muscle of the movement, not the brains. They were the ones on the front lines during a street fight, getting hurt, getting arrested. But you could never trust one of them to lead a political organization.

"You take what you can get," Wolfgang confessed. "Even crazy old kooks like John Ross Taylor who ramble on about astrology and UFOs. You don't turn people away because you never know where they might be useful. In a political movement you need bodies, you need votes. The trick is to sift through the muck and pluck out those who can serve the greatest purpose to your cause. You find them, hold onto them, and you run with it."

He reached into his pocket, fished around a bit, and came up with a tiny black box. He pushed it across the tablecloth at me. "I hope you like it."

It looked an awful lot like a jewellery box. My eyes grew wide. "I...you shouldn't –"

Wolfgang shook his head. "Don't refuse. We all pitched in on it and we hope you'll take it as a sign of our appreciation."

I scooped the box in my palms. At Wolfgang's urging, I flipped up the lid.

It was a gold ring. A heart wearing a crown, held together by two tiny hands.

"Go on, try it on," Wolfgang prodded me.

It glided on my finger like a dream. I said nothing. My cheeks burned red. *A gold ring!*

"It's a Claddagh, a traditional Irish ring. If you aim the heart toward you, it means you're taken. If the heart points outward, you're free."

I looked down at my finger. Unaware of the tradition, I'd placed it with the heart facing me. Wolfgang seemed pleased; I *was* taken. Taken by the Heritage Front, by himself.

He picked up his glass and prompted me to do the same. We clinked them.

"Happy birthday, Elisse. You're a unique asset to the movement."

Within a half hour everyone else had arrived: Nicola, her boyfriend Peter Mitrevski and Grant Bristow. My new family. They cheered me on and told me how remarkable I was for having progressed so rapidly in only three months. Nobody asked why I was with them tonight rather than partying with others closer to my age. Their silence on the issue was comforting; it required no explanations about my home life.

Halfway through dinner I tore into more presents that Grant had paid for: a delicate 10k gold bracelet, a blouse and skirt set. They must had noticed I didn't have any nice clothes.

"If the dress doesn't fit just give it back the next time we meet and we'll replace it," Wolfgang said near the end of the night, as Grant was handing his American Express to the waitress to cover everyone's bill. "Grant has the receipt."

Like an obedient daughter, I spent a lot of time at 2 North Drive that winter. The low-rise, mustard-bricked building was home to several people in the Heritage Front core. I would drop by Wolfgang's apartment on the second floor first to sort incoming mail and read him messages I planned to record for the hotline. Then we would go downstairs, where Donna Elliot made the best lasagna for her holiday parties. Nicola and Peter always showed up, as well as

Jack and Sabrina Prins, an elderly German couple close to Ernst Zundel. Despite his countless knee surgeries and the fact that he could barely walk, Jack's greatest pride came from having won an Olympic skiing medal for Nazi Germany.

Max French's apartment was on the third floor. Max had run in the mayoral race for Scarborough as a candidate for the Nationalist Party of Canada, advocating for a European homeland, and came in third place. He was one of the twenty Nationalist Party members who had travelled to Libya in 1989 on the 20th anniversary of Khadafy's revolution, hoping to score some cash to fund the white racialist movement in Canada, and followed Wolfgang into the Heritage Front after the mass exodus from Don Andrews' leadership.

Max shared custody of a cute three-year old girl with an ex-wife who was now carrying Don Andrews' child. Although the red-headed single father wasn't a Scotsman by blood, he fancied himself as one. He bought a kilt and had grown a bushy red bagpipers' moustache which he jelled and combed with a pink Barbie doll comb.

It was a family of misfits, to be sure, but it had banded together and adopted me. For the first time, I thought someone cared about me.

On a dazzling day in February, I stood in the middle of the Doc Martens shop on Yonge Street surrounded by a small group of Heritage skinheads. The time for my evolution had arrived: like a Selkie coming back into the fold, I discarded my coarse winter coat in favour of a shiny new flight jacket that moulded itself into my second skin. The skinheads cheered and smacked my back and I knew that the initiation was over. I was part of the pack. With our eight-hole white-laced boots and black bomber jackets, we were invincible – a Roman army without the laurel leaves, a horde of young werewolves howling at their first full moon.

The first thing we did was stroll ostentatiously through the Eaton Centre shopping mall, getting a kick out of the pinched looks on saleswomen's faces as they followed us in the isles. After a security guard started to trail us, we decided we'd had enough of the game and exited the mall through the back doors that led to City Hall.

Then Carl spotted the gigantic Menorah that was planted next to a permanent stone edifice erected in memory of the Allies. It had gone up for Hanukkah and nobody bothered to take it down yet. He pranced up to it and spat right on it. A thick gob of mucus slid down the metal shaft, provoking me and the other girl there, Maya, to groan in disgust. John and his buddy Dave started kicking over the wreaths, sending them careening down the marble memorial steps.

In the middle of all the fun, we heard a shout. We turned our heads to see a middle-aged woman set her shopping bags on the ground to glare at us. "Just what the hell do you hooligans think you're doing?" she demanded to know. "I'm calling the police! Get away from there!"

John started screaming, calling her a fucking Jew while the rest of us beat a quick retreat. It was City Hall after all – a cruiser couldn't be that far. We raced across Nathan Phillips Square, laughing, hooting, the wind beating against our flushed faces. Once we had climbed up to the roof stone-top terrace, we spied on the ground below until we judged it clear.

It was exhilarating.

TWELVE

ESCALATION OF COMMITMENT

The racialist uniform of bomber jacket and combat boots elevated me to a higher notch of revolutionary, but I'd read enough revolutionary propaganda to know that only after arms training could I graduate into a bona-fide guerrilla fighter. And just as he did for my birthday, Wolfgang wanted to give me a gift. This time, however, my present would be intangible. *Knowledge.* The kind of gift you couldn't buy in a department store.

"All women should learn to defend themselves," he'd said. "With all the muds out there, every girl your age should be carrying a gun for protection. Even if you'll never use it."

"Wait a second," I protested. "When the Race War breaks out I want to be on the frontlines, not bandaging amputees."

A small laugh got caught in the back of Wolfgang's throat; he always got a kick out of hearing me say stuff like that. That's when he told me I should ask Peter or Drew to let me tag along to a clandestine spot on the isolated hill where they went for target-practice. The setting of the training regimen was supposed to be a remote part of countryside, a property that started off of a dusty clay road and stretched up a hill toward a distant cliff where they could shoot their rifles unencumbered.

Nicola's live-in boyfriend Peter Mitrevski was a thirty-something Macedonian with eyes as dark as burning coals and a personality to match. He was nearly six foot tall, whale-boned and rippling with muscles. He looked as if he slept in his army fatigues and always had a rugged, five o'clock shadow on his square jaw. The sadistic glint in his eyes, the rolled-up sleeves that revealed heavily-tattooed hairy forearms, all added to the impact – he meant serious business. But as a misogynist, he was reluctant to have a female join them when they went shooting.

"Not even my own girlfriend has gone up there," he bitched to Wolfgang before finally suggesting that instead, he would start to teach me hand-to-hand combat. After all, learning how to shoot was useless if somebody just clobbered me in an alley before I could withdraw my revolver.

In the past, Wolfgang had arranged for about ten of us to get self-defence lessons from a judo expert at a dojo close to the Beaches, but after only a couple of sessions the guy decided he was uncomfortable training the Heritage Front. Being only 5'3 and of a slight build, I was glad that Peter was willing to take up the torch and teach me how to fight.

The next time I was over at Nicola's place, Peter gestured for me to follow him into the backyard. He made me stand in front of him while he showed me a few quick throws, and quickly became displeased when I showed no natural aptitude for combat training.

"Roll, goddammit," he said when I clutched my shoulder in pain, having crashed hard for the tenth time. "Don't just drop like a sack of potatoes. *Fuck*."

I gathered myself up, shook the kink out of my neck, nodded that I was ready for more. This time he went for my wrists, grasping them tightly, twisting them behind my back. He pushed higher still, bringing me down to my knees. He seemed to enjoy it immensely.

"Ouch," I yelled. "Let go already."

"If this was a real situation, I'd have you down on the ground by now," he replied. "It would be over. You've gotta be faster than this. Snap your wrists out of my hold at the junction where my fingers meet. Kick me in the nuts. Just try to defend yourself, for fuck's sake."

He must have thrown me a thousand times. My body was a mess of developing bruises, my hair had strayed out of the long braid that ran down my back, dirt and leaves stuck to me like they'd been super-glued on.

"If you want to be one of us, you've gotta learn how to fight," he sneered, watching me drag myself to my feet. "Don't expect I'm gonna take it easy on you just because you're a girl."

Yeah, I figured that already. I glowered at him, ready to claw his eyes out, and he just laughed. "Good. Come on then. Gimme all you've got."

My escalation of commitment paralleled the Heritage Front's escalation of influence in Toronto. We were in the news nearly every week, with ever-increasing number of supporters swelling our membership ranks. At our peak, we had close to two thousand people on our contact lists. But the most exciting thing was yet to happen: a new event was being planned that promised to put us in international spotlight. The Latvian Hall had been booked, the deposit paid, and the guest speakers were none other than Tom and John Metzger, the notorious father and son duo who lead White Aryan Resistance in the States.

With their criminal records, nobody thought they'd be allowed to enter Canada. Metzger Senior had been fined $12 million in a civil suit for inciting a skinhead to the point that the guy went out and attacked an Ethiopian exchange student in the street, beating him to death. Instead of paying the fine, Metzger surrendered his house, declared bankruptcy and moved to another state.

The WAR enterprise was a family affair: John was leader of the youth wing, while his daughter Lynn headed the Aryan Women's League. Their monthly newspaper WAR carried the most radical and unabashedly racist articles and cartoons I'd ever seen in my life. In spite of my familiarity with the publications that circulated in the far right, I never saw anybody come close to topping WAR in shock value.

The Front began fundraising for the event. A great sum of money was necessary: the Metzgers had to be paid in cash for their appearance and flown from California to Buffalo, where cars might have to be rented to get them over the border, and the list went on. There was no guarantee we could get them into the country, but Wolfgang was confident we could pull it off. How exactly we were going to smuggle them in was another story, one we still didn't have the answer to.

Having gotten wind of our planned rally, Canadian immigration had already issued a country-wide alert to stop the Metzgers if they attempted to cross any border. So a great plan was devised: several cars would drive down to Buffalo and act as decoys. Cars were in short supply though, so they approached Drew, who'd already pitched money into the Metzger potty. They asked him to borrow his new girlfriend's car and drive it down to Buffalo, where he'd meet up with the Metzgers and bring them over, somehow.

Gerry called me just after midnight, his excitement bordering on hysteria. "Guess what? We got them through. We got the Metzgers in!"

"How the hell did you manage that?" I asked in awe.

"You won't believe it."

"Tell me!" I pressed him.

"We smuggled them over the border dressed like rabbis. Can you freaking believe it? Orthodox rabbis. Fuck, you should have seen how they looked, jerry-curls and all! They got such a kick out of it!"

"The irony," I gasped. "Are you serious? *Rabbis*?"

"May a menorah strike me down if I am lying! Freaking rabbis. Customs waved them right through. Guess it would've been un-PC to frisk them? Un-fucking-believable!"

In such illustrious company, I could only accept the invitation to make a speech that night. I wrote and rehearsed it carefully, memorizing the whole thing. Whether I was going to go on after the Metzgers' talk or warm up the crowd beforehand, I had to get the blood moving in the room. This was much more than a gathering – it was a symbol that we had outsmarted the government: all the immigration officers, metro police and intelligence factions who'd tried to stand in the way of this evening. It would be the mother of all rallies.

On the evening of June 27, 1992, to much anticipation, the Metzgers made their scheduled appearance at the Heritage Front's "W.A.R. in Toronto" rally. Grant went up first, giving an impressive speech where he called the Human Rights Commission a bunch of parasites and enemies of free speech out to steal all our rights. He concluded the talk by shouting "WHITE POWER!" and getting the young skinheads all pumped up.

Then the Metzgers took over and made the fiery speeches they had been smuggled in for. They were greeted with a thundering ovation by the crowd of over two hundred. The cameras were rolling; videotapes of this rally were sure to sell out in pre-sales before the final mix even got released.

At the end of the night, as Tom and John were out in the Latvian Hall parking lot along with Wolfgang, a SWAT team stormed their car and they were all taken into custody. Wolfgang was released the next day while the Metzgers were charged with entering the country illegally in order to break Canada's hate laws. They were held at the Don Jail until their Immigration hearing the following week.

This was another publicity cash cow for the Front. Emergency rallies were organized, placards made, faxes went out to all media outlets. Starting the next day and lasting until the Metzger's deportation on July 2nd, we protested in front of the Don Jail, demanding that the government release the Metzgers at once. At first it was exciting, but by the third day we'd grown bored and the cameras had dwindled. By noon only six of us remained, holding the bulk of the picket signs. "Let's head over to my place to drop these things off," Drew suggested.

Forty-five minutes and two buses later, we got there. Before his mother could complain that her son didn't have time to do anything except hang out with skinheads, Drew whisked us up to his loft in the attic. The space was narrow and taken up with Drew's bed and a six-foot oak cabinet. Lost in the corner, a set of dust-covered barbells had seen happier days.

Me and the only other girl there, a bleached-blonde Chelsea named Jennifer, sat cross-legged on the bed while the guys plopped on the floor. Drew reached under the bed and pulled out his wide array of international far-right zines and an impressive collection of tee-shirts he'd traded with white supremacists all over the world.

Pumped up by our oohs and ahs, Drew grew more confident. "Ok, I'm gonna show you something else," he shushed us. "If my parents find out I've got these they'll kill me."

He walked over to the massive cabinet in the corner, creaked open the doors and stuck his arms all the way in, digging through a clutter of jeans and shirts. Finally, he pulled out a huge shotgun and two rifles with barrels that looked so shiny I thought Drew oiled them every night. The guys clucked their approval. "Fuck, man, this one's sweet," Chris said, holding the shotgun up in the air.

"A bit heavy, isn't it," I noted when my turn came to handle it.

Drew took back the shotgun and thrust one of the rifles at me. "Check this one out. Much more lightweight. A good starter weapon for a girl. Wanna buy it off me? Hundred bucks and it's yours."

"I'd rather have a semi-automatic Beretta," I said.

He scoffed. "Who wouldn't? But it would cost you a shitload more."

"You know they're soon gonna ban the buying of ammo in gun shops," Chris said. "A drag, now that my FAC was revoked."

Drew nodded. "Yeah, I've heard. I'm stocking up on as much as I can fit in this closet before that rule goes into effect. Everybody should be grabbing thirty-cartridge mags before they get banned altogether."

Suddenly, Drew's mother started yelling from the bottom of the stairs. Drew shoved everything back into the wardrobe and slammed the doors shut. "Hold your horses, Mom," he shouted down at her, then turned to us and whispered, "You guys sneak out while I keep her busy in the kitchen. I forgot to do my chores."

THIRTEEN

FULL STEAM AHEAD

By mid-1992, the Heritage Front was a household name in Ontario and Quebec. Our flyer campaign and the publicity generated from demonstrations, street brawls and counter-offensive anti-racist marches had done the trick. The Front's membership rolls began to soar to new heights. New rallies and concerts were planned with guest speakers like ex-KKK leader David Duke, who was running for governor of Louisiana; Dennis Mahon, head of the White Aryan Resistance chapter in Oklahoma and also a Klansman; and British-born David Irving, worldwide Holocaust denier, master revisionist and Nazi sympathizer.

Wolfgang invited me to speak at all those rallies. "Your speeches exhilarate the crowd," he told me. "Nobody can believe you wrote them all by yourself." In reality, I leveraged everybody's opinions when I wrote my speeches or articles for Up Front. The crowds liked that I used the knowledge I acquired from Ernst to tell inspiring stories about brave Nazis and their fight for an Aryan utopia. Skinheads in particular loved hearing that kind of radical stuff coming out of a girl's mouth. They all wanted their girlfriends to be that patriotic.

I was the perfect example of what an Aryan woman should be. At last, I had become the poster girl Wolfgang had always wanted me to be.

Keeping the Heritage Front in the limelight was fairly easy to accomplish, given the fact that whenever there's even the slightest possibility of street warfare, media channels flock to it like flies to shit. The crew they send remains the same: one gum-chewing cameraman paired with an overexcited frontline reporter itching to get caught in a brawl during a live broadcast. Like it or not, that's just the way things work in journalism, and Wolfgang made damn well sure that the Heritage Front did not disappoint. To him, appearances on the six o'clock news were free air-time, commercials we didn't have to pay for. There was no such thing as bad publicity.

But among all the reporters who doggedly pursued the Heritage Front, was only one journalist who knew the group nearly as intimately as an inside member: Bill Dunphy of the Toronto Sun. Dunphy was your old-fashioned type of reporter – as much persistent sleuth as gritty journalist, the sort of man who always carries a tape recorder in his back pocket, who intensely pursues any lead that comes his way and isn't afraid to get down and dirty with the best of them. Not shy to hound down anybody for an interview, he seemed at ease either in Wolfgang's apartment or chatting with Rodney Bobiwash outside a courtroom.

All the breaking stories that involved the Heritage Front were first penned by Dunphy. His editorials were biting, aggravating and shrewd, but no matter whether you loved or hated his style, you couldn't deny that you had to watch what you said around the guy. He didn't skip a beat.

On November 28, 1992, in a two-page spread that was the headline story of the day, Dunphy broke the history of the Heritage Front. Among the photos of its key players, which included Wolfgang, Grant, Peter Mitrevski, Max French and George Burdi, he described the Front as "the most powerful white racist gang to hit Canada since the real Nazis, back in the dirty thirties. They believe we're headed for a racial war – and some of them are getting ready for it by arming themselves and undergoing paramilitary training."

We had arrived.

At any given demonstration about two dozen of Toronto's finest trailed behind us. They were supposed to maintain the peace, keep the antiracists who jeered us from the sidewalks from murdering us and vice-versa. For the most part they kept their personal opinions to themselves, with the exception of the secret few who attended Heritage Front rock concerts and purchased videotapes at the back of the room.

Wolfgang had befriended more than his share of cops. He went about it quite pragmatically; he'd made it a personal rule to shake hands with them before the rally, and he prided himself on being on a first-name basis with quite a few.

"There's a strategy to this," he said. "Make them feel respected. Boy, do they get off on it. They go into the profession for the power trip, you know. If you want to get on their good side, you've gotta sugar-coat them with bullshit like, *What a fine job you're doing, officer*. So when they step in during a riot, who do you think those cops will side with? Who are they going to use their clubs on? Some filthy Anti-Racist Action street kid who hides his face behind a bandanna, spits on their uniform and screams *Death to Pigs*, or me – the nice guy who bought them their coffee this morning?"

Today's parade was winding along University Avenue. George Burdi, the muscular frontman of the ever-popular Rahowa band rock band, worked up everybody with a megaphone. "What do we want?" he cried out.

"Equal rights," chanted the crowd.

"When do we want them?"

"NOW!"

"And what is the only solution?" boomed George, the engorged vein in his neck throbbing as if a snake had just burrowed under his skin and started writhing.

"WHITE REVOLUTION!" the Heritage Front members screamed back in delight, getting off on the shocked faces of people who'd stop in place and shake their heads in disbelief. A Nazi parade, right along the main downtown artery. What was the world coming to?

This is when some of the braver skinheads, the ones who weren't afraid of their parents seeing them on TV, started pumping their right arms to their chest and outwards in a rapid succession of frenzied *Sieg Heils* that gave them the presence of insane marionettes.

People huddled on the sidewalks to ogle. They stuck their heads out their windows, gathered on their balconies, stared down at us with mouths agape. Their looks of consternation were no doubt stoked by the Nazi Republic flag being waved high in the air by a beefy, heavily-tattooed skinhead with no neck who stomped along in heavy-duty combat boots procured from a second-hand army supply store.

The guys were particularly thrilled when a non-white individual didn't make it across the street in time and ended up cowering under a store awning. Invariably one of the skins would race over to the poor soul and shout in his or her face "Keep Canada white!" before one of the police officers stepped forward to intervene.

After the rally we reconvened back at the Parkway, where I sat next to Wolfgang. We got into a conversation about how so many skinheads were enlisting in the Armed Forces so they could get military training.

"If I were to do things over again," he confessed, "I'd enlist in the French Foreign Legion. They're open to any nationality, don't give a shit about your past and affiliations, and you're not required to have any formal education. Best of all, they give you a comprehensive training that beats anything you'd learn in a boot camp here. Plenty of boys have gone on to bigger and better things after their stint with the Legion. Some of them even manage to score French citizenship after just three years of service."

"What bigger and better things are you talking about?"

"Let's just say they follow their entrepreneurial spirit and hire themselves out to the highest bidders. They *make* money, instead of constantly worrying about bills."

"Is everything okay?"

Wolfgang's shoulders slumped. "You can't imagine how much it costs to maintain basic operations. If it wasn't for Grant, who at least has a decent job, throwing in extra cash to supplement the cost of meeting halls, print runs, the lawyers' defense fund, we'd be up shit's creek. Never mind the cost of supplies. The trump change we collect from the rallies, subscriptions and tee-shirts don't even come close to covering my phone bill. You don't go into politics to make money, that's for sure."

I tried to keep up with Wolfgang's laments. He was going through a weird phase where he constantly brainstormed new ways of getting money. "One way people have done it," he articulated slowly, watching me out of the corner of his eye, "is by recruiting women to turn tricks for the organization. Lots of commie radicals in the 1970s did it – sold street drugs and made their cash from prostitution."

I glanced at him with disdain. "I think you'd have a hard time recruiting anybody for that sort of thing."

"Well, there goes *that* plan," he said, laughing. "Then there's the stuff Ken's going on about, holding up a gas station or convenience store. But armed robbery's tricky. There's always some camera rolling and if you get busted for that, you go in for a long time. Selling drugs gets you lesser sentences, but then you have to hash it out with the niggers and the bikers for a cut of their territory. It can get messy."

He fell silent. I remembered that he'd already done time over drug possession and didn't want to go that route again. Not when the Front was bigger than ever.

"So here's what I was thinking might work," he started to say. "Picture this: twenty people go on welfare and get five-six hundred bucks every month. If they turn the money over to me, that's ten grand with me sitting on my ass. Nothing illegal about it. Welfare fraud's one of the hardest things to prove. Worst case scenario, you get kicked off assistance. Who cares? So whaddaya think about that?"

"Might just work," I replied.

It was the sort of money-making operation he got a kick out of – an elegant, easy way to scam the system. Others did the deed while he profited without getting his hands dirty or having to regress to drug-dealing. But the best thing about the idea was the fact – oh, the beautiful irony! – that the Canadian government was bank-rolling our group. It didn't get any sweeter than that.

On November 29, in a cheeky, attention-grabbing headline that screamed *Racist Milks Us*, Bill Dunphy broke the story that Gary Schipper, the yappy, hyperactive new voice of the Heritage Front hotline, was on welfare while still earning an income as a telemarketer. By the time public outrage got Gary cut off from assistance, a dozen more of us had received welfare cheques and gave at least half the amount back to the HF. Nicola had written me a landlord letter so I could qualify, even though technically I still lived with my mother.

In return for agreeing to go along with the scheme, Wolfgang wanted to do something nice for me. "Peter and the boys are heading up to Michigan this weekend. They're having a cross-lighting celebration up there, a memorial for Christian Identity leader's Pastor Bob Miles, who helped found Aryan Nations. Why don't you ride along with them? Peter's just come back from another KKK event up in Georgia where he was spreading news of the Heritage Front. You've never gone to a Klan rally, have you?"

FOURTEEN

BOYS WILL BE BOYS

The road to Michigan was hemmed by a virgin forest that formed a groundswell of lush, verdant green. Musk from the pines coated my lungs with chlorophyll. The deluge that had accompanied us for most of the early morning had turned into a fine mist, and the sky, a brightening canvas.

We rolled into the compound around four-thirty in the afternoon, Peter pulling over for the compulsory inspection. Gruff-looking Aryan Nations-type guards in combat gear circled our car, hands clenched around the straps of hunting rifles draped over their shoulders. As their army boots came into contact with the wet earth, they made a sloshing, syncopated noise with every footfall, as if they were slapping the ground. Their hard stares bore into our faces.

One of the sentinels leaned over Peter's window, stretching his neck to see into the back seat. Max French and Drew Maynard didn't elicit any second glances, but when he spotted me he paused and scowled. It took all I had to keep my chin up and sustain an unwavering gaze. I knew that look. I'd gotten it before at some Front rallies: the man didn't think I was white enough. He appeared to be evaluating the proportion of my nose to the rest of my face and something didn't seem quite right to him.

My skin, usually sallow in an anaemic sort of way, always tans down to a golden colour in the summer. My eyes are a deep shade of brown. Every once in a while, after a speech, I'd notice some old man staring at me grimly. In those moments a certainty gripped my consciousness – I was an impostor. Like my father, I was the bastard child of my grandmother's past, and I feared the day when someone would call me on it: I didn't belong here.

I was the enemy – a mangy, starved coyote who's managed to crawl inside the chicken coop and disguised itself by rolling around in white feathers. Every time I applied red dye to my hair and waited several minutes longer than the directed twenty-five minutes it would take to bleach it, I was all too aware of the blackness of my roots.

Peter cleared his throat to get the guard's attention. "So we're good?"

The guard plucked out a cigarette from a crumpled pack in his back pocket and lit it. He took a long drag and blew out several chunky rings of smoke before he finally gestured to the others. "These folks are clear. Open the gates, boys!"

We were among the first to arrive – others had probably tried to wait out the storm that morning before getting on the road. Dogs barked and strained against their leashes as one of the Christian Identity soldiers gave us a perfunctory tour of the property, showing us to the cottage where we'd sleep. Lucky for us, being early meant we didn't have to pitch a tent outside. The 'lodge' was one big open space which held several cots. I took the cot against the farthest wall, plopped my sleeping bag on it to mark the spot and joined the others outside.

The streaming afternoon light and country air invigorated us after the long drive. We headed up to the main building, a spacious two-level farmhouse, to get something to eat. Several women rushed to serve lunch on a long, medieval-looking table that could easily seat twenty. They wore ankle-length dresses and styled their hair in long braids that dangled down their backs.

I watched them with curiosity, which gradually turned to irritation. They left the room every time the men started to discuss politics. Sure, it wasn't the first time I'd seen women defer to males in the movement, but their behaviour was so overt it made me wonder if there was some sort of unspoken expectation that I too should get up and join them in the kitchen. Feeling uneasy, I continued to eat my soup and pretended I didn't notice I was the only female in the compound who wasn't hovering over a stew pot or dangling a babe at her breast.

The only subject that preoccupied those women was children: how to have as many white babies in as little time as possible. They asked me how old I was, and when I said seventeen they exchanged glances and I could tell they thought I was just about ready to start popping them out myself.

How could they tolerate being treated as lesser by the men in army fatigues who marched around and demanded food and drinks without as much as a thank-you in return? And yet, performing menial tasks was a fate they seemed to have happily accepted. Worse yet, they were *proud* of their ignorance in political affairs. It blew my mind that someone should want to keep themselves that ignorant on purpose.

"Are they, like, part of a harem?" I joked to Peter under my breath. "Polygamists? Why are there so many women and kids living in the main house? Where are their husbands?"

He shrugged, tearing off a chunk of his cornbread. "Things run differently 'round here, don't they? Best you don't ask too many questions, you don't wanna piss anybody off."

By midnight, the clearing by the large steel gates had become a sea of cars. Dozens of intoxicated voices rang out into the night. I was heading back to the lodge when I glimpsed a cluster of men huddled between the trunk of a car and the outhouses. I squinted, discerning Peter among them. Their animated exchange was punctuated with nods and laughter. Then the voices lowered and I could catch only a few whispers over the crickets' hum.

I didn't need to hear their conversation to know what it was about. It suddenly dawned on me that most Canadian racists wouldn't have driven all the way here just to attend a cross-burning. If they wanted to partake in the experience, Martin Weiche's farm in London, Ontario was the place to go. In reality, this was a business convention for far-right paramilitaries and mercenaries-for-hire. The only difference between a holistic expo, psychic fair or a Soldier of Fortune convention was that here you didn't have to rent a table to display your wares. Deals were made left, right and centre – weapons traded or sold, orders placed for more exotic armaments, shit you wouldn't find in a Canadian gun shop even with a permit.

I rose to the sound of laughter and barking dogs. Sliding into my bomber jacket, I snuck outside. The sun was just starting to poke out and dozens of people were strewn across the grounds, smacking each other's backs in greeting. It looked like a science fiction convention where fans dress up like their favourite alien: there were skinheads in black bomber jackets and fourteen-hole Docs; survivalist Odinists with long hair and beards, wearing runes and Viking paraphernalia; Nazi punks in full retro costume; Klansmen who proudly carried white robes over their shoulders. You could tell each individual's affinity by the assortment of pins, patches, and Celtic cross badges they'd sown onto their clothing.

A beat-up bus pulled in, so splattered with mud and dead insects that you couldn't tell its original colour. The people who emerged were the sorriest-looking bunch of youngsters I'd ever seen – filthy, reeking urchins out of an Oliver Twist film set. To my horror, a couple of them walked up to where Drew, myself and five skinheads from Detroit were standing.

"We're the Posse Comitatus," said a rat-faced youth. "Branch of the Michigan Militia. We live in our bus." He gestured proudly toward the scruffy vehicle, whose stench had attracted a horde of flies. "Took turns driving all night from a rally in Pennsylvania to get here."

A guy carrying a black duffel bag came over. "Anybody wanna buy some mace?"

I fished out ten bucks and exchanged it for a small canister labeled CS Tear Gas. "You've gotta replace it every couple of years or it goes flat," he advised me.

"How do I know yours is fresh?" Drew asked. I could tell he really wanted to buy some, but ten bucks was ten bucks and he was paranoid about being scammed.

"Well," the guy laughed. "You're welcome to try it out."

Just as a salesgirl at the mall might get you to sample a new perfume by spritzing the air so you can smell it, Drew picked up a can of mace, shook it, held it at arm's length away from himself and squirted it high in the air. Unfortunately for him, and unlike a scent of perfume that you can walk by and ignore, when he tried to sniff the mace to test its potency, the tiny droplets of gas came after him like an army of angry hornets.

"Jesus fucking Christ," he exploded, batting at his eyes. The skinheads around him stepped back, doubling over in laughter as a thoroughly-shamed Drew handed the guy a ten-dollar bill and, without saying another word, took his mace and red-faced self away as fast as his feet could stumble.

"Holy shit, that dude just maced himself," a Posse fellow snickered. "Not too bright, that one."

The Posse Comitatus were big players in northeastern United States, particularly the Michigan-Pennsylvania belt. They struck me as ultra-radical and rabidly racist, guys who didn't just talk but planned future paramilitary actions because they had nothing to lose. Christian Identity played a big part of their ideological make-up, but the phrase Love Thy Neighbour wasn't in their Bible. They were the precursor of a new breed of underground, survivalist extremists calling themselves the Michigan Militia, who three years from now would come to be connected with the Oklahoma City bombing.

Just after noon the portable johns were dropped off. Almost on cue, Dennis Mahon arrived. He was immediately surrounded by an army of loyal sympathizers and I wasn't fortunate to get away fast enough. "Hello there, young lady," he called out, waving me over. "I know you from Toronto, right?"

I approached obligingly. Dennis didn't stop until he had me sitting on his lap. He looped one arm around my waist while using his other hand to play with my hair, twisting one of my long curls around his index finger. He hummed approvingly, an irritating deja-vu of the last time he was in Toronto and had insisted on doing the same thing.

"Isn't it interesting how there are so many girls around here with red hair," he mused. The men milling around him nodded in agreement.

I felt like a piece of meat hung up on a rack, surrounded by a pack of drooling hyenas. "Um, Dennis," I said, "Looks like the Metzgers have just pulled in. I'm gonna go say hi."

Not shy to hide his disappointment, Mahon released his iron grip on me but not before planting a wet one on my cheek. I waited until I was out of sight to wipe my face in disgust. When I turned around to make sure he hadn't seen me, I was relieved to notice he'd replaced me with another redhead.

The Metzgers couldn't stay for the entire ceremony but had just enough time to shake a few hands and kiss a few babies. What with the campground being split between Mahon and Metzger worshippers, I decided to explore the property and headed for the meadow that stretched beyond the makeshift campsite. Not five minutes later I came upon a clearing where I retreated to the shade of an elm tree and watched two beefy men struggle with a ten-foot cross, trying to plant it into a freshly-dug hole. So that's where the ceremony was going to take place, I noted, circling back to the encampment through a path that snaked through the wilted remnants of a cornfield.

At dusk, everyone lined up outside the shed and waited their turn for a bowl of potato and beef stew. As darkness fell, flashlights beamed grotesque outlines against the landscape and the dogs once again barked themselves hoarse. The men who'd brought their white robes went to change inside the converted shed.

When it was time for the procession, a horn was blown. I followed the others into the abnormally cold night, rubbing my hands together for warmth. We made our progress toward the clearing in the middle of the sprawling cornfield. I struggled to see where I was stepping. Somewhere up ahead, a voice boomed out, "Stay together, people, and watch out for the dogs. We turn them loose at night to keep trespassers out."

Then we were finally there, at the foot of that monstrous cross. We formed two circles: the robed Klansmen on the inside, the children and the rest of us who didn't wear robes on the outside. A song erupted as one of the men, face covered by a hood, walked around the first circle with a flaming torch in his hand and lit all the gasoline-drenched torches held by the rest of the Klansmen. One by one, each hooded man and woman stepped forward and placed their torch at the foot of the cross. In about thirty seconds, the whole thing was ablaze.

The bright flames licked and spat out glowing embers. They rose in a swirling orangey-red column toward the whirring sound of a helicopter engine, our sole link to reality and presumably the FBI. I looked into that star-littered sky and inhaled deeply, swallowing the aroma of burning wood. A part of my brain refused to believe this was actually happening. Goosebumps rose up along my arms. Being here took my teenage rebellion to a whole new level.

I would attend two cross-burnings during my time with the Heritage Front: the one tonight and another one in London, Ontario, at the farm of Martin Weiche, one of the other men who, along with Wolfgang, had tried to take over the island of Dominica.

But in this moment, as I looked to the somber faces of the children present, at the reflection of the flames across their widened irises, I wondered what their existence was like, being brought up by such radical parents. Would their lives be over before they even began?

The children stood stiffly and weren't the least bit afraid; they had done this before, they knew the drill. I thought back to all those books and films that had created a negative knee-jerk reaction in me, an apprehension at the sound of three little letters: K.K.K. It was strange to find emptiness inside me in place of where fear would have once resided. But I had crossed over. I was on the other side of the chasm now: vicious and powerful instead of vulnerable. Oppressor instead of victim.

Wasn't this what I'd always wanted?

As I scanned the crowd, I realized there were faces behind those letters. Faces that belonged to men, women and kids who lived in town and intermingled with the population, who lived such average lives that you'd never suspect, had you run into them at the grocery store, that they made a habit of gathering at the foot of a blazing cross.

The sound of voices united in song lifted high into the air, as if to accompany the smoldering flames. A wave of electricity passed over us: we were all one – one blood, one voice. We linked hands, feeling the vibration of energy build higher and higher, ascending with the flames.

Nothing mattered except the sensation of unity that radiated across people's eyes from behind their white hoods. In that moment, any man would have laid his life for the cause, for the kin next to him. This odd mix of love for one's own and total hatred for any outsiders mingled until it formed an indistinguishable column of smoke rising into the sky, diffusing, like the pungent odor of burning wood, across the blackness of the night.

The next morning, as we were packing our gear into the car for the long drive back to Canada, Peter pulled me aside and flashed a conspiratorial grin. "Come, I wanna show you something." He reached into his waistband and pulled out a pearl-handled gun. "Feel it," he instructed me, depositing it in my hands. "Feel that power."

It wasn't the first time I'd held one of his guns. I already admired his sleek black .45, which he had showed me proudly at Nicola's house earlier this summer after she had gone out to the park with the kids. He'd sworn me to secrecy, saying she was a party-pooper and a stickler for not wanting her kids to grow up in a house full of guns.

I looked down at Peter's new acquisition. An explosion of pure, unadulterated adrenaline surged through me, a fast-moving virus spreading in my bloodstream. It was a heavy, reliable gun. A gun that would kill with no reservations. When you fired a gun like this, you felt its heartbeat in your hands; you fused with the forged steel.

I held it for another moment, savouring the knowledge that with a gun like this I'd never worry again about walking alone through Regent Park at night, before giving it back to him. As he slipped the gun back in his belt, I was prickled with the sense that he was disappointed in me, in the fact that I didn't want to buy one from the shifty-eyed guys around the campsite. Aside from the fact that I couldn't afford it, the idea troubled me. Up till now, playing freedom-fighter had been an exciting pastime. But in this compound, with weirdos and arms dealers roaming all around, the game had evolved into a startlingly uncomfortable reality.

On the drive back, Peter was in the middle of telling Max French, who was sitting in the front passenger seat, that a friend or relative of his had "caught yellow fever and betrayed his race" when a screeching siren made it evident that we were getting pulled over.

I watched the policeman, a porcine guy pushing fifty accessorized with an obligatory salt-and-pepper mustache, get out of his cruiser and moseyed on over to us, hand dangerously close to his revolver. Drew, sitting beside me, kicked me in the shin.

"Ouch!" I exclaimed, ready to kick him back. "Watch it."

"Don't look so worried," he whispered anxiously, not heeding his own advice. "We're just gonna get a ticket. Act cool."

Why the fuck did Peter have to speed? Didn't he give a shit about being busted? Was he getting off on the thrills? Pissed off, I spat out my gum and wondered what the sentence was for being an accessory to arms trading. There were at least two guns hidden in the car: Peter's pearl-handled new baby, plus a basic rifle Drew had obtained from one of the Posse Comitatus guys.

Panting gruffly, the cop mentioned the speed limit. His attitude cooled when he took a closer look at Peter who, as luck would have it, had made the brilliant decision to wear a short-sleeved shirt that did nothing to hide the radical tattoos that coursed up his hairy arms toward his neck. "May I see your identification," he asked.

Peter took out his driver's license. "Here you are, sir," he said reverentially.

Drew and I huddled in the back seat, trying to look as innocent as possible. A threadbare green blanket covered up the bomber jackets laying across our laps.

"Take down your hair, Elisse," Peter had murmured just moments before. I'd untied my ponytail and allowed my hair to fall softly over my shoulders and into my eyes. With any luck, I could pass for thirteen. If the cop thought there were kids in the car, he might hopefully assume we were just another family out for a quick shopping trip over the border.

The police officer glanced at me, squinting. I did my best to force a sweet-as-sugar smile, which died as soon as he was out of my direct sight.

Then, joy of joys, we were waved along with just a warning.

It was a close call.

"You liked the rush, didn't you?" asked Wolfgang when we met at the Parkway for brunch the following week. Of course, he wasn't talking about the rush of almost getting busted for possessing a trunk-full of illegally-obtained guns. Afraid of his reaction, we had collectively decided to spare him the story.

"Those first few times you see a cross-lighting are magical," he said wistfully, adding another scoop of sugar to his coffee.

"But you don't attend them now," I said, stirring milk into my own coffee.

He threw his head back and laughed. "I'm just as radical as the day I was born. But the world doesn't respond to this kind of theatrics anymore. The time for people to march around in Klan robes and Nazi costumes is gone. Everybody's so conditioned to run the other way when they see that shit, it would be blatantly counter-productive. No, the thing to do is run for office. If you don't wanna start a group from scratch, you just infiltrate an organization and take it over from the inside. Remember how Grant and I were in charge of security at the last Reform Party convention? We were Preston Manning's own bodyguards. And that moron has no idea we're gonna take over."

What if they couldn't pull it off, I wanted to ask. Just when I opened my mouth to form the question, the waitress arrived with our plates of steaming food. I leaned on an elbow and watched Wolfgang devour his way through a stack of pancakes and bacon. I stared down at the fried eggs in front of me and realized I'd lost my appetite.

What if Wolfgang's plan was exposed by the media and all Heritage Front members ended up expelled from the Reform party? Would we be forced to turn to arms? Was that our backup plan?

Up until now, all of this – the intensive stints of hand-to-hand combat practice, all that weekend warrior shit – had been a fun, stupid game, like taking a paintball match to a whole new level. Best case scenario, we'd know how to defend ourselves when the Race War broke out. Having a registered gun in your underwear drawer wasn't a bad thing. But importing semiautomatic guns from illicit arms dealers was far from a tactically-defensive move.

The reality of how close we had come to getting caught sat like a bitter pill in my mouth.

What were we really gearing up for?

Peter Mitrevski and Drew Maynard were only two of the numerous other skinheads I saw or heard bragging about acquiring guns. The joke was, as long as you had a firearms license, nobody could bat an eye. Why should anybody be afraid? We had a perfect example of someone in the Heritage Front leadership who owned weapons and had beat the system: Grant Bristow.

Back in the fall of 1991, in the exact month I met Wolfgang and was introduced to the HF, Metropolitan Toronto Police Force agents had swept down on a car he was driving and arrested Sean Maguire, a top American White Supremacist in Canada illegally (and staying at Grant's place) on an Immigration warrant.

When they opened the trunk of Grant's car, they had found two guns in their cases: a 12 gauge shotgun and a semi-automatic rifle. Right after the arrest, a CSIS Investigator dressed in civilian clothes showed up on the scene. The police brought Grant to station 41 pending a decision on whether to charge him. While his car was being taken apart and various other police-type gadgets were being removed, a heated discussion took place among CSIS, RCMP and the arresting officers.

I wouldn't know the exact details of what had transpired in that precinct that day for another year. It was only after Grant Bristow was revealed to have been a CSIS agent that the ugly possibility of a cover-up emerged.

A former Immigration officer who was on the scene, Harold Musetescu, informed SIRC (the Committee who was appointed to investigate CSIS' actions in the Heritage Front affair) that there was a "heated discussion" at 41 Division about charging Grant Bristow for "dangerous weapons" and "unsafe storage of firearms". Musetescu said that the police thought that they had "got two birds with one stone", and were keen to lay charges.

But in the end, as they always did whenever their boy got in over his head, intervention from Bristow's CSIS handlers ensured that he was not charged.

One thing is clear: if Grant Bristow had been charged in September 1991 and Operation Governor ceased, scores of innocent people might have avoided becoming harassed, tormented and targeted for attack. The Heritage Front would not have had the guidance, CSIS protection and financial assistance to become the powerful organization that it was back in 1993.

The skinheads who looked up to Bristow wouldn't have been tempted to stalk their targets with a tactical precision emboldened by their new-found confidence and belief that they were part of a carefully-orchestrated "Intelligence Division" created and single-handedly spearheaded by Grant Bristow.

The lives devastated by stress, depression and assault may well have been spared. And the people who are no longer with us, whose health was severely impacted by stress and illness following these incidents, might be alive today.

FIFTEEN

STREETS OF FIRE
November 13, 1992

Situated at the corner of Queen and Gladstone Street, the Roma Banquet & Restaurant became the setting of a street riot that would bring the incendiary conflict between the Heritage Front and their opponents Anti-Racist Action (as well as mayor June Rowland's inability to resolve it) into the national spotlight. Because the Latvian Hall had come under considerable pressure to deny the Heritage Front's repeated requests to rent the space, this new site was chosen for our next meeting and concert. By eight o'clock, over a hundred and fifty HF members showed up in the banquet room on the second floor, far fewer than the massive crowd of anti-racists who had mobilized outside and taken over surrounding streets.

Hundreds of people had converged for this anti-fascist rally from as far away as Quebec. Inside the building, even with the windows closed, we could hear the demonstrators shouting, deliberately trying to make as much noise as possible to disrupt our meeting.

I walked to a window, lifted the corner of a shade and peered at the sea of furious faces below. Havoc had spilled over the roads. Placards were being waved around: *Anti-Racist Action is here to stay,* they said. *Death to Nazis.* The activists chanted singsong phrases like, *Hey-hey, ho-ho, the Heritage Front has got to go!*

Police on horses had begun to make their way through the swarm of bandanna-wearing protesters, waving their riot sticks in the air. We would need a lot of police presence to get out of the building at the end of the night, I thought. But like Wolfgang said, police these days were more inclined to smash in the heads of scumbag street youth who recited, *Kops and Klan go hand-in-hand*, than arrest us nice folks who flattered their egos with a *How ya doing, officer.*

The scared-eyed management of the Roma restaurant were rightfully beside themselves – afraid to kick us out and put themselves under attack by more than a hundred fierce-looking skinheads, while simultaneously terrified at the likelihood of propriety damage that could easily ensue if the activists outside tried to rush the building. As a compromise, they closed the bar at the back early to prevent a complete meltdown. It didn't matter; most of the guys present were already buzzed, having polished off enough beer at home to put them in the mood for a street brawl.

Whenever Grant took the podium, the audience was captivated; merely opening his mouth was enough of a net to reel everyone in. His opening speech tonight was no different. As he started the talk by addressing the situation raging outside, skinheads nodded and swilled back their beers. Enthralled, they gazed up at Grant with utmost respect. He knew the anger they felt inside. He was on their side. A natural-born *führer*.

"There's one little thing I want to discuss with you guys in regards to how you use the Heritage Front name," he said. "It's good to use it when we promote the concept of white separatism. We would appreciate it, however, if people didn't use the Heritage Front name when promoting death on the telephone against another individual, throwing objects on people's front porches or rocks through windows."

Stray laughter broke from the crowd. Grant continued, a sarcastic expression on his face. "We just had another visit from the police in relation to another firebombing they're trying to pin on the Heritage Front. When leftists do actions like that, they just make up a new name every time: one day they're out demonstrating and throwing eggs as the ARA, the next day they're Lesbians for a Free Guatemala. So, use your imagination…"

The advice generated spontaneous applause. People howled with laughter, nodding, *Duh*. Of course – when you kick somebody to death, make sure you don't leave your calling card at the scene. I wondered who had been stupid enough to spray-paint the Heritage Front's hotline number on the walls of the recently-firebombed abortion clinic. Glancing around the room at the skinheads shouting "White Power", it looked to me like there were a shitload of individuals present who were a few cards short of a full deck.

Grant pumped his fist in the air to an enthusiastic ovation. When the cheers died down, he added, "But we are NOT going to let the parasites at the Human Rights Commission shut us down. Help us tonight to fight these people by putting money in the collection tin that's being passed around. Show up at the courthouse and provide moral support. We're gonna stop them in Ontario. We're not gonna let them go to Quebec, the Atlantic provinces or Manitoba. We're gonna fight them every step of the way, and cost them a whole lot of money. *WHITE POWER!*"

Grant was a tough act to follow. After the speeches wrapped up, the chairs were stacked against the walls and George Burdi took the stage, opening with a classic Screwdriver song: *Nigger, nigger, get on that boat. Nigger, nigger, go go go*!

Rahowa's ear-splitting music resulted in spontaneous straight-arm salutes and mashing, an odd phenomenon where skinheads smash into each other like bumper cars. "Death to wiggers!" someone shouted from the crowd. Wiggers were what was known in the movement as white people who were wanna-be blacks. "Eighty-eight!" said another. 88 was code for the eighth letter of the alphabet, which in turn stood for Heil Hitler.

The meeting-slash-concert had been a complete success. The process of exiting was not so straight-forward, however. Wolfgang, always a junkie for an adrenaline rush, put his arm around me. *Are you ready for this? Stay close to me and whatever you do, don't get separated.*

It was one in the morning but the whole city had exploded in flames of shouting, broken bottles and horse hooves. As we squeezed through the barricades of riot police and screaming Anti-Racist Action members, SHARPs (Skinheads Against Racial Prejudice), communists, feminists, international socialists, hippies and every other group that wanted to tear a piece of us tonight, life took on the quality of a slow-motion reel.

Protesters were trying to hurl bottles at our heads. Hand-to-hand skirmishes erupted. People turned their placards upside down and tried to use the wooden sticks as weapons to jab at our group. Batons were flying through the crowds. I thought that at any moment they were going to break out the tear gas, and then we were all going to be fucked.

128

Hands tore at my clothes, my hair. Everything became a blur. I was going underwater, and any second now I was going to drown under the weight of the violence around us. And then Wolfgang shoved me forward. I could feel the heat of his laughter close to my ear.

This is what he lived for.

SIXTEEN

THE PUPPET MASTER

In the winter of 1992, about thirty of us in the Heritage Front core had gathered at the Parkway. The only thing we knew was that the meeting had something to do with the direction of the HF. What were we going to do next? Somebody thought maybe we should plan another concert, or go distribute flyers in the Beaches. Wolfgang said nothing, smirking his usual Cheshire cat grin.

Around 10:30 PM Grant made his entrance, briefcase in hand, file folder under the arm. We all turned to him expectantly, eager for instructions.

Wolfgang cleared his throat. "Grant and I have been speaking about the direction we should take the Heritage Front. As I've said before, we'll continue to have the HF as the political arm of the organization, like Sinn Fein has done in Ireland, and keep our noses clean in order to infiltrate the Reform Party. But we've also decided to take a step in a different direction and create a Heritage Front Intelligence Unit. Grant will take on the role of Director."

An intelligence unit? Was he going to train us to be spies? We simultaneously turned our attention to the Director in question, waiting for an explanation.

"Folks, it's time," Grant said with a twinkle in his eye. "Time to ramp up the fight against those who want to shut us down. Time to fuck with heads and make them shit their pants."

He paused to scan our faces, building up the suspense. Finally, he took a deep breath. "As you all know, I'm a licensed private detective. I have a certain skillset that is in high demand. After discussing things with Wolfgang, we both agreed that we need to form an Intelligence cadre in which all of you will play a role. I'm going to teach you the tricks of my trade and how to fight back against the enemies of freedom. How to put degenerate faggot scumbags like Kevin T., his fine-feathered friend Rodney, and despicable commie dykes like Ruth M. out of their misery. How to push them until they self-destruct."

He paused to let the news sink in. "There's only so much we can do without wiretapping, unless we recruit someone who works for the phone company. But there are always ways to find out who these communist degenerates are."

Grant' list of alternative data-gathering means was straight-forward. In no particular order, we would be taught how to:

1) Use special tricks to crack into anti-racist groups' answering machines, starting with the Native Canadian Centre on Spadina Road and the Anti-Racist Action Hotline. When we had gathered enough data, we'd break into the answering systems of those who had left their numbers on the original machines.

2) Use reverse directories to track home addresses. If an address was unlisted, use other deceptive ways to get it, such as calling to pretend the target had won something and offering to mail out their prize.

3) Impersonate the target, then spread rumours about the target.

4) Impersonate reporters and call up various ethnic and Jewish organizations to conduct mock interviews for the purpose of gathering information.

5) Attend anti-racist rallies in disguise and wait in cars equipped with police scanners, thus intercepting any demonstrators' information that cops might radio back to headquarters.

6) Use Hydro utility directories and voters' registries to identify all residents at a particular address. Follow people to and from work. Watch and photograph targets.

It was a game in which we competed against one another in who could be most clever, gather the most addresses and phone numbers. My biggest competition came from The Fischer brothers, an interchangeable pair of meatheads who constantly vied for Grant's attention. One year later they (along with Drew Maynard) would be arrested and charged with the kidnapping and torture of one Tyrone Mason. Already teased mercilessly by the other skinheads for having a "black guy name", the poor bastard had been accused by George Burdi of stealing a computer that contained the full membership list of the Heritage Front. Even though he denied it, the guys decided to drive by Tyrone's place in a white van, pull him inside, beat him up for over three hours and threaten to inject him with a syringe filled with Windex.

Aside from providing security at Heritage Front and COTC events, both Erik and Elkar "Carl" Fischer were members of the Canadian Airborne Regiment, a unit of our armed forces that would get disbanded in 1995 after the Somalia Affair (and the leadership's attempt at a cover-up). The Somalia Affair would be seared into the collective memory of Canadians for decades to come because it involved the brutal beating death of a Somali teenager at the hands of two Canadian soldiers deployed to serve humanitarian efforts in Somalia.

Instead of sticking to their peacekeeping duties, Cpl Clayton Matchee and Trooper Kyle Brown caught their victim, Shidane Arone, in the vicinity of their compound. Without any evidence to back their charge, they accused him of trying to steal army supplies, proceeded to beat him, sodomise him with a broomstick, burn his genitals, and take "trophy" photos of the torture. The killing took place weeks after Canadian soldiers shot two other unarmed Somalis in the back, killing one of them. In that incident, allegations were made that trophy photos of the corpse were also taken. Two additional Somalis had been killed on that tour of duty.

Aside from thrill-kill murderers, or boneheads like the Fischer brothers, who gave Church Of The Creator skinheads weekly paramilitary training and had now been recruited by Grant Bristow for the *It Campaign*, the Canadian Airborne Regiment was rife with other neo-Nazis like the eight soldiers who attended a Nazi rally in Metcalfe, ON, and the unforgettable Matt McKay. Posing in front of a Nazi swastika banner hung in his army barracks, Winnipeg-born McKay gave a straight-arm Seig Heil salute while wearing a Hitler tee-shirt – a bit of an overkill, but his desire to make sure the world *really* knew he was a Fascist added to then-Defence Minister Kim Campbell's and Canadian Armed Forces' decision that the Airborne Regiment was a lost cause and needed to be kyboshed before it caused further embarrassment.

Incidentally, Cpl Matt McKay was an associate of Aryan Nations Canada leader Terry Long and a past member of the Manitoba KKK and the Final Solution Skinheads in Winnipeg. He was quoted as saying that he went to Somalia to *"shoot me a nigger,"* and was caught on video saying, *"we ain't killed enough niggers yet."*

The Dirty Tricks, a preamble to what would come to be known as the *It Campaign*, got underway that winter. It essentially marked the commencement of psychological terror tactics against community activists, Anti-Racist Action and Toronto Coalition Against Racism members, and organizations such as the Native Canadian Centre – its executive director Rodney Bobiwash being a particular target given that he ran the Klanbusters Hotline and had lodged a Human Rights Commission complaint against the Heritage Front Hotline (or HateLine, as opponents called it).

It started with threatening phone calls. At least a dozen people were targeted further, having their workplaces called by Heritage Front members directed by Grant Bristow to use every pretext in the book to get targets fired from their jobs. He had a short target list of ARA protesters and Aboriginal rights activists he hated more than anything in the world. One of them, Kevin Thomas, had been targeted mercilessly and at one point topped the IT Campaign list.

Grant, who often called male ARA activists *faggot* as a rule of thumb no matter what their sexual orientation was, boasted of having phoned Kevin's workplace in an attempt to get him fired. Using a three-way conference calling system, he ensured that I listened in on some of the calls as 'examples' of what I should say to managers. " Did you know your employee is engaging in political activity on company time?" Grant cackled. "Did you know your employee is a pedophile and procuring children for sex? Were you aware that your staff is involved in bestiality?"

Wanting to push the envelope on the bestiality angle, Grant had ordered a box of live gerbils to be delivered to another activist's workplace, cash on delivery of course. Later I would be told by Rodney Bobiwash that they often had pizzas and weird knickknacks delivered to the Native Centre – he'd even received a large doll that had been delivered in his name.

For extra kicks, Grant would tell another frightened Human Resources personnel that the employee in question was "a virulent white supremacist." It was the office's duty, therefore, to stop him in order to save children from the Nazis who would use them in various sexual perversions. He especially got a kick out of that line, *Save the Children.*

Answering machines were broken into and phone numbers lifted. The list of people to be terrorized was passed around at the Parkway to skinheads who bragged about it afterwards. Anti-racist activists, along with those unfortunate enough to have left their personal information on those answering machines, were stalked.

Along with handing out telephone numbers indiscriminately and rattling off the names of enemies who were out to shut us down and needed to be neutralized, Grant instructed members on how to use the Freedom of Information Act and easily-accessible sources – reverse-directories, water bills, voters' registries, drivers' licence bureaus – to track down people who could be targeted for future actions. He taught us how to spot and avoid surveillance and how to get around police questioning.

Even though I had no idea what Grant was going to do with the information we fetched and delivered like trained dogs, I forced myself not to think about it. Wolfgang had drilled it into my head that it was best not to ask questions – ignorance would never be incriminating.

This was only a game.

As the only female at the Parkway the night our Intelligence wing was born, Grant had a special request for me. He scrawled a name and number on a notepad and ripped out the page, pushing it over to me.

"I want you in on this one, Elisse. Start by calling some personal sex lines," he said, eyes shiny with glee. "Like the ones listed in the back of *Now* Magazine. Record a personal ad saying your name is Ruth M and this is your phone number. Say that you're into real hard-core masochism, that you'd love to be raped by blacks and beaten with chains. Say that they can call you any time, day or night. The later the better."

I didn't do it, but I kept her number. His odd request made me wonder who Ruth was and why he had such a hate-on for her. This was a side of Grant I'd never seen before. I wasn't sure how to react to the ever-widening gap between the dignified Grant Bristow, respected leader in the Heritage Front, and this new man who delighted in tormenting people arbitrarily. He boasted of having directed a small group of skinheads to show up and pound on her door in the middle of the night. After the police was called and the skinheads had scattered, he'd waited an hour before calling to say, "We're still on our way."

If anyone else had any qualms, they certainly didn't reveal them to me. Everyone was careful not to question him.

Moving forward, I resolved to put any misgivings out of my head. To be on Grant' good side meant getting swept up into an exciting cloak and dagger operation. He was training us to be spies. I marvelled at Grant' ability to hack into any answering machine. His talents were incontestably brilliant. You'd never want to go against him; his intense hatred, even among white supremacists, was scary. He did all this with flair and persuasion of a thousand men. Nobody could say no to Grant. He was god.

Months later, in a moment I would recall vividly in one of my affidavits, I would summon the courage to ask, "Why Ruth?"

Grant would shrug dismissively. "Collective guilt   collective responsibility. She must be punished. And to think, the miserable bitch hasn't even thanked me. Not even once, after taking all this time out of my busy day to deal with her."

He burst into hysterical laughter. "I want to pound Ruth's head in. I want to give her a facial massage with a sledgehammer."

SEVENTEEN

REALITY CHECK

On the rare occasions when I wasn't meeting the boys at the Parkway, riding around town with Wolfgang on his bailiff runs or helping Ernst at the Bunker, hanging out with Nicola was the only way to relieve my boredom. And for whatever reason, Nicola seemed to enjoy my company. She saw me as a little sister she liked to fuss over. "You're so rough around the edges," she'd complain. "Why don't you let me do your hair? Don't you care how you look? God knows you're old enough to start dating."

She talked me into spending the odd Sunday evening at her house where, as promised, she trimmed my split-ends and put highlights in my long hair. The process took a couple of hours altogether what with the application of the dye, the waiting, the rinsing and the drying afterwards. Wolfgang's new girlfriend Marque sometimes came over, and after Nicola's little ones went to bed the two of them sipped their white wine, bitched about men and teased me.

"Good to get out of the Bunker once in a while, isn't it?" Marque taunted. "Surely you want more for yourself than to be folding pamphlets when you're eighty, like Alfred-the-Owl. What do you *really* want to be when you grow up?"

"I want to be a terrorist," I said.

Nicola furrowed her eyebrows. "Seriously, is that what you *really* want?"

I nodded. "It's not really terrorism anyway. It's being a freedom-fighter. I've been reading all about it. Women in the IRA, the RAF, the Red Brigades, forming underground cells...."

"Elisse dear, those are all Marxist guerrilla movements," she sneered. "They tolerate women's participation more than the right-wing. You bought into the wrong cause, sweetie. And even *if* you were a leftist, those groups are also dominated by assholes on a power trip. The only use they have for women is to sleep with them. Come *on.*"

Marque frowned. "Since when did you decide on this career path?"

"Since she's been hanging out with the boys, what do you think?" Nicola scoffed. "She's getting far too radical, too fast."

She turned to me and shook her head. "Where's this gonna lead? Getting killed, blowing yourself up, becoming some sort of martyr for the cause? I can't even imagine the kind of shit they're filling your head with. But guess what? You're still a kid and ultimately you have no clue as to what's important in the grander scheme of things. Wait until fall in love, have a child, have something to live for. You won't be so eager to go out and take others' lives or put your own in jeopardy."

I stood against the Formica counter and sipped my coke, reflecting on their words. I resented their opinion of my radical trajectory in the movement, yet there was a grain of truth in what they said. When I first joined the Front, it had been the comradeship and late-night political discussions at the Parkway that had hooked me. By the time I realized that they didn't see me as an equal it was too late, I was all too determined to prove myself. I saw us fighting for a mutual, glorious cause. But imperceptibly, over the last few months, the focus had shifted from advancing our cause to something entirely different.

I was irritated by Nicola's unspoken indictment, her thinking something was wrong with me. It's not like I wasn't trying. I kept waiting for "it" to happen, whatever that meant. At first patiently; then, as time went by, with annoyance. More than once I caught myself gazing toward the doorway of the Parkway, hoping that someone would walk in and miraculously stir a feeling in me where there was none. I sensed the pressure from others; it was as though I was the spoiled daughter of a fairytale king who was about to be given an ultimatum – make your choice of a husband or be given away to the first peasant who walks through the village.

Ernst Zundel himself, who didn't fancy himself as a matchmaker, had decided to set me up with Eric Hartmann, an enviable prospect in the movement considering his pedigree as the son of Rita Ann Hartmann, the virulent anti-abortionist and founder of the Northern Foundation (where core members of the Heritage Front had congregated in the years preceding the inception of the HF) and REAL Women of Canada. The Northern Foundation had many notable members in its heyday: Wolfgang Droege, Nationalist Party's Don Andrews, Paul Fromm, leader of what would evolve into the neo-Fascist Western Guard and CFAR, Preston Manning, head of the Reform Party, as well as many veteran Heritage Front adherents. But none was more famous than Canada's current Prime Minister, Stephen Harper.

For once, I agreed with the set-up. Eric's genes were Aryan gold – over six feet tall, with striking blue eyes and flaxen hair, he was sure to improve on my darker, Mediterranean complexion if we had kids. Above all, I thought Eric would make a fabulous boyfriend given the fact that he lived in Ottawa, a five-hour bus ride from Toronto, and was only in town for the big rallies. He'd be out of my hair most of the time.

And yet, after two dates and lots of encouragement from both Ernst and Wolfgang, the closest I came to being intimate with Eric was holding his hand as I walked him to the Greyhound station where he would catch the bus back to Ottawa.

I knew he had a huge crush on me by the way his eyes softened as he listened to me harp on about political subversion and revolution. With his strong-willed mother, he was used to being dominated by a matriarch. He was kind-spirited and never pushed me, which was odd for someone who was a leader among the skinheads of Ottawa. But in private, he was a softie. Secretly, I wondered if he would stay that way; this movement had a way of hardening people, sooner or later.

Just before he got on the bus, he leaned down and kissed me on the right cheek. It was such a gentle, respectful peck so unlike anything I had anticipated from a skinhead that I smiled back at him and thought, *I can do this. I should try harder.* And yet, as I stood on that platform and waved at him while the bus pulled out of the station, my eyes watered. I didn't want to continue this terrible game with Eric. He liked me too much, and I was frozen inside. Completely unable to reciprocate. A deep-set fear crept into my chest, constricting my ribs.

I knew people were starting to talk behind my back. I could feel it. And Marque confirmed my suspicions when she announced that she'd had enough. "I'm setting you up with David," she declared, with Nicola tittering in the background. "Before you say no, you should know he's not some loser skinhead. He's educated and well-spoken. To top it off, he's seen you around and wants to know you."

I rolled my eyes while she nudged me. "Come on, you have to start somewhere. If I wasn't already dating Wolfgang, I'd go cougar on David. He's the type of guy who knows how to treat a girl right, has a decent job and can take you out for dinner. You could do a lot worse. You just need a fling to lose your virginity and get the ball rolling. Trust me, he's the perfect guy to have for your first time."

On paper, David Earle was a dream. A youth leader in the Progressive Conservative Party and an active participant on Jean Charest's election campaign, David was blond, blue-eyed and oddly evocative of Rolf, the mailboy-cum-fascist in *The Sound of Music*. He was about twenty-two and certifiably English, having mapped out his heritage all the way back to the Crusades. In private, however, David was a tad more radical than Jean Charest or Preston Manning would have been comfortable with. You could say that David's fetish went far beyond collecting Nazi regalia – he was enraptured with the SS, boasting that he met all the requirements for recruitment into their elite ranks. To prove what a good SS officer he would have made, he planned to get the tell-tale tattoo received by men admitted into the SS, two black lightning bolts, tattooed on the inside of his left bicep.

On our first date he picked me up in his minivan while I waited for him near the Queen street and Shuter intersection, at the north-end corner where all the prostitutes hung out in the evening. I hopped from foot to foot and prayed he'd get there before I got propositioned. When he finally showed up, I jumped into the passenger seat while he leaned over to give me a peck on the cheek and all I could think was, Jesus, take it easy with the cologne.

"Have you eaten?" he asked, checking me out while pretending not to. I nodded yes. Truth was, I wasn't comfortable with the idea of him taking me out somewhere and paying the tab. I'd feel like I owed him something afterwards.

He looked pleased to skip the formalities. "You don't mind if we go for a drive?"

"Not at all." So much for Marque's promise that he'd wine and dine me.

"How about coming on my father's boat? It's docked along the marina and we can really get comfortable there. It's got a stocked bar."

A warning flag popped up in my head. No way was I going to go to some shipyard at this hour of the night. I didn't really know this guy. What if he spiked my drink or something? "Uh, maybe next time," I said. "Let's just drive around."

"You'd like it," he insisted. "I take all the girls I'm dating there."

I bet he did. He probably thought the peer pressure effect might whittle down my reluctance to go to the marina. He didn't know me very well. Revulsion spread over me as he threw his arm around my shoulders in one of those pretend-to-yawn moves. Common sense interfered, however, and I ignored the pressing temptation to shake him off.

Half an hour later we were parked in the shadows of a massive tree and he was latched onto my right breast with the voracity of a newborn infant who hadn't nursed in days. "You like this, don't you?" he breathed in my ear when he came up for air. "Are you wet yet? Am I turning you on?"

"Umm, I think so," I said so he wouldn't feel bad. Taking that as encouragement, David's fingers found their way to the crotch of my jeans. His tongue felt foreign in my mouth, a slippery eel trying to ram itself down my throat. I felt like my face was being scraped by sandpaper. Gingerly, I reached up and rubbed my cheek.

David read my mind. "I should have shaved today, huh?"

His breath smelled like sour beer and cigarettes and I hated that he was a sloppy kisser. As he reached to unzip my jeans, I stopped him. "Let me touch you instead," I offered. A gesture of appeasement. When I'd recount this night to Marque, I didn't want to be accused of not being forthcoming enough.

He unfastened his pants and guided my hand down to his crotch. "Like this," he showed me. "Up and down. That's right, you're doing great," he moaned, throwing his head back against the seat.

I thought his pale, fat penis, which glowed grotesquely in the moonlight, was just about the ugliest thing I'd seen in my life. But better I handled it with my hand, at arm's length, than have it come into contact with more intimate parts of my body.

He came in less than five minutes. Panting heavily, he grabbed a Kleenex box from the dashboard and stepped out of the van to get cleaned up. I wiped my hand on the side of my jeans, over and over. If this was what dating was supposed to be like, I was in serious trouble.

Marque scrutinized my face closely the next time we had our girls' night at Nicola's house, searching for evidence of deflowering. Finding none, she frowned. "What? Don't you like David? Did he make you feel uncomfortable?"

"No, not at all," I stammered. "I just didn't want to do it with him."

"Well, you don't have to, not on your first date. Of course not. Just go out a few more times, have a couple of drinks and let it happen naturally. That's how I lost *my* virginity. *Thank God* I was drunk," she laughed.

According to her, my only problem was that I was really uptight and I should just get drunk and get it over with. But the thought of having sex with David turned my stomach.

"Elisse." her voice now turned insistent, serious. I glanced up. Her eyes burned into me. "You're not...I mean, you don't...""

She hesitated. I arched an eyebrow, prompting her to continue. She took a deep breath. "It's not because you like girls, is it? You're not like that...are you?" her voice trailed off.

I choked on my coke. "Of course not. Jesus, that's disgusting."

Nicola leaned into me and grasped my arm. "I've heard that Grant put you up to crank-calling some of them," she said in a hushed tone. "You have to be careful, you know. Those kinds of people, they recruit youngsters like you."

"You mean, recruit like the Heritage Front does?" I started giggling. "Is there an incentive plan? A toaster or something?"

She squeezed my arm to shush me. "Come on, I'm not joking. A pretty young girl like you has to watch herself around people like that. Don't even walk on Church Street. I've never understood Grant's idiotic plans to target queers."

"Okay, all right," I said, willing her to stop.

"Elisse, look at me." Her gaze went through me like a needle, leaving me cold. "You'd tell me if you were...if you were like that. Wouldn't you?"

"But I'm *not*." I shook myself free of her grasp. "Let's just stop talking about this." I avoided her stare and prayed that she wouldn't notice the deep blush that had started to spread over my cheeks. My fingers twisted in my lap.

Nicola's voice nudged me back to reality. "Sweetie, they're starting to ask questions. You've been in the movement for more than a year and you've never had a boyfriend. That's not *normal*. All the other girls in the Front are busy trying to make little Aryan babies. That's just how it is. I'm just trying to help you out here. You know that, right? *Right?*"

Nicola's insistence made me think back to a joke someone had made behind Gerry Lincoln's back, about how he'd been spotted walking past the gay bars on Church Street, the *de facto* gay area in Toronto's downtown. The next time Gerry called me to shoot the breeze, I let the conversation drift to his queer rants before I broached the subject. "What should someone do, hypothetically, if they thought they were gay?"

"If they can't make themselves lead a straight lifestyle, the only honourable thing is to kill themselves. Why do you ask?"

"Just curious. They say that homosexuality isn't a choice, it's something you're born with. What do you think about that?"

He snorted indignantly. "We all have free choice as human beings. We can choose to suppress the urge for an unnatural lifestyle."

"What about all those evangelical preachers who keep getting caught with young guys? They say they couldn't help themselves."

Another grunt. "You know what, Elisse? You think too much. Why don't you get yourself dolled up and forget about politics? With a skin-tight pair of jeans and a tighter top you could recruit guys a whole lot better than engaging in pointless discourse."

"I'm not going to whore myself to get new recruits."

"Who said you have to fuck them? Just put some makeup on, let your hair down. You get more flies with honey than by being a shit-disturber. Men are natural breadwinners, women are child-bearers and homemakers. Girls should start having children by age sixteen instead of polluting their minds with information that won't be useful to them in the home. Remember the old German saying: *kinder, kuche, kirche* – children, kitchen, church."

"Give me a break. You'd rather have me barefoot and pregnant."

"Darn right. You can't hide what you are. You don't have a dick between your legs so don't act like you do. By the way, you're welcome to come over and watch Ilsa with me."

Oh no, not *Ilsa, She-Wolf of the SS*. It was Gerry's favourite porno flick. It had blonde, sadistic Nazis with huge fake tits and black leather chaps, and once he got going, that was all he could chat about until I hung up. *What was I thinking, asking Gerry, of all people, about this?* It wasn't like I could really talk about it with anyone. I didn't even want to admit it to myself. But gay people made me curious. Nervous.

Between morning rallies and evening meetings with comrades, I spent long afternoons wandering along the alleyways near Church street, spying on gay bars, looking furtively at passersby of the same gender holding hands.

I hated them. They were perverted and weak, giving in to instincts that should have been controlled, overcome somehow. *Why couldn't they be strong?* I stared at women who exchanged kisses on the patios of restaurants, and butterflies churned in my stomach. The thought of a woman touching me like that repulsed me.

Once in a while, gay activists recognized me from a rally. They crossed the street angrily to confront me, an obvious intruder on their turf. The fact that I always wore my black Docs and bomber jacket didn't do anything to conceal my identity as a neo-Nazi. Today it would be a heavy-set activist who glowered at me from across the street. She waddled over, fuming. "Get out of here. We don't want your kind making trouble."

I laughed in her face. "I'm not doing anything," I said, holding my palms up. "See? I'm just standing on a sidewalk watching the fruits mill about."

She shook her head in frustration. Coarse dark curls flew into her eyes. She brushed them away swiftly, scowled at me one last time and disappeared into a watering hole I recognized as a lesbian hangout that someone in the HF had suggested should be firebombed.

I laughed again and turned away, failing to notice the dark figure coming straight for me. Before I could react, a woman wearing a black leather jacket had materialized out of nowhere. She grabbed me by the collar and threw me against a wall. Her right hand pressed over my neck while her left arm was drawn back, fingers tightened into a fist.

I stood as still as I could, my gaze darting from the fist that hovered an inch away from my head to her furious eyes and back again. I winced, anticipating the blow.

"Just what do you think you're doing here?" she yelled in my face. "Anyone else with you?" She took a glance to the left and right, then glared back at me. "There's lots of people here who can really fuck you up, you know," she hissed.

I continued to say nothing. My heart pounded hard in my throat. I was certain she was going to strike me. The funny thing was, a part of me actually wanted her to hit me, more than anything.

Her grip loosened imperceptibly. "What, you don't wanna fight?" she mocked me. "Look at me when I'm talking to you." She jerked my collar hard, forcing me to stare directly at her.

I caught my breath. She was taller than me, probably about five-seven. Her blue-black hair was pulled back in a taut ponytail. I glanced away quickly. My cheeks burned. A heat wave coursed through my entire body.

She continued to watch me. "What are you, sixteen?"

"Seventeen," I managed to whisper.

"Seventeen," she repeated. "And this is what you're doing with your life. Pathetic."

Out of the corner of my eye I noticed two of her friends run over to us. ARA activists. "Nope, there aren't any more of them around. Looks like this one came on her own," one of them said, cocking an eyebrow. "Cruisin' for a bruisin'. She giving you any trouble?"

The woman scrutinized me for another moment. My heart stopped. Suddenly she let go. "Nah. Just go home, kid." An unreadable expression came over her face. Her lips twisted in a disdainful smile. "Don't get caught around here again. You never know who else will see you. Some of your friends maybe? Next time you might not get off this easy."

Mortified, I slinked away from her, turned and walked fast, then broke into a run. I heard the women's laughter rise up behind me. Later that night as I tried to fall asleep, I replayed the whole thing in my head, imagined those hands pinning me back, this time not letting me go. I started crying underneath the bedcovers. I had never felt lonelier.

EIGHTEEN

THE LEAFLET

It was a starless night, murkier still after the earlier downpour, and the wet pavements stunk of petrol and smeared mud. As was his habit, Wolfgang dropped by my building complex unannounced, buzzing me from downstairs just as I was getting ready for bed. Within ten minutes I was dressed and in his car, waiting for him to tell me what was up.

I rolled down the window to get some air only to be hit with the stench of decaying leaves overflowing the gutter. I thought he was turning toward Parliament Street when he took a sharp detour, turning the wrong way. "I need to grab some files back at the office," Wolfgang said, noting my questioning glance.

"It's close to midnight," I complained, stifling a yawn.

Wolfgang laughed. "Since when have you ever gone to bed before three?"

It was probably quarter to one when we pulled into the deserted parking lot in front of the bailiff's office Wolfgang shared with Al Overfield. I'd been there only twice before, but had waited in Wolfgang's car while he'd gone in to get his files. This was the first time I got to peek inside.

All in all, it wasn't a large space so much as an efficient one. You stepped through the unassuming door into a vast open room. I noticed the absence of formalities such as a welcome desk or the kind of cheaply-upholstered chairs that are perennials in a standard waiting room; this office was not intended for outside visitors. The walls were stark white, bereft of wall-hangings. Along one wall were a couple of large steel filing cabinets, a heavy-duty, industrial-sized photocopier and an elongated table next to it, loaded with office equipment. The centre of the room was occupied by an oversized desk and a telephone switchboard system.

Wolfgang grabbed the files he had come for, and on our way out he took up a thick stack of flyers next to the photocopier. We got back in the car and drove back to my building. When he'd pulled over to drop me off, he impulsively reached over the dashboard and handed me a batch of the freshly-printed leaflets.

"So? what do you think?" He looked giddy as he watched my face for a response.

My eyes scanned the flyer. It was a cartoon likely lifted from one of Tom Metzger's White Aryan Resistance zines, featuring a split view of a black man and a gorilla. Running underneath the cartoon titled Animal Life Series No. 1 was the full name of a woman named Celeste, along with an address and telephone number. I had no doubt that it was her home number, though it was listed as 'Association for the Advancement of Simian Intelligence'.

"You like it?" Unable to contain his amusement, Wolfgang started to laugh. "The niggers are going to be hopping all over her for this."

I stared at him with incredulity. "Who's Celeste?"

He shrugged. "Who cares? Some ARA bitch."

I blinked. "You're going to pass *this* out?"

He laughed. "Not only are we going to, but you'll be taking a bunch home yourself. Post them around downtown and in your area. I want your Regent Park neighbours to see these. A couple of skinheads have already committed to taking them over to Jane and Finch."

This was the only flyer I'd ever received that I was reluctant to pass out. It crossed an invisible line in the sand. Celeste's home address and phone number had been brought into Overfield's office by Grant Bristow earlier in the week, along with the cartoon itself. But despite all the harassment and stalking of antiracists that Grant had already directed, witnessing Wolfgang's eagerness to go along with this new dirty tricks scheme was chilling. The cold reality that he was setting someone up for a beating or worse struck me like a fist against bone. Until now, we had been revolutionaries training to defend ourselves in the fight for a greater cause. But this wasn't a fair fight. Not even close.

Someone could really get hurt here. What did this Celeste ever do to deserve this?

Moreover, what was *I* going to do about it?

The answer came to me a few days later, as I was getting ready to attend my weekly Irish Gaelic night class at Brockton High School. I had been tense all day, thinking of the two Anti-Racist Action activists who were enrolled in the same class. We had tried to ignore each other but I knew they were watching me like hawks, anticipating that I might cause trouble.

Give it to them! the nagging voice inside my mind wouldn't be quieted. *They know Celeste, they'll warn her. It's the only way.*

That night I would indeed pass out a flyer, but not in the way Wolfgang had intended. And unknown to me at the time, giving those women the Animal Series flyer would set in motion a series of events that would change my life, and the Heritage Front, forever.

During the mid-break, with the two activists scowling at me, I fished the flyer out of my pocket and handed it to the one named Edan. "This is what they're doing now," I said.

The taller of the two, Shannon, peered over Edan's shoulder. "What is this?"

"Do you know Celeste?" I pointed to the name printed underneath the cartoon.

They nodded in unison.

"Would you give it to her?"

Shannon cleared her throat. "Why...why are you giving us this?"

"Look, she has a right to know what's being passed around. It's got her name and number right on it, see?"

"I see."

"I – I think she's being harassed and I don't think she deserves this."

"What's it to you?" Edan snapped, folding the paper and slipping it into her pocket.

"It doesn't feel right." It was lame, but the only thing I could think to say.

The women exchanged glances, and the second one snickered. I took that as my cue to turn on my heel and sprint away as quickly as I could down the school corridor. Edan's footsteps rang behind me and she chased me into the women's washroom.

What followed was an intense conversation that left both of us shaken and me in tears. Edan insisted that I leave the Heritage Front, while I shook my head in desperation. "They're my only family," I insisted. "I can't."

"Then maybe you should find a new family," she replied, not missing a beat.

What nobody knew then, not even myself, was that a great chasm had broken inside me. I was no longer certain of whether I was revolutionary or victim, a Heritage Front member or a girl without any identity of her own. A girl whose entire self was molded by a hateful ideology, but who was as hollow as a bullet on the inside. The imaginary line I'd drawn between myself and the antiracist women targeted by the Heritage Front had gone from blurred to virtually nonexistent.

When our war of ideology had begun to fade out and the faces of real, living and breathing people appeared in its place, people we were supposed to target simply because of their different beliefs, gender and skin colour, everything ceased to be a game. I saw, in full and bleeding Technicolor, the entire future trajectory of the Heritage Front. The destruction and horror that lay full-steam ahead.

And now, half of me stood on one side of the precipice, political manifesto in one hand, naïve ideals in another.

Across the great and dark abyss, a newer-born fragment of my consciousness was shaking, empty-handed, peering stubbornly into the void below in search of a glimmer, an infinitesimal spark of something that she herself didn't know if she could recognize.

NINETEEN

THE IT CAMPAIGN
St Patrick's Day, 1993

In a world where nearly every Heritage Front member had a criminal record, news of my arrest, about a week after I had warned the ARA activists, made little splash. Everybody assumed I had been caught putting up a flyer at Brock and that Celeste contacted the police because her name was on it. It would have been inconceivable to imagine I had done something that could be considered a profound betrayal of the Heritage Front. When Max French, Gerry and Wolfgang himself pleaded with me to tell police that I had fabricated the flyers and take the rap for Wolf, I refused. "You won't do any time," Wolfgang argued. "You've just turned eighteen, you're a girl and don't have a criminal record. You'll get probation."

I may have been willing to go along with the Heritage Front on almost everything, but this was one sticking point I wouldn't budge on: lying to save Wolfgang's ass. As far as I was concerned, he should have been happy that I hadn't ratted anybody out. But I'd rather have gone to jail forever than admit guilt when I was innocent.

Now that I couldn't go over to the Bunker or hang out at the Parkway without breaking bail conditions, finding things to occupy my days became increasingly difficult. I looked forward to the St. Patrick's Sunday afternoon parade to see if I would run into my Gaelic teacher who, after my arrest, had decided to have me kicked out of her class. I figured she owed me an explanation.

A ten-foot tall leprechaun wearing an enormous hat with a gold buckle sauntered by, throwing strings of green beads at the multitude of watchers. I stuck my hand into the air and snatched it, pleased as punch that I had beaten a pudgy seven-year old boy to it. I slipped the necklace around my neck and scanned the crowd for familiar faces.

Further along the street, a black bomber jacket gleamed in the sun. It belonged to a skinhead with white power patches sown on. He was standing next to someone I assumed was his girlfriend, a tall strawberry blonde with a Chelsea haircut.

I walked over to them. "Hey, guys."

His face brightened. "I know you…Heritage Front, right?"

I smiled. "Yup. You guys up to something or just hanging out?"

"Just chilling," he said. "I'm Dave. I saw you on the news. Meant to go down to the last concert but I was in lock-up."

"You're not members of the HF, are you? Bail conditions, you know."

He nodded sympathetically. "Nah, it's cool. We don't have membership cards or nothing like that. Actually, the only group I'm a member of is the local Imperial Knights of the KKK, but doesn't look like I'll be staying."

"Oh, yeah? Why?"

"I haven't gone to the last bi-weekly meetings and they have this retarded rule that if you skip three meetings, you're out. They're assholes about it. Found out the hard way that they don't let their people go easily. I've already been in one fight and they're following me and Holly around now, can you freaking believe it?"

"No shit."

The girl piped in. "Wanna come to the Eaton Centre with us? We're headed there now."

As we hung out for the afternoon, I realized that Dave suffered from the classic "I-wanna-start-my-own-group" syndrome. "What I'd really like," he confessed, "is to have a heart-to-heart with Wolfgang and share some of my plans with him. You think you could fix it for me? And can you ask him if I can get in without having to pay ten bucks for membership? We're two months late on the rent already and the landlord is gunning to evict us. So you think Wolfgang might let me in? I really think he'd be interested in some of my ideas…"

Before I could answer, he went on. "Oh, I do realize he is quite busy. I approached him at a rally but he was so ambushed by all these people, I barely had the chance to say hello. But who knows, if you put in a good word for me…"

I kept my face impassive. "I'll see what I can do."

Holly looked pleased. "We live down on Sherburne and Parliament, you know the area?"

"That's just around the corner from where I live."

"Cool, we were just heading back. Wanna walk over to our place?"

Over the next few weeks, I got to know Dave and Holly well. They were former street kids who'd pulled their shit together just enough to get into a basement apartment in a hooker building that always smelled like piss and stale cigarettes. But they were ten minutes away from my building on Shuter street, and hanging out with them kept me from going crazy.

Their scene differed immensely from the Front. For them, life wasn't a political debate – it was gritty, hardcore reality. Street kids didn't give a rat's ass about ideology. Skinheads drifted in and out of the left wing. It wasn't unusual to have friends on both sides, as friends were made while food was scavenged and shared. No one in their right mind would turn their head when offered a drag from a joint just because the offer came from an anti-racist. Their motto was simply, *Don't fuck with me and I won't fuck with you.*

The thing that made them most appealing to me was that they knew a lot of people in the ARA. Holly in particular had gone back and forth on the scene, depending on which boyfriend she'd had at the time. We started to talk about anti-racists when Holly casually mentioned, "Yeah, I know a few of them."

It caught me unprepared. "W-what?"

"I know some of those people. I used to volunteer at the 519, the gay community centre on Church Street. Why? You think it might be important?"

I took out my notepad. "We need to talk," I said.

As it turned out, she was a goldmine of information on the left-wing. I knew I'd hit the jackpot. No sooner did I get home that I called Grant. He insisted on taking me out for lunch at the Parkway to discuss a strategy, right then and there. Only an hour later, I was sitting across from him – the first of several private meetings we would have over the months to come. He handed me a stack of grainy prints taken from rally videotapes, mostly of youth with bandannas obstructing half of their faces.

"Try to get her to identify some of these fuckers," Grant said. "You'll be doing me a huge favour."

He fished around in his pocket and came up with a twenty-dollar bill. "Make friends with this girl, take her out or something. Get her talking and scoop her brains. Find out everything – where the street kids hang out, where they're squatting, who's in charge."

I was elated. Sure, I couldn't attend rallies or work at Ernst's Bunker, but the honour of working behind the scenes on intelligence matters with Grant surpassed all other duties in importance.

That month, true to my word, I became Holly's best friend. I told her the Heritage Front Intelligence needed her assistance and how important she was to us. She was flattered, so much so that she helped me identify more than half of the grainy stills. She also gave me the address where the ARA held their meetings, along with the names of everybody who lived there.

The information I collected from Holly would, in turn, bring me closer than ever to Grant. I met with him weekly, and he fed me further questions to ask. "You're doing good work, real good," he praised me. "This shit really gets into your blood, doesn't it? And you have a real knack for it."

I nodded. Making Grant happy gave me a good feeling. I was of value to him.

He smiled generously. "Didn't you once go to a meeting with the Irish Freedom Association?"

"Yeah, but it wasn't too exciting. Just a bunch of middle-aged people who get together for pints of Guinness and listen to depressing ballads."

"Doesn't matter. Think you could go there again and get me some names? You know that IFA group is a bunch of commies, don't you? You'd be doing me a big favour."

"Of course," I said. "Anything."

"And keep holding that Holly girl's hand," he added. "Buy them a six-pack, see what comes out when they get drunk."

Girls made more money panhandling so lots of times Holly and me sat on the sidewalk on Yonge Street and begged for spare change. Dave kept watch across the street in case anyone hassled us. When hunger forced us from the curb, we made our way to the Evergreen youth drop-in centre or the soup kitchen on Dundas street. Why bother wasting our newly-earned money on food when we could get meals for free? I let them keep my share of the panhandling money since they were always on the brink of running out of smokes or falling back on their rent.

"There's a trick we use mostly in case of emergencies," Holly said. "You know that cruising spot near the corner of Dundas and Shuter street? The one where all the hookers and pimps hang out at night? I go there sometimes, real late, and wait for some loser john to approach me. I lead him down this alley and tell him to wait a sec because I have to go check that there's no cops. Then I hide while Dave and his buddy Mike come out from this fire-escape ladder where they hid and jump the guy. They beat the shit out of him and take his money."

"For real?" I looked at her quizzically. She stared back and laughed.

"Hey, it's not like we do it that often – only in case of emergencies, you know? Those guys are total creeps. One time, one of them tried to rape me before Dave kicked his head in."

Although they were on welfare, it wasn't enough to cover Dave's hash addiction. He had some debts Holly wouldn't tell me about and the situation was dire. "He thinks our only choice is to move north to Sudbury and live with his mom. Maybe I could get a job at the mall or the local diner. Who knows, right?" she shrugged, lighting a cigarette.

A couple of months later, they did just that. There was nothing left for them in Toronto. All their friends were broke and squatting in abandoned warehouses. Dave's best buddy Mike was in jail again, this time for aggravated assault. And everybody was pissed off at Monica, a girl who had crashed at their place for a while and now was talking to the cops about the firebombing of the Youthlink group home on Runnymede, which she claimed to have information about.

Apparently some skinhead she knew had done it. And because everyone was out to get Monica and she was known to have stayed at their apartment, Dave and Holly were getting hassled left and right. The last straw came when another friend of theirs who lived upstairs had his throat slashed and had lain in a pool of his own blood for two days before the smell of his decomposing body forced the neighbours to alert the police. That Monday, Dave and Holly were gone.

I didn't have time to miss them. Grant was hot on another anti-racist's trail. Phone calls to be made, answering machines to be broken into, houses to be watched, that sort of thing. I quietly took notes. My Intelligence notebook was filling up fast.

One afternoon when we had met up at the Parkway, Grant unexpectedly took a notepad out of his back-pocket, scrawled half a dozen names, tore off the sheet and pushed it to me. I recognized some of the names: one person was in charge of a local gay youth drop-in group. Another name belonged to a woman who had been on the news recently as the founder of a Native rights group. I would follow through with the usual stuff – track down their addresses, then check the voter registries of those addresses to get the names of the other individuals who shared the residence. I'd forward everything to Grant and wait for further instructions. But before I did, I asked him why he targeted women more.

"They're the easiest targets, the first to break," Grant answered. "They're more emotional, much more likely to totally lose it."

The more Grant trusted me, the more he let his guard down and bragged about his latest actions, such as the women he'd had followed to and from work. One woman had skinheads dressed in military fatigues posted outside her workplace for days on end, doing nothing but staring at her through the windows. What could she do to stop them? They were just standing on a public street, doing nothing illegal. Other than fuck with her head.

"Who's Sister Ruth?" I asked Grant, noting that name again on his updated hit-list. I hoped he wouldn't remember that I was supposed to have impersonated her on sex hotlines.

"Oh, just your average dyke activist. She's this fat, ugly woman – the type of lesbian kike who fights for a free Nicaragua or starts a collective for feminists from El Salvador. A hard-core communist. The fucking bitch really has it out for the Front and wants to shut us down."

"So what do I have to do?"

"Oh, nothing much – just make her wish for death." A giggle escaped his lips. "But seriously, call her at work and at home, the later the better. Use a phone booth or call-block so she can't trace your number. There's this exchange router in Toronto – let me write it down for you – where if you call it, a different number shows up on her call display screen. So if you don't want to bother going to a phone booth in the middle of the night, call her through this system.

Make sure you use chewing gum or muffle your voice to get rid of your accent."

"But what do I say?"

"Tell her she's being watched. Make the stupid dyke so paranoid she'll turn on herself. Don't worry, I'll show you how. When we call her, just stay on the line and say nothing. I'll do all the talking."

Tethering on the verge of uncontrollable laughter, Grant couldn't keep his voice straight. "By the way, remember our buddy Kevin Thomas, ARA's spokesman? Things aren't going so well for our little friend. I called his landlord last week and asked him, what's he doing renting his place to a child molester? Oh, and did you know he's a heroin user with AIDS?"

Choking on another giggle, he cleared his throat. "Fucker totally bought it. Man, I wish I was a fly on the wall when our boy gets his eviction notice."

"Wow," I said. Where did Grant get his creativity? There didn't seem to be any limit to how low he could go. An unease in the pit of my stomach spread into my chest.

"Going back to Ruthie," Grant said, starting to breathe heavily. His eyes glossed over, giving him the appearance of someone aroused. "She's *this* close to the edge. One more tiny push and she's going over. I'm gonna make her shit her pants and have a total breakdown. She's *It*, you know. Like in tag. Last time I called her up, I said to her, My name is Marcus, and from here on I am your closest friend. You have been selected to be 'IT'. If you don't want to be 'IT', all you have to do is give me the name and phone number of someone else so they can be *IT*.'"

The ins and outs of this new technique would involve mobilizing everyone in the Front's Intelligence network to go after one person at a time. Unlike before, where the target was random and people were making crank calls indiscriminately, this was a specific tactic that was designed to break down the intended mark faster. Grant called this evolution *The It Campaign.*

When someone was made *It*, that person's life would be made miserable. They were to be harassed 24 hours a day. One would not be able to eat or sleep in peace. The goal was to make *Its* life miserable, get *It* fired from *Its* job and made to fear one's own shadow. The only way an individual could stop being *It* was by giving up someone else's name and phone number, so that new person was going to take *It's* place.

"Ruth's going to regret the day she was born," Grant giggled. "You watch and see."

One night Grant called me up. "Wanna do something fun?" he asked. Sure, I was game.

"Ok, just listen quietly and don't say anything," he said, breathing heavily. "Watch and learn."

A few clicks later, and suddenly a tape began to play. I listened intently, trying to figure out what was going on. Then it hit me – this was somebody's answering machine. Another click, and we were in. Grant chuckled softly. Then, presto! The messages were all wiped out. He hang up that line and came back on with me. "Remember that recorder gadget I told you to get, the one where you plug one end into the receiver and the other into a cassette recorder? Well, I just got all of Klanbusters' voice mails and they didn't. Wanna see something else?"

I marvelled at his ability to crack into electronic gadgets. Of course I wanted to learn more. "Ok, check this out," he said. "Just keep quiet, ok? Don't make a peep. This one's a real nasty piece of work. Fucking piece of shit kike. A total useless waste of human tissue."

"Hello?" a female voice called out on the other end.

Grant said nothing. Just kept breathing heavily, trying to stifle his snickers. After a moment, the woman slammed the phone down. Grant burst out laughing. "Man, you should see how she's freaking out right now."

The It Campaign elevated the psychological warfare against Heritage Front opponents to a whole new level. It was the logical progression of Grant's training, which up until now had involved impersonating reporters and putting on different guises in order to fish for information on unsuspecting citizens, information that could be later used to terrorize them.

Front members were getting bolder. Grant's mentoring had boosted their confidence. The fear they now elicited from community activists empowered them, made them feel downright invincible. Rallies grew larger. Concerts attracted hundreds of attendants.

We owned this city. We had the cops on our side. This was the year of Dudley Laws and the Black Action Defence Committee's organized marches against the police, whom they had accused of targeting black women for unwarranted strip searches. The boys in blue were tired of being called racists. Even the head of the Hate Crimes Unit was chummy with Wolfgang. He'd gone over to his place for coffee, Wolfgang told me, and they spent more than an hour chatting about how violent the ARA was. They looked at video stills of protesters in order to ID them and discussed who among the activists should be arrested during the next riot.

Over the winter, the It Campaign escalated in viciousness. The streets were run by violent left and right factions whose actions were inflamed by the targeted attacks. One female ARA activist, a friend of Ruth's who had also become the target of a terror campaign, found the personal attacks worse after she adopted a black baby. All her car tires were slashed and she was left messages that said she was a race-traitor and both herself and the child would be swinging from a pole when the Day of the Rope came.

Then the Morgentaler abortion clinic blew up. Just in case the media failed to connect the dots, a clue was left behind: the Heritage Front's telephone number spray-painted in life-size numbers on the wall of a building directly across the street from the clinic, with the caption underneath reading '*Peace, Love and White Power!*'

Spray-painting was a favourite activity for HF skinheads: aside from synagogues, the Native Canadian Centre on Spadina Road and a local left-wing bookstore on Bloor Street, Pathfinder, were both targeted on the same Friday night. The Native Centre had a black swastika painted on its front steps, while the bookstore was marked with a Star of David.

A Jewish activist's home in Kitchener, Ontario was firebombed, not once but twice. Her name was Mona Zentner, a Canadian Jewish Congress member and professor at the University of Waterloo who had demonstrated vociferously against David Irving when he made his appearance at the European Sound Imports store – a talk I had been kicked out of because Michael Rothe, the store owner, had freaked out when he took one look at me and screamed at Wolfgang that he had brought a Jew, a fucking goddamn Jew, into his store.

I remember asking Wolfgang about Zentner's house right after it happened. He had shrugged and flashed his usual grin, and even though this wasn't an admission of culpability, I couldn't shake off the feeling that he knew who was behind those arsons.

In May 1992, a Rahowa concert scheduled at the Boys and Girls Club in Ottawa led to a massive confrontation directly in front of Parliament Hill between some six hundred Anti-Racist Action and Heritage Front members. The incident, which made international news, led to lead singer and Church Of The Creator "reverend" George Burdi kicking a female activist in the face and breaking her nose (a brawl recorded by CTV cameras). One of four HF members charged with assault after that riot, Burdi would be convicted and sentenced to a year in jail.

Then the street attacks began. Three South Asian men were beaten within a short period of time: two of them died, including 32-year old Gunalan Muthulingam. A third one, a 41-year old Sri Lankan Tamil immigrant, former science teacher and father of three by the name of Sivarajah Vinasithamby was punched and kicked in the head so violently that he became brain damaged and paralyzed. The last attack happened right after a RaHoWa concert had let out, and the skinhead convicted, Jason Hoolans (one of three skinheads responsible for the attack) was a card-carrying Heritage Front member.

One of the most vicious incidents involved Runnymede House, a Youthlink group home for runaway girls. The home had been firebombed after one girl, whose boyfriend was a Heritage Front member, was evicted for wearing white supremacist paraphernalia and putting up racist Heritage Front posters in her room. The onslaught of accompanying death threats led to the staff and remaining girls having to be relocated under police protection.

The HF tried to spin the whole thing as bullshit, but I knew it was true. The fourteen-year old girl who had instigated the attack was dating one of Holly and Dave's skinhead friends. Dave himself had told me that the teen's boyfriend was itching to get revenge and was asking around in the Heritage Front for assistance with a plan of attack.

Soon thereafter it got out that one of the female staff members at the home was black; perhaps that was the reason they singled her out.

The teenage girl held her responsible for the eviction. The youth counsellor was targeted with threatening calls involving the word "nigger" and followed to and from work multiple times by a white van that would drive slowly beside her. She sought refuge at a friend's place out of town, but that place was also broken into and death threats scrawled on the refrigerator door.

The culmination came when she was a skinhead broke into her apartment, beat and raped her with a foreign object. When she called police to report the sexual assault the cops argued she had done it to herself, arrested and charged *her* two days later with public mischief. Although Dave and Holly had told me that a Heritage Front cell was responsible for the attack on that group home, I wouldn't discover the specifics of the incident, how vicious the assault had been, until much later, when told the horrific details by the woman at the top on Grant Bristow's hate list.

The blatant escalation to violence left me unsettled. The fact that the majority of targets were female was sickening. Judging by the sexual nature of the attacks, the victims' race or political bent was only an excuse for being targeted. No philosophy or ideology, no matter how radical, could justify this.

Of course Wolfgang denied any connection to the attacks, but I couldn't ignore the fact that the leadership believed in setting up covert cells of HF members who were never to intersect. At any moment a cell could be activated and directed to do a job at the leadership's request. It was more than possible that the people responsible for the attacks were in some way connected to the Front, if not part of a cell itself. The fact that the flyer I'd been arrested for had also listed a female target, only served to embolden my suspicions.

This thought haunted me, turning into an obsession. I needed to know the truth.

"Is it really true? Is the Heritage Front behind that youth counsellor's attack?" I decided to ask Wolfgang one night. "Because if it is, it's all fucked up. What's all this got to do with patriotism? With revolution?"

I watched his face in the gloomy twilight, silhouetted against the darkening café window. "Do you really want to know?" he asked me. "Because I don't think it's a good idea for you to ask too many questions. At this point, we need to operate on a need-to-know basis."

TWENTY

THE CURTAIN PARTS
June 11, 1993

By mid-summer the Heritage Front had bigger problems to worry about. Aside from the usual legal issues related to Rodney Bobiwash's complaint to the Human Rights Commission and the injunction to stop the Heritage Hotline from operating, the It Campaign had struck bone. Community activists and anti-racists had had enough. Within two months, word came down that another street brawl was unavoidable. Judging by the posters littering downtown, Anti-Racist Action was planning to have a major rally on June 11, 1993. The actual route of the march had not been disclosed. In fact, the only detail posted on their flyers was the meeting point, Allan Gardens, but based on proximity and the statement on the ARA hotline that they were going after '*a major centre of Nazi operation*', Wolfgang and Ernst figured the target had to be the Bunker on Carlton Street.

The city centre was brimming with cops, both uniformed and undercover. I'd tied my red hair into a fast bun and pulled a hoodie over my head to appear inconspicuous. Hands buried in my pockets, I strolled to the outside perimeter of Allan Gardens and watched as the group of people gathering inside the park grew larger. The park wasn't very big, just a few benches covering a grassy area that enclosed a botanical garden housed inside a huge solarium. There wasn't enough space for HF members to hide and not be spotted by the ARA scouts who trolled the area in search of suspicious activity. If anyone resembling a white supremacist was spotted, a mob brawl was likely to erupt.

Wolfgang's plan was to keep the HF split in small bunches all through the surrounding streets and alleys. The point was to lurk and observe the anti-racists as they came down Carlton Street, then spring up on them and attack before they made it within rock-throwing distance of the Bunker.

My eyes scanned the side alleys, the awnings of nearby stores, the bus stop at the corner of Gerrard Street. At each station, I caught sight of one or two guys standing stiffly, grim-faced, pretending they were just hanging around. Every loyal member on the Front's membership list had been called in to defend their race from socialists, just as the anti-racists had mobilized some of their most radical bunch.

Bandanas covered people's faces. Pockets bulged with an invisible arsenal of bottles, sticks and rocks. No matter which side of the fence you happened to fall on, the thing that seemed to inspire most of those who showed up was the idea of a savage, bloody riot on downtown's streets. Both sides looked like they were out to draw blood. Heads were gonna get bashed in. From the way it was playing out, I calculated about five anti-racists for each HF skinhead. This was going to get ugly.

I took off down a side street and made my way to the Bunker. A group of Heritage Front guys were waiting up front, ready to fight back the ARA mob. They had been there since yesterday, after Zundel appealed to Wolfgang for help in protecting his townhouse from being egged or firebombed. With the help of tall ladders and a gigantic plastic wrapping, five or so skinheads had managed to pull what looked like an enormous condom over the entire building. But their efforts had been for nothing. As they kept waiting, and waiting, for the ARA mob to materialize, a collective thought struck everyone's minds: *This was a set-up. Zundel wasn't the real target.*

I ran back to the park, racing through the alleys that led to Carlton. By the time I got to Allan Gardens, the ARA had vanished. Within minutes, HF members had congregated in the gardens. The skinheads were fuming over the deceit. *We've been played, what the fuck's going on,* seemed to be the question on everybody's lips.

A car circled the park and pulled to the curb. Grant and Wolfgang jumped out. Grant was holding a walkie-talkie and had it tuned to a police frequency.

"They've gone after Schipper's place," he shouted at the crowd.

Pandemonium. From his police scanner, Grant had learned that two hundred anti-racists had marched eastward to Gary Schipper's rented house at 97 Bertmount, where they'd thrown rocks and excrement onto the front porch. They had managed to smash all the windows before being cordoned back by police units called in by terrified neighbours.

Poor Gary! A twitchy, balding little telemarketer who had recorded animated daily rants on the HF hotline for over a year, he was Wolfgang's lapdog and so loyal to his boss that I couldn't help but wonder if he might have prostituted himself if he believed it could advance the racialist cause. I also wondered if he was permanently high on cocaine because he could never stand still. Gary had been adopted and raised by a Jewish family (although he swore up and down that he didn't "have a drop of Jewish blood in me"), which made it all the more weird that he was such a rabid white supremacist. Then again, with my father's heritage, I wasn't one to throw stones.

Or excrement, that is.

The Heritage Front gang was enraged. In the mayhem that erupted, a hundred voices had a hundred different ideas of how we could retaliate. "If that's the way they want to play the game, that's fine. We're gonna track those motherfuckers down," Wolfgang said.

Grant's eyes bulged out of his head. He shouted at the crowd until his voice grew hoarse. "It's payback time! We've gotta go to their houses and workplaces and give them a taste of their own medicine." He rattled off a number of addresses that included Ruth M's house on Clinton Street and Kevin Thomas' office. He was so angry that he began to shake, unable to physically contain himself. Gobs of saliva sputtered from his mouth. "We'll go smear shit on *their* front porches, smash their fucking windows in, blow the whole thing up. Let's go *right now*!"

"No," George Burdi interrupted, holding a megaphone to his mouth to cut off Grant. He turned to address the skinheads, who all looked up to him. Fearsome and meaner than a junkyard dog, not only was George the lead singer of RaHoWa and the Canadian branch of the COTC, he had been in so many brawls that he'd earned their unequivocal respect. "No, let's regroup. We need to be strategic. We'll wait until they're in their vipers' nest, celebrating their victory. By tonight they'll be at Sneaky Dees, getting wasted. We'll track those fuckers back to their watering hole and take care of all of them at the same time."

Fast-forward three or so hours later. Under the cover of night, more than forty Heritage Front members entered Sneaky Dee's bar. I tailed behind them, keeping close to the front door. The skinheads stomped toward the rear of the bar where, in slow motion, I watched as a flurry of arms, legs and tables overturned on top of each other.

All hell broke loose. Bottles went flying through the air; shards embedded in people's skulls. Women started screaming. From out of nowhere, sirens resounded and uniformed police burst through the front doors. I slinked along the wall and slipped back outside, my heart pounding so hard I thought it would burst.

I had to find a place to hide, and fast – the brawl was spilling into the street. The sound of shattering glass followed me as I raced across the busy intersection, dodging the flow of cars and motorists who honked at me furiously. Taillights reflected in the glistening wet pavement – it had rained earlier, and the dampness in the soggy air carried the stench of blood pouring from people's wounds.

From the other side of the street, I watched in horror as about thirty men started punching each other. A couple of skinheads fled down College, followed by six ARA members. One younger guy wasn't so lucky. About a dozen ARA people swarmed around and knocked him to the ground, kicking him in the head, shoulders and spine as he curled into a fetal position. They were going to kill him, I thought. They weren't going to stop.

A dark car came screeching around the bend and stopped right in the middle of the road. The doors flew open, and Wolfgang and Peter sprung out. Wolfgang was carrying a heavy flashlight in his hand and a devilish grin on his face. "You motherfuckers," he shouted in glee as he stormed the mob that was attacking the skinhead.

The metal of the flashlight baton made contact with bone, likely splintering somebody's nose and knocking teeth out. Peter's elbows were flying in all directions; his fists were pummeling heads indiscriminately. Wolfgang's knee dug into somebody's solar plexus, cracking a rib. And suddenly the cops were there, with their batons drawn, and Wolfgang was now flat on the pavement, his cheek squashed into the dirt, a cop's knee digging into his back. But the shit-eating grin on his face refused to go away.

Police and bar patrons streamed into the street. Traffic had halted in several places and was down to one lane. A yellow cab was rolling by slowly when I waved him down. The driver stuck his head out trying to decide whether he should stop, and when he saw I was a girl his expression relaxed. "Get in," he gestured with his thumb.

I opened the door at the same time as a couple of skinheads hopped across the road. One had looped the other's arm around his neck and was dragging him along. We made eye contact. "Come on," I yelled at them. "Hurry!"

The door was flung open from the other side and the two guys shoved their way in. "The closest hospital," one of them said. "As fast as you can."

"St. Mike's?" asked the cabbie. I rapped the back of his seat, "Yes, that's fine. *Go!*"

The skinhead beside me collapsed on my lap. I glanced at the other guy. "What's wrong with him?" I asked, smelling the blood before it coated my hands.

"What do you *think*? They broke a bottle over his head," the guy said. "You were there, weren't you?" He looked antsy until we had turned off of College. "Stop here," he demanded.

"Where are you going?" I asked him as he hurriedly stepped out of the taxi. "What am I supposed to do with *him*?"

He shrugged. "Drop him off at emergency, I suppose. I'm getting the fuck outta here."

The wounded skinhead moaned. "Please hurry," I said to the driver, trying to ignore the blood oozing all over me. "We'll be there soon," I whispered.

I half-carried him into Emergency where an orderly took over, ushering us to a stretcher edged by a crudely-drawn curtain. While we waited for the doctor on duty to arrive, the guy managed to lift his head and peeked at me, grimacing in pain. "What's your name?" he asked.

"Elisse," I said. "And you?"

"Joe," he answered, scooting onto the bed.

"I think you'll be okay now," I said. "It's getting late, I'd better go."

I turned to walk away. "Elisse," he called out.

I spun back around. His eyes were wide and fearful. "Stay with me?" he pleaded.

Fine. I stood in the corner with my arms crossed, trying to avoid the sight of the ER doctor hovering over the guy's skull, and the big, bloody shards of glass he extracted and dropped into a liver-shaped tin.

"Just the stitching left," the doctor said. "Hang on a second," he added, sauntering away.

Joe tilted his head up toward me. "Could you do me a favour?"

"What?"

He hesitated. "Could you hold my hand? I don't know if I can handle this."

"All right, but don't make me watch, okay?"

I grasped his hand and turned my face away just as the doctor came toward him holding what looked like a humongous staple. *Clunk. Clunk. Clunk.*

"*OW*," Joe yelled, gnashing his teeth. "Fuck, man, it hurts!"

He clenched down on my fingers each time the staple made that awful sound against his scalp. *Clunk. Clunk.* Again and again, something like twenty times. Finally, it was over.

I stayed half the night trying to keep the moron awake like the doctor had said. It didn't seem right that I should just leave him. It took another fifteen minutes in the washroom to rinse the congealed blood off my clothes. No matter how hard I scrubbed my hands under the scorching hot water, the acrid smell wouldn't come off. I blotted at my jacket and pants with paper towels, trying to get as much of it off as I could. Then I paced the sterile corridors back to the bed where Joe was snoring.

"Wake up," I said, shaking his shoulder. "Doc said I shouldn't let you fall asleep."

He grunted, turned over on his side, grunted again. "They really got me, eh?"

"You'll be fine," I said. "Worst part's over."

I rubbed his back until he calmed down. Suddenly he grasped my wrist. "You know," he said, "you're a real nice person. I don't even know you, and you're here with me. The guys I came down with ran off and left me to those assholes."

A memory from a lifetime ago flooded my consciousness: the night at the Parkway where a drunk young man named Zvonimir

166

broke down in tears while talking of how his comrades had let him take the rap for spray-painting a synagogue. I told Joe the story. "And you know what else he told me?"

Joe's eyes bulged out. "What?"

"Nobody ever visited him in prison, that whole year he was doing time."

"*Nobody*? Really?"

"Really. Look at what happened tonight. Did your buddy come with you? Did he hold your hand when you got stitched up? They can't even take care of their own. Nobody gives a shit about each other in this movement."

He closed his eyes and let out a big sigh. "I have a lot to think about, huh?"

A long stretch of time passed. Finally, he spoke. "I think I want to go up to Sudbury to stay at my sister's for a while. She's always telling me I can crash on her sofa. I could stay there till my head heals up. But I have to get the Greyhound to get there. Nobody will pick me up if I hitchhike looking like this."

I fished around in my pockets until I found a twenty-dollar bill, the only money I had on me. His eyes watered. "I'll get this back to you when I –"

"Whenever," I said, cutting him off. I knew I'd never see the money again, but that wasn't the point. "Take care of yourself. *Do* something with your life. Something positive."

It was nearly dawn when I left the hospital. After an evening of intermittent showers, the sky was still heavy with rain clouds and a new drizzle had just began, but the drops were so faint, so refreshing on my tear-streaked face, that I welcomed it. I buried my hands in my pockets and walked briskly, the rapid pace keeping me warm despite a breeze that seeped through the lining of my nylon bomber jacket.

I felt like a hypocrite. I'd encouraged Joe to leave the far-right, but what about myself? I'd grown up inside the movement. Pathetic, yes, but they were the only family I ever had. From that first night, a whole underground world had opened up to me, welcomed me with open arms. For more than a year I'd lived and breathed the ideology: spending my days slipping flyers under the windshield wipers of cars in parking lots, working afternoons at Ernst's place, going out in the evening with the boys.

Even as this world had become increasingly suffocating and dangerous, even as I wanted desperately to cut the cord that tied me to them, a cord that twisted around my throat and restricted my voice, it seemed impossible. Without my group identity, I didn't know who I was.

How could I get away? Where would I go? Who would I be?

Without a Cause to fight for, I was nothing.

TWENTY-ONE

CROSSROADS

A vivid light pierced my eyes. I tried to move my head away but the entire world seemed frozen. Tentatively, my senses sought to touch the unfamiliar surroundings, and yet my mind refused to process anything but the shock of brightness against my retina. Gradually, sounds turned into voices. My eyes focused on the faces around me. I was in a bed, not my own but a stretcher in a hospital room, surrounded by two white-clad women and a man with a stethoscope around his neck.

"She's coming around, look," someone said. The attempt to twist my head in the direction of the voice caused a sharp pain to flow up from my stomach, engulfing my chest.

"No-no-no, don't you move," said another voice.

A face came into view, a grey-haired man wearing thick wire-rimmed glasses. "Relax." He sat on a low stool next to me, his nose inches from mine. "Elisse. Do you remember what happened?"

I shivered and shut my eyes as tight as I could. The throbbing in my abdomen was excruciating.

"We'll give you more charcoal for that. And just so you know, we're required by law to keep you here for observation for forty-eight hours."

I opened my eyes and looked straight at him. "But I'm fine," I said. "This was a mistake."

"You didn't just try to kill yourself tonight?"

The thought of being locked up in a mental ward for two days straight sobered me up instantly. I shook my head. "No, of course not. I guess I took too many pills to fall asleep, but I didn't mean to do it. I just want to go home."

He frowned. "I don't know if I can do that. You took enough Tylenol and sleeping pills to make yourself quite sick. You'll have to stay put at least until everything clears out of your system. Do you want us to call someone for you? A family member?"

"No thanks," I said. "But I'll take a telephone if you have one handy."

"All right, I'll see that the nurse brings you a phone."

I spent the next hour throwing up a disgusting mixture of liquid charcoal into a liver-shaped tin the nurses had thoughtfully placed in my hands before I knew what it was for. The spot where the iv had been inserted into my wrist started to sting; a tiny drop of blood had backed up through the needle and was now stuck in the surgical tape that kept the tubes attached to my arm. I couldn't stand to look at it. I wanted, more than anything, to rip out all those appendages, the iv and the heart monitors that were affixed all over my chest and ribs, and just run out of that room without looking back.

A half hour later, a nurse came in carrying a handset and laid it on the pillow next to me. She took the foul liver-shaped container from me and put it on a counter.

"How's the stomach?" she asked. "Still vomiting?"

"No," I said. "I'm feeling better. Do you think I can go home now?"

"I'm not sure we can do that. Perhaps if a friend came to pick you up…"

She looked down at the phone next to me and I knew right then that if someone came to get me tonight, they were going to let me out. She walked off and left me to my call, and I desperately began to rake my brain. Was there *anybody* I could reach out to?

A cold sensation descended over me. The reason I was here was to get away from them. The memory of what happened earlier rushed back: I'd retreated to a secluded spot of Allan Gardens and tried to separate myself from the Heritage Front in the only way I could think of.

Before I could stop myself, I reached for my bomber jacket, which someone had folded on the chair next to my bedside. I fumbled through every pocket until I found what I was looking for: a crumpled piece of paper I'd kept since Grant had given it to me at the Parkway months ago. As my fingers began to dial the number, anxiety gripped my chest, rendering me breathless.

"Hello?" a light voice answered. A salsa rhythm bounced in the background.

"Ruth?"

"Uh, yes. Who's this?"

"It's Elisse. Can you talk?"

Silence. Then she cleared her throat. "What do you want to talk about?" she tried to sound unperturbed, but her voice took on a strained note. The music shut off. I heard a rustling noise; no doubt she was reaching for a tape recorder.

"I'm in the hospital."

"You're in the hospital?" she repeated, like she didn't trust her own hearing. "Uh, what's wrong? What happened?"

"Do you think you could meet me?"

"Like, right now?"

"Yeah."

Ruth gave a funny laugh. "Is this a joke? Because if you're setting me up, I'm going to call the cops."

"It's no joke." I hesitated. "I'll tell you anything you want to know."

A long pause. "Where are you calling from right now?"

"Women's College Hospital. Emergency department."

"You all right?"

"Not really. I have to talk to you."

"You *have* to talk? *To me*? And why is that?" she asked doubtfully.

Oh God, she didn't believe me. "I just have to. I don't have anybody else..." my voice trailed off. I didn't have the energy to insist. I was about to hang up when I heard her sigh.

"Give me a minute. I'm going to call the hospital front desk and get them to patch me through to you. Just to confirm this is for real. Can you hang on?"

I closed my eyes. "All right."

It took Ruth under an hour to double-check my story and get here. I was still propped up on the bed when she appeared in the doorway. A short-haired, dark-eyed woman about ten years older than me, I had seen her at demonstrations before, had crank-called her house (though too sheepish to ever say anything) and walked by her workplace since Grant had given everyone the address. But we'd never actually talked face-to-face.

She just stood there, looking at me. I felt both awkward and shy under her scrutiny.

"Please close the door," I said. I couldn't think of anything else to say.

"Right." She did as I requested. Then she pulled up a chair next to me. "You know," she said, an odd expression on her face, "I've gotta tell you, it says a lot for your comrades that I'm the only person you can rely on right now."

"Pathetic, isn't it." I felt horrible for dragging her here in the middle of the night. Before I could tell her that, she put up her hand to stop me. "Does anybody else know you're here?"

I shook my head. "No, nobody."

"Ever done this sort of thing before?"

"Nope."

We didn't have a chance to speak further before the doctor came back into the room. I repeated my story that the whole thing was a misunderstanding, an accidental overdose and no, I hadn't really wanted to die. He took my blood pressure again and sighed. "Well, if you think you're well enough to leave, I guess you're free to go."

Ruth waited outside the room while a male nurse removed my IV and monitors. I changed back into my street clothes and came out wobbling. She gripped my arm as I stumbled over my own feet. "You okay?" she asked.

"Yeah. Let's just get out of here." Silently, I added, *Before they change their minds.*

Outside the double entrance doors stood a tall, short-haired blonde woman I'd never seen before. She walked over to us. "This is Annetta," Ruth said. "A friend of mine."

"How do you feel?" Annetta asked in a strong German accent which gave me pause. For a moment, I wondered if she was a neo-Nazi. The only Germans I knew were all fascists.

"Dizzy," I finally answered.

The earth was spinning under my feet. Ruth didn't release her grip on my arm until we were in the parking lot. I climbed into her car's back seat and put my hands over my face.

"If you feel you can handle it, I thought we could go somewhere and talk," she said, watching me through the dashboard mirror.

"I'd like that," I said.

Annetta climbed into the passenger seat, and then we were off. As she drove, Ruth rolled down her window. The rush of cool air felt good, dampening my nausea.

We went to Fran's Diner on College street, a 1950s-style burger and fries place complete with black and white checkered floors and chunky booths made of turquoise vinyl. I slid into a booth while Ruth and Annetta took the opposite side, waiting for me to speak. I said nothing.

"Want to order something?" Annetta offered. "Something to eat, maybe?"

"Nothing. Just a coke, I guess," I said, thinking it might help with the queasiness.

They ordered beers for themselves and we sat in awkward silence for a minute before Ruth began to question me. "I can understand why you're stressed. Everybody in town has heard about your arrest. But why call *me*? Why not get your boyfriend to pick you up tonight?"

I stared at her blankly. "What? I don't have a boyfriend."

"Marc Lemire, aren't you dating him? I saw a picture of you together in the newspaper."

I shuddered in disgust. "He's *so* not my boyfriend. That was just an interview we did with the Toronto Sun. But no…I don't have anybody like that." Tears began to brim behind my eyelashes. "They want me to, though. They're pushing me to date somebody. But I...I can't."

I must have spoken louder than I thought, because when I looked up again both Ruth and Annetta were staring at me fixedly.

Ruth sat up in her seat. She cleared her throat. "What do you mean by that?"

I shook my head, flushing. "Nothing."

"Why can't you date any of them?"

"I don't want to. I…I can't."

The two of them exchanged looks. Annetta's blue eyes softened. She opened her mouth as if to say something, but changed her mind.

She leaned forward slightly, watching me intently. I looked away immediately.

"I'm sorry I ever crank-called you," I said, choking on a sob.

Ruth frowned. She was determined to pursue this line of questioning. "Why did they make me a target? What did they tell you about me to get you to call and harass me?"

I looked back and forth at her and Annetta. It must have been obvious that Ruth had been targeted for being a lesbian. The people who had stalked her over the past year had made it clear enough through their insults and threats. Why did she have to force me to spell it out?

"That you...you're a...." I couldn't find the words.

"Say it," Ruth demanded.

"No. I can't."

"*Say it!*"

I hung my head down, my cheeks burning with shame. I couldn't even say the word *gay*.

"Is that why you called *me* tonight? Why you did what you did?"

I started crying. I covered my face, wishing the checkered floor could have opened up right there and there and swallowed me whole. "I don't have anybody else."

"But –"

"All right, all right," I heard Annetta say, interrupting Ruth. "Enough already. You don't have to say any more, Elisse."

They dropped me off in front of my building and watched until I made it safely through the bulletproof front doors. From that day on, Ruth telephoned every day. With all the guilt I felt over having been involved in the crank-calls, I was still too shy to dial her so I waited by the phone until I saw her number pop up on the call display.

"Promise me you won't go to any more rallies," was one of the first things she insisted on. "You don't want to get in any more trouble already."

"I won't, I promise."

"Maybe we can get together this week," she suggested. "I'd like to see how you're doing."

A few core members of the Heritage Front found out about the suicide attempt within a couple of weeks, after Marque had begun to grill me. "What happened to you last weekend? You've been acting strange since. You haven't called me or Wolf, or even your buddy Gerry. What's up with you?"

I told her what I'd told the emergency room doctor – that I'd been so stressed, I impulsively took some pills to numb myself and ended up in hospital.

She freaked out. "What were you thinking? Why didn't you call anybody?"

"I did. Nobody answered."

"Did they keep you for observation? How did you get home?"

"No, I got out that same night. I took a cab back."

"Jesus. Swear you'll never do anything like that again until you talk to me."

"Can't we just drop it? Please don't tell anybody."

Of course she had to go tell her best friend Nicola, and Wolfgang himself was bound to eventually find out – after all, Marque was staying over at his place most of the time by now.

Wolfgang was so pissed off at me for going the way of Ken Barker (who, only months earlier, had sliced his veins open from wrists down to elbows) that he didn't speak with me for a month afterwards. Peter, on the other hand, called me up right after Nicola had spilled the beans. He yelled at me for half an hour straight. It was his own special, tough-love way of showing his concern.

What kind of a racialist are you, doing this sort of thing? he insisted to know. If I wanted to die, there were better ways. I could strap a bunch of explosives to my body and take out a whole synagogue of Jews while I was at it. Why waste a perfectly good suicide just on myself?

TWENTY-TWO

DEPROGRAMMING

I met Ruth again one week later, on a sunny afternoon in the off-leash park behind her house in the Annex. She introduced me to Mr. Muggs, her gigantic five-year old sheepdog. Muggs ran up to me, panted and slobbered on my hand, and Ruth laughed and said that I was good with animals. We sat down on a grassy mound and then she turned to me abruptly.

"Who's responsible for the harassment campaign, Elisse? I deserve to know why I was targeted, who put them up to this. Is it Wolfgang?"

I shook my head. "He thinks all this is funny. But he isn't the one giving out the target names. It was Grant's idea to start the It Campaign."

A puzzled look crossed her face. "Who's Grant?"

"Grant Bristow. The other leader of the Heritage Front. He runs things from behind the scenes. Wolfgang's the external leader, but anything major goes through Grant. It was his idea that we establish an Intelligence Division and go after our opponents."

She nodded slowly, processing the information. Then she stared into my eyes. "Why are we really here? You want out, don't you? Isn't that why you came to me?"

"I don't know if I can leave. I don't have anybody else..."

She put up a hand to interrupt me. "Fine. I'm not going to demand that you leave the Front right this second, but there is one condition I will insist on – you must let me know if there are any big actions coming down. Deal?"

"Deal," I said, and we shook on it.

"The other thing I'm going to ask is that you tell me the names of everyone on their target list so we can make sure this doesn't happen again."

Our meetings were a long, grueling process. At first they took place in the park behind her house; later on, as she grew to trust me, in her own living room. She demanded to know everything about my past and home life, everything I loved and hated about the movement. She asked me things like, *Why do you feel the need to depend on them? Why do you think you have to hate everything and everyone in order to survive? Why do you only feel strong when you hate someone?*

I had no answers, only more and more confusion. It felt like my brain had gone into hibernation and couldn't be thawed out. I recognized everything that came out of my mouth as ideological bullshit, lines that Wolfgang and Ernst had spoon-fed me, but there didn't seem to be anything left of my old self. It had been eradicated, stripped off. I was a shell with a tough exterior, but as scrambled as an egg inside. Who *was* I? Could I actually formulate my own opinion about anything, without parroting propaganda?

The net was disintegrating. Little flashes of insight blew craters into my weak arguments. It was as if two giants were fighting a mortal battle inside my head, and the old me was wounded and bleeding to death. Every question Ruth asked led me to formulate a new analysis. Whenever I repeated my standby question, *But what do YOU think?*, Ruth laughed at me. "You have to think for yourself. Come on, It's not that hard. Can't you feel your brain creaking back to life?"

Why did we try to get the police on our side, if secretly we believed in overthrowing the government? Why did we compromise our beliefs by stating that minorities and race-mixing white trash were the only ones who took advantage of the welfare system, when our own people were encouraged to go on social assistance and "milk the system" to fund our actions? Up until now I'd been too blind-sighted by loyalty to assess the strength of the mortar that held together my shaky ideological foundations. I had no arguments to counter Ruth's words.

"It's so simple to shut your eyes and say '*I hate them*,'" she said. "'The immigrants, the illegal refugees, they're taking jobs away from OUR people.' Whose jobs are they stealing, anyway? They get the most menial, demoralizing, underpaid positions. The kinds of jobs someone's gotta do but we think we're too good for."

I shook my head. All my life I'd reached toward others like me – who looked like me, who hated like me, who wanted to hide behind a flag and impose their authority on others. I wanted to fight for a utopia, a heavenly Paradise, a totalitarian bliss where we could all be happy and free to do as we pleased. Where we could experience the peace that we lacked within ourselves. But how could we even know what we wanted, when we had never experienced inner peace? Contentment? Joy?

"Do you really think they wouldn't lie to your face to get you to buy into their bullshit? All their 'facts', the 'proof' of Jewish conspiracies, is based on erroneous data. Zundel's so-called evidence that there were no gassings at Auschwitz is ridiculous. The chemical tests he refers to were not carried out using scientific means and were categorically refuted by scientists years ago. But I guess they didn't tell you that, did they?"

It was frightening to think I might have been wrong. My belief system was my identity. I couldn't remember who I was before I joined the movement. Everything I did depended on what they'd found acceptable – what clothes to wear, what music to listen to. I saw that same glow of adoration on the faces of young skinheads who had joined only a month earlier and were already recruiting others. I saw it as plainly as someone must have seen it on my face a lifetime ago.

"What do *you* like?" Ruth asked me, narrowing her eyes. "What do you actually like to do with your time beside going on marches? Can you actually pick a book you'd like to read without asking them first if it's okay? Can you make any decision *at all* without asking, *What do* you *think*?"

I looked down in shame. Apparently not. The twig at the end of the branch cannot shake the tree. It depends on its sap not to wither away. If my entire artificial self collapsed, what would replace it? I needed an ideology to fill the gap.

"It's *easy* to start hating, but overnight you become so full of hate that you end up eating each other alive. Selling one another out. You are an addict and their camaraderie is your drug. Hating is just a fix, it keeps you pumped up and going, keeps you away from facing your past. Without them you go into withdrawal. You don't have a mind of your own."

"They are my world. I can't imagine being without them," I heard myself saying. "And hatred is pure. It's the most honest emotion. It keeps you intact. Love doesn't create civilizations – hatred does. It sparks revolutions, motivates mankind, enables the survival of the fittest."

"Hatred destroys. It corrodes you from the inside. It murders your true identity. You don't need the movement. You *think* you do, but really you don't. You have survived this long by taking one breath at a time. You're stronger than you think."

I shook my head silently. She didn't get it. A moment passed like a shadow between us, and Ruth finally lost her cool. "Sometimes I just want to shake you. What *happened* to you? What's made you so fucked up? Where does all this hate come from?"

"You're confusing pride for hate," I retorted. "It's got nothing to do with hate – I love my race and only hate those who want to mess with me."

Ruth's eyes flashed with annoyance. "That's total bullshit and we both know it. This is all about wanting to get the upper hand. The only way you feel better about yourself is by putting down someone else. Hate is the only fire that's raging in you. So I'm going to ask you again, where does this come from? What happened?"

I wrenched myself away from her. "Nothing, okay? Fuck off already."

She shrugged, made a point to glance at her watch and leaned back, crossing her arms. Her expression said, *We have all day.*

I chose my next words carefully. "It's better to be the aggressor rather than the victim. If you had to choose, would you rather be the powerless guy in the prison camp or his commanding officer? I mean, if you had only these two choices, would you choose to survive at whatever the cost or be killed? Would you side with the authorities like the kapos did in the Jewish ghetto, would you wear a uniform and pretend you were one of *them*, or hang on to your ethics and go to your death holding your head up? I refuse to be weak. No matter what, I won't be a victim. Not anymore."

"Interesting. Where did you first come up with this idea? Don't shake your head, think back to when this belief took root."

I shrugged. "My father used to beat my mother when she got out of line, and she in turn took it out on me. If I'd been older, stronger, I could have hit back."

"Okay, what else?"

"Isn't that enough for you?" I protested.

A curved smile emerged on her face. "Maybe for a group counselor, but I want you to dig deeper."

"Not if I don't want to. Just drop it."

Ruth leaned into me. "Whatever's just crossed your mind right now, I want to hear it. And I'm not letting you off the hook."

An image I'd been trying to block out for years forced itself into my consciousness. My shoulders sagged under the weight of the memory. "I was fourteen. My social worker had placed me back home temporarily, and my mother decided to take us back to Romania so she could visit her relatives. I begged her to let me stay behind in Bucharest with my best friend Pereta. I hadn't seen her since we'd emigrated, and my mother agreed."

Ruth's voice was soft, almost inaudible. "What happened that summer?"

"It started the first night, while we were sharing the bed. When we were kids, Pereta and I had always fooled around, pretending to be knight and princesses. That night she spooned me like she always had during our childhood sleepovers, but this time I felt her trying to kiss me. It freaked me out. I shoved her away and was so mad I hardly spoke to her the next day."

I'd had no words for what that feeling was. In the make-believe world we'd created as children, certain words, paragraphs, definitions had been purposefully omitted. But now our former games were discarded like old clothing, and in their place was the sensation that something was different. Something that a huge part of me was trying to deny. I resented this intrusion, and I resented Pereta for ruining the innocence of our childhood games by escalating them into something more. Something dirty.

But we couldn't be mad at each other for too long. By the end of that week everything had gone back to normal and we walked down the streets of Bucharest hand-in-hand, just as we'd done when we were little girls. And then...

"What happened, Elisse?"

"We were walking on a side street close to where my old apartment used to be when a group of older teenagers emerged out of nowhere. They saw us holding hands and started to call us horrible things that made me want to run away. But Pereta sprung forward to defend us. A fight broke between her and the leader of the pack."

I stared down at my lap, where my hands were resting limply, palms upward. "Instead of stepping in, I froze. I watched his fist make contact with her face. if it wasn't for an elderly woman carrying groceries who just happened to walk by, he may not have stopped hitting her. But the woman put her bags down and called out to the boys, shouting that they should be ashamed for beating up on a girl. An *old woman*, but at least she'd had the guts to do something. I...I did nothing."

Pereta never questioned why I hadn't helped her fight back against our attackers, but the shame I felt inside was as palpable as a shout. A chasm divided us now. I could not forgive my inaction. I couldn't look at her, I couldn't kiss her. How could we ever pretend that we were just kids fooling around, when the world saw right through us? When it attacked us for being something else? As I helped her clean up, I pressed a cloth against her bruised face and a voice resounded in my mind: *You have but one of two choices – become the enemy, or be broken.*

When I returned to Toronto I didn't respond to her letters. I cut off the part of me that had reacted when her lips had touched mine that night when we had lain in bed together. I forced myself to forget the sensation of her hands on my body. The only sentiment I allowed myself to feel was contempt for the world, for anything weak, for any vulnerability. I had to hide behind the armor of my hardened emotions, or I would die.

"It wasn't your fault." Ruth's voice, quiet as it was, injected itself into the memory, bringing me back to the present.

"Of course it was. I learned a lot about myself that day. For example, that I'm naturally a coward. When shit goes down, my instinct is to run away."

"You were fourteen. A kid, for Christ's sake. You got scared, who wouldn't? Don't judge yourself for something you couldn't have controlled. *You* didn't hurt your friend, those boys did. *They* were the assholes."

"But I think people don't really know themselves, who they *really* are I mean, until they're in a situation that brings out their true self. Then the way they react tells you the strength of their character."

"And you think you're a coward because you didn't step in and get your head kicked in also? It's hard to break out of our sense of self-preservation. Being scared to get hurt doesn't mean you've done something wrong."

I gazed right at her, my eyes wet and glowing. "Yes, I did. Don't you see? By doing nothing, I did wrong. That day I became one of *them*."

She released a great sigh. "We need a break. Let's go for a walk," she said, picking up the dog leash and shaking it. Muggs ran to us, tail wagging, and the three of us headed over to the community park that stretched behind her house.

Once there, Ruth bent down to unclip Muggs's collar, letting him scatter off to greet his doggy pals. We sat in our usual spot, a grassy mound under a vast oak tree whose wide branches provided soothing relief from the scorching sun.

"You haven't told me everything," Ruth said.

I turned to glance at her. "What do you mean?"

"Why did you run away when you were thirteen?"

"I already told you. I lived with a crazy bitch."

"You know you can tell me anything, right? *Right?*"

Mr. Muggs ran up to me panting. I got on my knees and clung to his shaggy neck. I sniffed his doggy sweat. "You need a bath," I said, laughing. He slobbered over my hands and I wiped the slobber back onto his fur.

"Elisse ..." Ruth started again.

"I don't want to talk about it."

"I remember you telling me that when you were at the group home, you shared something with a staff member and they called the cops. They were going to arrest your mother. And then you recanted the charges, just so they wouldn't prosecute her. What was that about?"

"I told you, I'm not talking about this," I snapped.

"Whatever she did to you, it wasn't your fault. No child deserves to be hit."

I kept running my hand through his shaggy mane. He was such a beautiful dog, it choked me up. "Nobody gets it, because nobody thinks mothers can do that to their children."

"Women are just as capable of horrible things as men," Ruth said. "Sometimes worse, because we are supposed to trust our mothers. They're our caregivers from birth..."

"Not mine. I hate her. I'll always hate her."

She touched my shoulder. I smacked her hand away. "Don't touch me! Just...don't."

I started to cry. She waited a few minutes, then scooted closer to me. She wrapped her arms around my shoulders and this time she didn't let go.

Later still, after we dropped Mr. Muggs at home, Ruth took me for a walk along Cherry Beach. The languid waves of Lake Ontario spilled softly onto the shoreline. We took off our shoes and walked barefoot in the sand. We were silent as the sun sank lower and lower into the water, and the sky grew purple against the horizon. She touched my arm. "Let's sit here," she said, pointing to a spot on the sand.

We sat and stared at the waves for another minute before she turned to me. "*Now* will you tell me?"

"I don't know what you mean."

"Oh yes, you do."

"I think..." I stopped myself. I inhaled sharply, and tried again. "I think I'm..."

"Say it. Just say it out loud and get it over with."

I frowned. "You don't even know what I was going to say."

She grinned at me. "Wanna bet?"

"So *you* tell me, then."

"Nope. You have to do this on your own."

"Ruth." I closed my eyes. She was right, I had to rip off this Band-Aid that was keeping me stuck. And it was now or never. "I think I'm gay," I blurted out.

She started laughing. "Come here," she said. She pulled me into a hug so tight I couldn't breathe. "I'm so proud of you."

I pulled back to look at her. "What? You knew already?"

"Of course I knew, silly."

"But...for how long?"

"Right from the beginning."

Oh God, was I that obvious? As if she could read my mind, she laughed again, "Relax, nobody knows. Just the three of us. Annetta, me, and Mr. Muggs of course."

We stood there, staring at each other. She threw her arm around me. "What do you want to do now?"

"You mean, do I want to leave the Front?"

She nodded.

I bit my lip. "That would be a waste."

Her eyes narrowed. "What do you mean?"

"Ruth," I started to say. "I'm so deep in this shit already. I know so much, I have access to so much information…."

Her face took on an expression of recognition. She understood. "Say no more."

Yes, I could have simply walked away from the movement. With time, perhaps I could have picked up the tatters of my life and started again, while the boys kept accumulating weapons and getting ready for Armageddon, for the Day of the Rope when all the race-traitors in the world would be executed. But in the meantime, how could I live with myself? How could I have contributed to that flame of hate, and just walked away? I had to undo any harm I'd caused, and the best way to do that was to leverage the power I still had in the far-right.

I had to hit them from within.

I was too angry to slink away now. I wanted to retaliate for everything that had been done to Ruth and Annetta, Celeste and Kevin, Merle and all the other innocent people who had been targeted for attack. Looking at Ruth now, seeing the kindness and humanity in her face, brought on a breath-taking guilt that threatened to choke me. I was furious that so many other teenagers like me had been used as pawns by people like Wolfgang and Ernst, deliberately desensitized and reprogrammed to the point that we had become human explosives, infused by hatred and rage.

I wasn't going to let them get away with it.

"Can you help me get out? Can you arrange it?"

She reached for my hands and squeezed them. "I personally can't help you do this, but I know someone who might be able to. Someone who has the necessary connections to make things happen. It's either him, or you can go to the media."

"Who is he?"

"An old friend of mine. Someone very much respected in the anti-racist movement, with a long history of activism. But you have to give me permission to tell him about what is going on and that you're ready to do this. If you give him what he wants, he might be able to help you get out."

TWENTY-THREE

PAY IT FORWARD

His name was Martin Theriault. A Montreal resident, he headed up a watchdog group called the Canadian Centre on Racism and Prejudice, CCRP for short. For the last five years he had spearheaded investigations into extremist movements worldwide, provided research data to the appropriate authorities, and published articles in the renowned anti-nationalist British publication *Searchlight*.

Now he wanted to speak with me.

We first met in an Annex café close to the Native Canadian Centre shortly after Ruth contacted him to arrange a meeting on my behalf. After a brief discussion, Martin proposed that in order to ensure this wasn't a Heritage Front setup, I would have to meet him in Montreal, on his turf. And that I should bring as much information with me as I could carry to prove I was sincere.

For this first in-depth meeting I took the first bus at dawn and arrived in Montreal by noon. I waited anxiously in a crowded café across the street from the Greyhound station, forcing myself not to crank my neck or swivel around too many times trying to figure out who was supposed to pick me up.

Though it felt like an hour, no more than ten minutes had passed before a twentyish guy with a shock of curly red hair eased himself into the empty chair across from my table. He smiled. "Hi Elisse, I'm Daniel. How are you?"

"Nervous. Is Martin here?"

"No, we will go and meet him. Are you ready?"

We cabbed it to the secret location, a two-story warehouse in an industrial district. The room Daniel ushered me in was large and starkly lit. The only furniture consisted of a large table running down the centre of the room, flanked by four wooden chairs. Aluminum file drawers lined the walls and space under the windowsills. The air stank of cigarette smoke and aging newspapers.

And there, standing in the corner with his arms crossed, dressed in a black turtleneck and dark blue jeans, was Martin. He was tall, in his late thirties or maybe just turned forty, with jet black hair parted in the middle and a pale complexion. When he saw me, he walked over and extended his hand: "Elisse. Good to see you made it."

We shook hands. "Let's sit down," he said, in a guttural voice tinged with a heavy accent. "Get comfortable, we'll be here a while."

Daniel rushed to set food trays in front of us, two takeaway boxes from a fried chicken restaurant close-by, along with fountain drinks. He smiled at me again. "Need anything else?"

"No, thank you," I said. "I'm all right."

He looked at Martin and they exchanged a few words in French. Daniel nodded and left the room, pulling the door firmly shut behind him.

Martin grinded his cigarette butt into the ashtray next to the dossiers on the table. He flicked a tape recorder on and checked that it was rolling. Then he leaned forward on his elbows and peered at me through the thick lenses of his glasses. "Just for the record, why do you want to do this?"

"Because I want to stop what the Heritage Front is doing. I want to take advantage of what I know and my position in the organization."

"You understand that I am not the police. We cannot guarantee that your charges will be dropped, or that you will receive a new identity. We can only help by getting you a new attorney, who will still need be paid through Legal Aid. We don't want to make this switch too early though, as it would be an obvious red flag to the boys if you fired the official Heritage Front lawyer right now."

I nodded. "Understood."

"We will also connect you with our lawyers so that you can make sworn statements, after which time we will initiate contact with the appropriate authorities. You are doing this of your own free will, without any expectation of recompense?"

"Yes. Leaving the Heritage Front isn't enough. I want to do something more – I want to leverage my knowledge."

"In that case, let me explain what's going to happen. The first thing I need to ensure is that your information is genuine. That all this isn't some elaborate set-up on the HF part. Are you okay with this?"

"Yes. What do you want me to do?"

He pushed a yellow legal pad over to me. "You can start by writing down the names, addresses and telephone numbers of everyone you have met in the last two years."

"That might take a while."

"That's fine. Take as long as you need. Whatever information you cannot recall from memory, I trust you have brought with you."

I snapped open the buckles of my knapsack. My hands shook slightly as I pulled out the papers I'd packed and slid them across the table. "It's all I have. But I can get more."

"Do you have access to the complete Heritage Front membership list?"

"Yes. I help with the mail-outs, write the addresses on all the envelopes we send out."

"You do this for Zundel as well, right?"

"The mail-outs, yes. The computer, no."

"Can you get his list? Make a backup of his hard drive?"

I had to think about it. "It's too difficult. Nobody is allowed near Jürgen's computer. Drew had started to do some data entry for Ernst, but only under Jürgen's supervision. I've never even sat in front of a computer, I wouldn't know what to do. But I can try to get as much as I can when the address labels are printed prior to the monthly mailings. I can't guarantee it'll be the entire list though."

He nodded, not at all phased. "So the way it's gonna work is, we will get right on top of verifying the accuracy of your information. We will double and triple-check your facts. If my sources in the movement come back and vouch for what you're telling me, we're on. Any questions?"

"What happens if they find out? Can you protect me?"

"*If* your information is genuine and you deliver what we want, I give you my word that we will help you when the time comes. This will involve contacting the Ontario Provincial Police and the RCMP. But first, you'll have to pass a test to prove that you're not a plant."

"—But everything I'm telling you is true…" I interrupted.

He waved, cutting me off. "Please. Spare me the bullshit. Do you think we would be having this meeting if I thought you were pulling my leg? The reality is, I have to do my job. Before I get involved and risk my reputation, I have to make sure you're legit. You need to convince me that you have something that will be useful to police. We already have people on the inside providing us with Intel, so why should we work with you? Can you give us something we don't already have that we can use to shut them down? That enables us to go after them in the court of law? And I'm sorry, miss, but the test to prove your commitment will be done on my terms, not yours."

I stared at him in consternation.

As he reached for a fry, he cracked a smile for the first time. "Try the chicken," he said. "It's from the best barbeque place in town."

I didn't make a move. He shrugged, shoved a few more fries in his mouth, then sat back and crossed his arms. "Relax," he said. "For now, you're going to play along with them and pay it forward."

I shook my head. "Come again?"

"Pay it forward. Just like Grant Bristow taught you to hack into people's lives without a conscience, you will now turn around and do it back to them. It's the law of the jungle. It's how you'll earn your stripes."

TWENTY-FOUR

THE PLOT THICKENS

The names and addresses I gathered from the Heritage Front's and Zundel's mailing list were in Martin's hands within the month. "It's all a matter of connecting the dots," Ruth told me when we met in the park behind her house. "With these guys, it's a domino effect – you knock down one and watch the rest fall, one after the other."

She studied my face for a moment before frowning. "What is it? What's wrong?"

"Ernst never did anything to me," I answered slowly. "I know he's a Holocaust denier, but as far as I know, he never physically harmed anybody. He needs to be taken down, but…"

She sneered. "Never underestimate the power of words. That man is vile. The damage he does to people's minds by twisting history around is inexcusable. He makes up facts, Elisse. Fabricates lies that fuel people's hatred. He may not hold a weapon in his hands, but he's far more dangerous than someone who sleeps with a gun under his bed. Wanna know why?"

I chewed on the inside of my cheek. "Why?"

"When that skinhead goes out and bashes somebody's head in with his steel-toed boots, he justifies it with Ernst's words. Ernst takes all that enormous anger and rage inside an alienated young man's heart –" Ruth's hands ballooned out to form the impression of a huge sphere, then smashed together in a fist – "and shapes it into purpose. Whittles it into a weapon. A motive and a cause to kill for."

She was right, as usual. "When will I hear from Martin?" I asked her.

"I assume as soon as he's had a chance to review your information. Don't think about this anymore. Go back to them and pretend everything's the same. Act normal. Don't give them any reason to suspect anything."

We got up off the ground and brushed the grass off our clothing. As I turned to walk away, she reached for my arm and pulled me into a hug. "Take care of yourself," she whispered in my ear. "Everything's going to be okay."

For the first time since we'd met, she sounded uncertain.

Our sense of foreboding was proven correct when my doorbell rang early one morning weeks after my initial meeting with Martin. Through the peephole, I saw Detective Murphy puffing hard, looking as if he hadn't had his donut and coffee yet. I could have pretended I wasn't home, but that would postpone the inevitable. If Murphy was at my door, something had to up and I'd have no choice but to deal with him, now *or* later.

With trepidation, I creaked the door open. He stuck his hand out and I saw that he was holding a piece of paper. "Take it and sign right over here," he said.

"What is it?"

"You're being charged with an additional offense."

"Why now, all these months later? I didn't do anything."

He scowled at me. "It took that long for the Attorney General to approve this charge. You are being charged under Section 319 of the Criminal Code: willfully distributing hate propaganda."

I stared at him incredulously. "You had to get permission from the *government* to charge me with this?"

"Just take it," he snapped. "Your bail conditions remain the same. We've just tacked on this on top of the other charge. If I were you, I'd get on the phone to your lawyer."

He turned and walked back toward the elevator, his footsteps echoing across the dirty linoleum parquet. My heart was pounding as I walked back into the living room, clutching the papers I'd just been served. Why was this happening? *I have to get a hold of Ruth right away*, I thought, fighting back the shock that was spreading through me.

With shaky fingers, I rushed to dial Ruth's work number. She had to pick up, she just had to. Finally, she answered, and I burst out in an incoherent torrent of words and tears. She could barely understand me. "Calm down, calm down," she kept repeating. "Come meet me at five o'clock outside my office. We'll talk then."

I was there by four-thirty. I waited impatiently, hands buried deep in the pockets of my sweater, fidgeting from one foot to another. After what seemed like forever, she emerged through the front doors of the non-profit organization she worked for. She took one look at me and gestured, "Ok, let's go to my car."

We walked toward the parking lot at the back of the building. I got in while she put her briefcase in the trunk and came around to the driver's seat. She made no attempt to start the engine. "What's going on?" she asked. "What happened?"

I told her. She closed her eyes and took a deep breath. "Well, this complicates things just a tad, doesn't it?" she said.

I looked down in misery. She reached in the back seat, fished out a Kleenex box and thrust it at me. I blew my nose forcefully. "Let's go back to my place and talk," she said.

She dropped me off at the end of her street and told me to walk up the rear alleyway behind Clinton street and knock at the back door. In case any of Grant's cronies were watching her place, we didn't want to be photographed out front together.

Annetta greeted me at the door with a hug. Her face was clouded with worry. "Are you all right?"

"Not really," I said.

"Ruth's calling Martin," she said. "He'll know what to do."

"It's really bad, isn't it?"

She averted my questioning glance. "Let's just see what he says."

After a minute, Ruth came back in the living room. "I left him a message," she said. Then she looked at me and her forehead wrinkled in confusion. "So let me get this straight." She paused, as if going over it again in her head. "The Attorney General gave the go-ahead to charge *you* with hate propaganda? What does that even mean – you're like the fourth person in Canada to be charged with this?"

Looking at me with pity, Annetta nodded. "Yes, I think she is. Only Keegstra and a couple other guys were ever charged before her. Pathetic, really. Zundel's been here in Canada for twenty years, cranking out the presses and mailing out his 'Holocaust is a Hoax' drivel all over the world, and where was the Attorney General then? It's a fucking joke that they now decide to charge an eighteen-year old girl with this and not an asshole like Zundel or Droege, who recruit and manipulate kids like her all the time. Just goes to show you how the government wants to make themselves look good and say, *Hey people, look, we've charged somebody under section 319,* but wash their hands of the responsibility of going after the real hate-mongers."

"They're afraid of going after Zundel," Ruth said. "He has a lot of support and resources on his side. He's been doing the same thing in plain sight on Carlton street and they can't seem to stop him, or they don't want to…who knows? But Elisse is a patsy for both sides. It makes the government look good in telling everyone that they're enforcing Section 319, while the Front washes their hands of the flyers they've been putting out. It's a win-win situation for all. They want to make an example of someone and she's perfect."

"But I didn't make the flyer," I insisted.

Annetta laughed hollowly. "Jesus, Elisse. You still don't get it. Do you think it matters to anybody what you really did or didn't do? The people who run this country are more interested in looking good. The policies this government proposes every year are geared to ensure they win the next election. They don't operate by what is fair and just, but by what will earn them another run in Parliament.

It's time you wake up and realize that nobody actually cares whether you made that fucking flyer or not. Nobody wonders how a girl who doesn't own a computer or printer, who doesn't have any computer skills at all, could have put together something like that while a guy like Zundel has a half-dozen printing presses in his basement. What matters is that you have no money and no adequate legal defense, whereas Zundel gets donations from Nazi supporters from all over the world and has the ability to tie up the case in courts for years."

TWENTY-FIVE

THE MONTREAL INCIDENT

Weeks after I'd returned to Toronto Martin called to give me my next assignment, which doubled as the last test I would receive to prove my authenticity. If I failed it, our deal wouldn't be worth the tape it was recorded on. "A racist rock concert is being held in Montreal next weekend," he informed me. "It's organized by the Northern Hammerskins and they're flying in Aggravated Assault, a virulent white supremacist rock band from the US. So far the exact location is still unknown. A large contingent of anti-racists are planning to demonstrate and shut the venue down, but nobody knows where it's going to be, not even my local sources."

I took a deep breath, anticipating his next words.

"You will go to Montreal and find out where this concert is being held."

"And you think I'm going to find this out, how?"

"You're a smart cookie. Do whatever you have to do to get yourself there. You'll find a way to acquire this information from them. You do this, and I give you my word that we'll do everything possible to get you out when the time comes."

Adam H., the leader of the Northern Hammerskins, along with a couple of his scary-looking buddies, met me at the Maisonneuve Central bus terminal. Wolfgang had called him to ask if he could pick me up, as a personal favour. He hadn't had to ask twice; the guys were dreadfully excited at the prospect of hanging out with Heritage Front 'elite', not to mention the fourth person ever to be charged with hate propaganda. It was a depressing, deeply embarrassing fact for me, all the more so because I'd been charged with a flyer that I had sought to warn others about, but for them it was a sensational feat that couldn't match their existing rap sheets, which were filled with more generic forms of violence such as assaults, mischief, the odd weapon possession charge thrown in for kicks.

Adam towered over six feet in height and was a scary specimen of Aryan genes, complete with icy blue eyes and a buzz haircut. He loomed over his buddies psychologically as well as physically and I had little doubt, even with my rudimentary knowledge of pop psychology, that he was probably a born psychopath.

I soon discovered that Montreal skins were a raucous bunch. As we walked back to the parking lot, the guys weren't shy to holler at people they thought looked at them in the wrong way. They kicked parked cars indiscriminately, using their Doc Martens to dent doors and crack side mirrors. Martin had been elusive when he'd described them; perhaps he had tried to spare me the nervousness of what lay ahead, but he hadn't done me any favours. All he'd said was that they were cut from a different cloth than the Heritage Front skinheads, who had pretty much fallen in line with Wolfgang's orders to stay out of trouble. These Quebecers were a different breed altogether – much more radical and defiant, they reminded me of the glazed-eyed Aryan Nations types I'd seen at the Miles compound in Michigan.

We piled into a ratty car driven by Dan, a stocky skinhead who was Adam's best pal, and headed to Mirabel Airport to pick up members of the rock band No Remorse. "They're coming in from Michigan," Adam explained. "Aggravated Assault, the other band we booked for the concert, is flying in tonight. I reserved all the rooms at this motel close to my dad's place just to make sure we had enough places for everybody who's coming from out of town."

They planned to hang out there the rest of the day, get wasted and party till dawn. The motel was next to the woods, in a remote spot that ensured privacy for the guests. *Great*, I thought uneasily. *Impossible to get away without a car.*

After picking up the band members uneventfully, we crashed at Adam's parents' house in St. Anne de Bellevue for an hour. The sun was beginning to set when Dan's girlfriend Alana arrived with a van to take us downtown so we could grab the musical equipment for Sunday. As we loaded the van, I memorized the exact address as well as the license plates of the handful of vehicles parked on the street. The more info I had, the better I'd do in Martin's test.

"Hey man, I saw you on TV last month," one of the guys said, smacking my back. "That's a pretty cool charge, hate propaganda. All I ever get busted for is assault."

He stared at me with a puzzled expression, until I realized that I hadn't looked sufficiently proud of my notoriety. "Oh, yeah," I said half-heartedly. "It's too stressful to get excited about it. What with the jail possibility and all."

He brightened up. "First time being charged with anything, eh? I remember those jitters. You'll be fine, kid. You'll be fine."

After we dropped the equipment at the motel, we headed to the airport to pick up the second band flying in, Aggravated Assault. About a dozen of us made up the welcoming committee; we waited for half an hour past the flight's arrival time, and nothing. All other passengers had already disembarked but the band was nowhere in sight. "Doesn't look good," muttered one of the skins, shaking his head. "I hope they didn't detain them at customs."

Finally, band members started walking through the gates, cursing the 'assholes' who'd held them up. The skinheads around me breathed out in relief. Still, no sign of the lead singer.

The reason for their delay became self-evident as soon as I looked at the band. Two out of the three guys were wearing short-sleeve tee-shirts, which anyone with an iota of common sense would recognize as a no-no – could they have been less inconspicuous going through customs while brandishing multiple Hitler and Klan tattoos? Of course they had been pulled aside and questioned, and of course they had been stupid enough to admit that they were in town for a gig, which set the radar on overdrive. They were lucky to have gotten through at all. But no such luck was to be had for the lead singer who, upon an immigration check, was found to have a criminal record. It was highly unlikely he'd be singing anywhere Sunday night except in a cell block.

"Fuck," Adam exploded. "I paid for their flights, man. Money down the drain."

I spent an interminable night crouched in a grungy motel armchair after refusing a band member's invitation to join him in bed. He swore up and down that he'd never touch an Aryan sister. Yeah, right. Besides, his buddies said he had bugs and kicked as a mule when asleep. When dawn finally broke through, Adam showed up in a

196

car he'd borrowed from his father. We all piled in, fitting eight people by having all the girls ride on someone's lap. We hung on for dear life as Adam cut sharp corners and nearly crashed into the windowpanes of the local McDonalds. As we settled around a plastic table with our McBreakfasts, I felt a twinge of anxiety rumbling deep in my stomach. No matter how plastered Adam had been last night, he wasn't talking. He hadn't so much as hinted the location to the other Hammerskins. It didn't look like anybody besides Dan and a couple of close buddies had a clue.

Unlike me, nobody else gave a shit about where it was – the only thing they were interested in was having a good time. I looked at my watch and frowned. It was eleven AM. The show was scheduled for tomorrow evening at seven. Between now and then I had to find a way to somehow divine the location of the concert and notify Martin, who in turn was going to get his people ready to cancel the event, and I had to do all this with enough time to spare.

"Adam," I started, "I'm really nervous about tomorrow night. I told you about my bail conditions, how I'm not supposed to associate with anybody in the movement. Do you think there'll be police outside?"

He waved dismissively. "No worries. Nobody knows where it is. You'll be totally fine."

"But what if they spot me? I can't go to jail. It's freaking me out."

"Half the guys coming are probably breaching their bail," he laughed. "Including yours truly. So trust me, it'll be okay. Just put on a baseball cap so you don't stand out."

"That's a good idea," I said, dipping a nugget into a packet of honey. "But if you're heading over there early to set up, couldn't you take me along? That way I can plan an escape route in case we get busted. Figure out the back-door exit, that sort of thing."

"It'll be *fine*. Just relax," he said. "Nobody's going to spot you." His cold blue eyes indicated that was the end of that.

I had to drop it. Any further questions and he might get suspicious. "Okay, if you say so," I said dubiously, turning my attention to Alana. "Any other girls coming?"

"Oh yeah, lots of people you should meet," she answered brightly. "They wanna meet you too. Everyone's so excited that you know Wolfgang. They'd love to talk to you about what the HF is up to in Toronto."

"Cool, I can't wait," I said, finishing my last nugget.

Back to the motel, the band members were just starting to stir awake. Adam and Dan heaved box after box of Molson's beer and stacked them inside each room. All the rooms that faced the parking lot had been occupied by out-of-town skinheads who were exceedingly thirsty. Barely past noon, the party got underway.

I sat on the living room sofa of Adam's suite and watched Jerry Springer. People milled in and out, grabbing beer and pizza slices. The all-too-familiar buzzing of a tattoo gun resonated from next door. Chairs were moved out to the parking lot and the tattooist-in-residence chipped bearded Vikings, crowns of thorns and swastikas on the beefy shoulders of skinheads who chain-smoked and chugged back on alcohol to take the sting away.

Then, a lucky break. Around four o'clock, Adam returned from dropping off the musical instruments at the mystery location. He stood in the threshold of the motel suite, holding what I knew instinctively to be the hall rental agreement. He paused in mid-motion, looking confused, and absentmindedly put the folded paper on the cabinet next to the phone. "Have you seen Dan?" he asked.

"He might be in there," I said, pointing to the bedroom. "With the band members."

Close to a dozen guys had snuck into the bedroom earlier, carrying long, skinny bags I recognized as rifle storage cases. Given the fact that last night, at his dad's place, Adam had brought out six rifles to show us, I suspected that the guys who'd just arrived were involved in trading or selling arms.

"Cool, thanks," Adam said. He went into the bedroom and closed the door behind him.

If not now, I might never get another chance. Without hesitation, I leapt to my feet and raced to the cabinet. I took a deep breath and unfolded the paper. There it was, the information I was here to get....and it was all in French!

My eyes scanned the paper desperately, searching for a street name. I forced myself to memorize it all. My eyes kept darting to the bedroom door and back to the paper. My heart pounded loudly in my ears. Blood rushed through my head. Finally, I'd memorized the hall owner's name and telephone number. I refolded the paper and placed it back exactly where Adam had left it. I went into the bathroom and turned on the faucet, scooped out a tiny notepad from my back pocket and quickly jotted down the details. I flushed the toilet and came back out, bracing myself for what was still to come.

A dozen upturned faces greeted me. The skinheads had moved into the living room and now sat around the dinette table. The paper was laid out flat in the centre. I fought the urge to throw up. "Am I interrupting?" I asked nonchalantly.

"No, not really," said Adam. I knew he didn't care whether I was there or not, but some of the other guys might have an issue with a female being within earshot. It was time for me to get out of there. "That's okay," I said. "I'll leave you guys to your business. Have fun."

Stepping out of the room into a wash of cool air, I wondered how on earth I was going to contact Martin's people. Cellular phones hadn't come on the market yet, and from the band members' griping I knew that outgoing phone calls cost 75 cents and were itemized on the final bill. I wasn't about to call from a motel room and have Adam go berserk when he saw the CCRP's number on the invoice the next day.

I decided to circle the motel instead. The late afternoon sun threatened to blind me as more and more cars pulled in. A sense of danger pulsated through the air. Voices got progressively louder: *Gotta get rid of those mutherfuckin' muds, man.* With each beer bottle they got meaner and I had no doubt that before nightfall someone was going to get beaten up.

I walked around to the check-in entrance, but the front door was locked. After renting out all the rooms, the manager had promptly shut down for the night. *Shit.* How the hell was I going to find a phone?

One of the Aggravated Assault members came up behind me and tapped my shoulder. "Wanna come see a movie? There's a documentary about dykes in the 1950s called *Forbidden Love* playing downtown. Might be fun to go stir up the theatre."

"Oh, really?" *I thought everybody had already opted to stay in and get pissed drunk.*

"Yeah, man," he said, his eyes glossy. "I'll see who else wants to come. Otherwise we'll just party down here."

"Maybe order some in-room movies?" I hinted. That brightened him up more.

"Oh, yeah. Something with lesbians would be fun," he said, taking a gulp of his beer.

"By the way, I just remembered I have to call my mom," I said, fishing out a calling card out of my pocket. "Forgot to let her know when I got here yesterday and she's probably freaking by now."

"Freaking mothers," he said sympathetically.

"You know where I can find a pay phone?"

"Yeah, I remember seeing one next to the convenience store up the road. Just follow the trail of people heading there for more beer," he laughed.

"You're a lifesaver. I'd better get a hold of her before she has a fit."

By the time I reached the phone booth, my wristwatch said 6:45. I glanced around. Half a dozen skinheads had just entered the convenience store to get liquor. I went inside the booth, pulled the glass door closed, picked up the receiver and dialed the number Martin gave me.

"Yes Roxanne, I was expecting your call," a woman's voice answered in a thick Quebecois accent. "Where are you right now?"

I told her the address printed on the book of matches I'd lifted from one of the rooms. Then it was time to tackle the concert location. "This is what I have," I started, reading off the information I'd jotted in my notepad. I kept my eyes aimed at the narrow path. A couple of tattooed bald guys were slowly approaching.

"What did you say was the street name?" She was unclear as to which was the owner and which was the address. I hadn't the slightest clue.

"The form was in French, I just copied whatever was written. I'm not really sure," I said brusquely. The skinheads were coming closer; they were now staring at me through the smudged glass of the phone booth.

As though sensing my apprehension, the woman asked, "How's the situation? Is it safe?"

"Yes, for the moment it is," I said, but my voice must have been a little shaky because she replied with, "You're doing a good job, hang in there."

There was no doubt in my mind the two were coming straight for me. "Ok, I've got to go, Mom," I said. "They're coming."

"Good luck," she said before I slammed the phone down, took a deep breath and stepped out. "Hi." I waved to the guys who stopped in front of the booth. "Wanna use it too? I'm just about done."

"Hey," one of them said cheerfully. "How'd you guess?" I relaxed, smiled at him. *They just want to use the phone. They can't read your mind, they're clueless. Just keep repeating that and you'll get through this.*

I walked over to the convenience store and bought a bag of Doritos and a coke so I'd have something to justify being gone. I allowed myself to let go of the tension that had gripped me the entire day. It was out of my hands. Martin's people were either going to make sense of what I'd given them, or they were not. But there was nothing more I could do at this point. For better or worse, my task was completed.

Forty-five minutes after my call, a car cruised slowly through the motel parking lot. It pulled in front of Adam's suite for a moment, backed up and circled the place again. Intuitively, I knew it was there because of me. I tried to spot the driver through the reflecting windshield but the dark tint made it impossible. I was grateful that everyone else was too busy guzzling their booze that they wouldn't notice such an overt inspection.

At nightfall, Adam and Dan started a barbecue in the wooden lot next to the motel. "So what's the HF up to these days?" Dan asked as he flipped a hamburger on the grill.

"Not that much," I replied. "Lately everybody's getting charged with something or another so we're keeping a low profile."

"I don't think much of them honestly," he confessed, "but I do have respect for Wolfgang. Despite the bullshit hierarchy. But they're just too mellow for me. They wanna go political or something. Too much talk and no action." He glanced at me. "Know what I mean?"

I nodded. These guys wouldn't have wasted a minute of their time on Preston Manning. I'd never seen a more violent bunch of Canadian extremists than the Northern Hammerskins.

"Our guys are willing to put action where their mouth is. Ain't that right, Carl?"

Carl was one of Adam's best buds. He was a light-haired bonehead with a lazy eye, which gave him the appearance of a pecked chicken. "Fuck, yeah," Carl said. "Remember Adam's AK47? We practice it all the time in the forest behind his dad's house."

It was fascinating to me how these guys couldn't care less about breaching their probations. Never mind that semi-automatic weapons were restricted in Canada and Adam was banned from owning as much as a Swiss army knife or a pair of Doc Martens on account that he'd once kicked a guy's head in with his boots. They believed themselves utterly above the law.

Carl called out to Adam, beckoning him over. "Hey Adam, next time you wanna try out the new M16 or stick with the AKA47?"

"That's a tough call," Adam said, taking a swig. "Depends on which takes out more monkeys and JDLs."

"Do you think a 22-calibre rifle would be an okay weapon to start with?" I asked. "Because that's all I've been able to get."

"Oh, yeah," Dan nodded. "Light enough for a girl. Simple to operate. Basic, but baby steps are okay. Good for starters." He reached for a paper plate. "Anybody up for a burger?"

"I'll take that," Adam said. Then he looked at me again. "You should really see my whole collection. My dad's totally cool with it. We have a shitload of stuff stored in our basement."

His girlfriend Julie came over to us. She smirked at Adam, who turned back toward the barbecue. Several skinheads were beginning to swarm around the food. I stepped off to the side. Julie wrapped a sisterly arm around my shoulders and whispered in my ear, "I'm getting the hell out of here before they get out of hand," she said. "Wanna come along?"

Julie was in a foul mood since she'd just found out that Adam, who she'd been dating for the last three months, was still seeing his ex.

"How bad is it gonna get?"

She rolled her eyes. "That's right, you're from Toronto. Bet you haven't seen people party like they do down here. Trust me, they get pretty rowdy. They get loud and mean, and I don't plan to stick around when the fists and beer bottles start to fly."

Couldn't blame her. "What do you have in mind?"

"I figure we go back to my place, call some friends and hit the bars in the historic district. You're welcome to crash at my apartment.

You can take my bedroom if you want. I have a nice pull-out sofa for when people spend the night."

My back still ached from contorting myself to fit the armchair I'd slept in last night. I surveyed the scene around me. Empty beer cans were scattered all over. Everyone was completely wasted and well on their way to passing out by the side of a tree. I doubted anybody would miss me if I snuck off with Julie and checked out downtown Montreal. "Ok, give me a second to grab my knapsack."

A tipsy Dan drove us to the closest bus station, and from there we made it to Julie's place some twenty minutes later. She lived in a narrow one-bedroom basement flat that seemed extra cozy because of its unduly low ceilings.

"I'm going to call my friend Christine," Julie called out from the kitchen. "We'll take the subway downtown."

I liked Julie well enough. She seemed stable, held down a full-time job and had been introduced into the racist movement only recently by her soon-to-be-ex-boyfriend Adam. Already she showed signs of having soured on the whole thing.

Downtown Montreal was dazzling that Saturday night; flashing red and orange neon lights accentuated the Mardi Gras atmosphere. Young people milled about everywhere, spilled out of cafés and pubs, laughing boisterously, flicking cigarette butts against the cobblestones and proceeding to immediately light up again. Every bar had a long line-up of party-goers in tight pants, chic leather jackets, big puffy hair and designer purses.

Julie's friend Christine was holding a place in line for us at their favourite discothèque when we arrived. Even though I wasn't carrying any photo ID and the drinking age was nineteen, the girls sweet-talked the bouncer into letting me in. We continued down a series of steps to a massive underground dance floor filled to the brim with sweaty, gyrating people. The strobe lights could have provoked an epileptic fit and the base was turned up so high it shook the building walls. Lots of skinheads were there, dancing wildly and smashing into each other to the reggae rhythms of UB40. They were all francophone, so Julie and her friend took turns as translators.

"This girl's the first person in the country in eleven years to be charged with hate propaganda," Christine boasted to one of her acquaintances, a dopey-looking young skinhead who flashed a toothy grin and smacked my arm in congratulations. *"C'est bien,"* he repeated, trying his best to come across as charming.

"He wants to know if you want something to drink," Christine hollered in my ear.

I shook my head no. "I'm so tired, if I drank anything I'd probably pass out."

"Try some of mine," she offered, holding out a test-tube filled with a viscous pink substance. It tasted like mashed strawberries. Not too bad. You could drink a lot of those and not feel anything until it hit you like a ton of bricks.

We left the place sometime after two in the morning. The 19th century cobblestone walkway that led to the all-night bus stop was lined with quaint little shops. The town square still brimmed with people and it had a kind of carnival-come-to-town feel. A couple of skinheads so smashed they could barely stand staggered behind us to the bus stop. Every two seconds one of them would stop dead in the middle of the road and shout out 'Sieg Heil' or variations on that theme.

"Shit," Julie muttered, scowling over her shoulder. "I hope they don't pick a fight."

The bus arrived and us girls plunked down in the back, pretending not to know the skinheads who had started to run up and down the length of the bus, screaming drunken obscenities in both official languages. Half an hour later we ambled into Julie's apartment, giggling in relief that we'd finally gotten rid of our unwanted companions. I sat at her kitchen table and started unlacing my boots when Julie noticed the message light flashing on her answering machine.

"Who could've called at this hour?" she frowned, pressed the Talk button.

The voice that boomed out of the machine was frantic: "Julie, are you there? Pick up the phone, goddammit! *GET RID OF HER!* She's dangerous! She's a viper! Before it's too late, GET HER OUT!"

I froze. Julie and Christine both emerged out of the bedroom, looking perplexed.

"Are they talking about *her*?" whispered Christine, glancing to Julie.

"What the hell?" Julie stared at me. "What did you do to get them so mad?"

I froze, momentarily speechless. It felt like a bucket of cold water had just been thrown on me. *Thank God the message had been in English*, I thought. I didn't know what had gone down but I needed to get the fuck out of there. Without saying a word, I struggled to put my boots back on, trying to keep my hands from shaking. Julie paced the length of the apartment and exchanged a few rapid words in French with her friend, something to the tune of *'What was that about?'*

"Now wait a minute," she said, noting my stricken face. "Just calm down and we'll figure this out."

"What if they're going to come over? I have to go."

She crossed her arms and shook her head vehemently. "They would've come by now, while we were out. It's a good thing we weren't here. By now they're in no state to go anywhere, trust me. And do you think I'm gonna let a bunch of drunken assholes into my place to attack you when they aren't even coherent about what they want? If they come by, I'm not opening the door." She kept shaking her head. "They're nuts. They get really scary when they drink. No, we'll wait until morning to speak to Adam and clear this whole thing up. You know, if they really think you're a rat it pisses me off that Adam didn't warn me before I brought you home."

"Right now, you're safe here," Christine added. "It's four a.m., the transit's stopped running. There's nowhere for you to go. We'll drop you at the subway in the morning. Julie will iron everything out with the guys."

I somehow doubted it. The girls replayed the message, struggling to understand what was going on. I, on the other hand, knew exactly what had happened – Martin's people must have cancelled the concert venue. I'd heard helicopters in the background, circling the motel. The skinheads had caught on that someone must have talked. And outside of Adam, Dan and the band members who were going to perform – guys who'd known each other for years and could vouch for one another – nobody but me had been inside the room.

Naturally, they suspected me. My saving grace was that the message had been so slurred by alcohol and paranoia that Julie chose to believe me over them and took no immediate action.

"Let's just go to bed," she said warily. "You'll be fine. This is *my* place, they can't force their way in." To accentuate this, she slid the deadbolt across the door. "Okay?"

We all went to bed or at least they did, sharing a pull-out sofa in the living room.

I closed the bedroom door behind me and went through my pockets, pulling out every bit of incriminating information I was carrying – the number Martin had given me, the pages with all the license plates I'd seen for the last two days. I tucked them inside my bra, wondering if I should destroy them altogether. I'd gone too far to get rid of all this information now. But what if they showed up before dawn and decided to rough me up? What if I ended up like Tyrone, suspected of informing by Drew and his buddies because the COTC computer had been stolen. They'd pulled him off the street, tied him up and tortured him for hours. I wasn't naïve enough not to know what they would do to a female.

I stretched out over the covers of Julie's bed, keeping my clothes on, even the boots. I had to think of a way to get out, and fast. I couldn't just sneak out through the front door because the girls were sleeping out there. Julie had insisted I take her bedroom, possibly as a way to keep me from running away until the issue was ironed out.

I'd never felt more terrified in my life, not even when I was ten years old and huddling on a street corner in Bucharest one night, hungry and scared, having been locked out of my father's apartment once again, when a strange man had come up to me and tried to drag me away with him.

My eyes grew accustomed to the shadows reflecting weird, gigantic shapes against the furniture, brushing against Julie's dresser, nightstand, and coming to pool at the foot of the bed. I turned my head toward the window, trying to make out the source of light streaming in from the alleyway. The sliding panes were quite oversized for a basement flat with such a low ceiling.

That's when the thought struck me. Taking care not to make anything creak, I stepped onto the bed, reached up on tiptoes and slid the window as far as it would go. I studied the gap and thought, *Yes, it might just work*. I turned and moved the clock radio and various junk from the dresser onto the floor, then took a deep breath. I couldn't afford to drag the dresser along the parquet in case the floorboards squeaked so I wrapped my arms around it and lifted it off the ground, groaning as I deposited it directly underneath the window. I had to hope it would sustain my weight.

I stepped on the bed and hopped up to the dresser, which creaked painfully but didn't split. I reached through the open window and smashed out the screen with my fist, locking my fingers against the outside windowsill. I braced myself, held my breath and leaped as high as I could, as if emerging out of a swimming pool. For a second I thought I wouldn't make it. My muscles shook violently. Gritting my teeth, I hoisted myself through the tight gap. I knew I had cleared it when my cheek scraped against a gravel pit. I was halfway out and there was no turning back. I took another deep breath and pushed up with all my might, landing hard on my knees in the alleyway and scuffing the side of my jeans for good measure.

I ran as fast and hard as I'd ever ran in my life. When I was about a mile away, I hid in the alcove of a nearby shuttered restaurant and waited for a bus. I sat on the ground and put my head against my knees. *Just hurry up already*, I thought. About a half hour later, when the bus headlights beamed orange across the wet roadway, I leaped forward and waved to the driver, who pulled over to let me climb aboard. I dropped some coins in the ticket slot and prayed the guys hadn't discovered that I'd gone missing.

I had nowhere else to go but home, and braced myself for the confrontation to come. The bus came to the end of its route minutes later and the driver forced everyone to get off. By the time I made it to the Maisonneuve station, another hour had passed.

No sooner had I started making my way across the platform that I spotted the bleached locks of a Chelsea and her skinhead boyfriend. I darted behind a brick column and aimed for the restrooms. Barely undetected, I slinked into the women's washroom and crashed against the wall, feeling nauseous. A cleaning woman hovering over a vomit-streaked toilet bowl raised her head to stare at me suspiciously. She probably expected I'd stick a needle in my arm. With my pale face and tousled hair, I must have looked the part. Ignoring her, I leaned over the sink and splashed some water over my face, tried to smooth my hair.

Afterwards I returned to the platform and lined up for the bus back to Toronto. The white-supremacist couple were nowhere in sight but I didn't breathe a sigh of relief until the skyline of Montreal had vanished from sight.

I knew that as soon as I got in the door, I'd have to deal with the repercussions of this hellish weekend. Adam would have called Wolfgang to share his suspicions before my bus had even pulled into the downtown terminal. Undoubtedly he'd demand to know why Wolfgang had okayed a potential informer to attend a Northern Hammerskins event. I might have passed Martin's test, but my credibility was completely destroyed in Montreal. *I hope it was worth it*, I thought ruefully. *I hope he sticks to his side of the bargain and helps me disappear if it gets to that.*

Despite the mess, I was confident that I could wiggle my way out of this. I planned to deny everything and blame the whole misunderstanding on the unprovoked paranoia that had set in once the Hammerheads had gotten pissed drunk. If the concert venue had been found out, it wasn't my problem. How could I have spied on them? I didn't even speak French! But I also knew that once a rumour like this begins to fly, it has the ugly tendency to gather steam. I had to make sure I proved myself loyal, and I had to do it fast.

Just as I'd predicted, I could hear the phone ringing before I even turned the key to get inside my apartment. "I heard you bad-mouthed the Front in Montreal," Wolfgang's voice resounded. "At the crack of dawn, my phone starts ringing off the hook. Before I even open my eyes Adam is on the line, totally hysterical, wondering what's up with you."

"I don't know what the hell's wrong with the guy," I said calmly, having rehearsed this conversation for the last five hours. "I didn't do fuck-all to him. His girlfriend and I left the motel and went downtown to the club district. When we came back to her place, all hell had broken loose. It's still a mystery to me."

"Did you know that their concert venue got cancelled? They've been planning this for months. It was top secret, and the night before the event the hall owner calls them up wanting to cancel it. Adam freaks out and tells the guy he had to abide by the contract or else. And when they finally show up for the concert this afternoon, there are hundreds of anti-racists and riot police everywhere and the hall owner refuses to grant them access."

"So why would they blame me? I was in town only two days and they kept me in the dark about the location, just like everyone else. What proof do they have that I magically divined their location and told everybody?"

Wolfgang paused. "They have no proof." A lengthy sigh. "I straightened the whole thing out with them. I had to give Adam my personal guarantee that you were cool, Elisse. But you should know that I don't appreciate having to do this kind of damage control. My reputation is at stake when people start mouthing off about the Heritage Front and say we sent our own people to spy on the Hammerskins. It doesn't look good on me, does it?"

"I'm sorry, Wolf. I had no idea how deranged they would be," I said sheepishly.

"I knew you wouldn't fit in with that bunch," he said, more appeased now. "Don't worry about it. Like I said, I cleared it up. Told them it was just a misunderstanding. But don't go anywhere else again without talking to me first, okay?"

As soon as I hung up on Wolfgang, the phone rang again. It was Grant, and he was fuming. "I *TOLD* you not to go to Montreal," he shouted. "But you just didn't want to listen."

"Well, I made it back alive," I joked.

He didn't appreciate the humour. "Did you really want to get arrested for breaching your bail?"

"Come on Grant, how the hell was I supposed to know those guys are psycho fanatics? Jesus Christ, Adam was waving around an AK47! They're beyond radical, they're ready to start the race war tomorrow."

Grant snorted. "And when guys like that get it in their heads that you're an informer, guess what happens?"

"Fine. Don't say it. I shouldn't have gone to Montreal," I admitted, feeling touched by how much Grant seemed to care that I don't come across as an informer.

He sounded just barely placated. "Next time you should listen to me when I tell you something."

TWENTY-SIX

TURNCOAT

The Montreal incident didn't go unnoticed. I might have been able to appease Wolfgang, but I knew that once started, rumours like this have a habit of gathering steam. What the Fischer brothers had done to Tyrone Mason could happen to anyone. This was a dangerous time for anybody trying to shut down the Front.

I spied on the Heritage Front for three more months. I unloaded whatever information I could come across: the names of every individual I met, lists of people who had left their information on the hotline, license plates, addresses, everything. When I was at Wolfgang's place, I jotted down the names of all the contacts listed in his rolodex. Whenever I went over to help Ernst with his mail-outs, I recorded the names of his international contacts and also sketched out a map of the Bunker for Martin.

My international contact list was extensive. Over the last two years I had corresponded with leaders of various racist associations in Japan, Australia, the U.K., South Africa, Norway, Poland and the US. I had four regular pen-pals: Vicky, the twenty-year old head of the Dublin chapter of Women for Aryan Unity; Greg and Eddie, two Protestant UDA members from Northern Ireland, and Gareth, a Welshman who put out a zine called *The White Eagle* and was a top leader in his country. He had visited Canada two years ago to shoot a video with Ernst to be distributed across Wales. I piled all those letters into a box and handed it off to Ruth, who would forward them unto Martin. As soon as they were out of my hands, I felt lighter. I had absolute confidence that the plans and information detailed in those letters would find their way to the appropriate police departments.

At my next meeting with Martin, I slid two pieces of paper across the table: the birthday card I'd received from Grant, which included a personalized note, as well as his handwritten target list for the It Campaign, the one that had Ruth's name along with several other people's names and telephone numbers.

Martin took a Ziploc bag out of his drawer and carefully placed the items inside. "His fingerprints and handwriting on a hit-list are a good start," he said. Then his forehead creased. "Bristow has a lot more power than I'd given him credit for."

"He's very afraid of the limelight," I said. "Because of his job. He doesn't want to be caught on tape when he makes speeches. He even asks to be edited out of rally videos."

"I know that already," Martin said. "But I'm wondering what else he's up to." His eyes lingered on a fixed spot on the wall. "What else can you tell me?"

"Wolfgang typically answers to Grant," I said. "Not always, but he takes his suggestions most of the time. The longer I work with Grant, the more I realize that he likes to run the show from behind the scenes."

Martin nodded. "Rodney and I have been watching him for a while. He's very secretive, yet holds an incredible amount of clout and control over the Heritage Front. Everybody else in the group has rap sheets a mile long, but this guy's different – he keeps his nose clean and likes to provoke other people to do his dirty work. Do you think you can get more on him?"

Sure, Grant's handwriting on a hit list was worth its weight in gold. But if we were to build a case of criminal activity against him, as Martin was suggesting, we would have to go further.

Since I'd never been invited to his place, I couldn't steal mailing lists or other information as easily as I had done at Ernst's or Wolfgang's apartment. I would have to do this the old-fashioned way – digging into Grant's past the way he'd taught me to do to others, taking notes whenever he asked me to listen in on his harassing phone calls, and hope that he was too cocky to cover up his tracks.

September was a month of tremendous activity: I signed dozens of affidavits before a Montreal lawyer and witnesses. I rattled off descriptions of weapons that included Peter and Drew's arsenal. Surely now that Martin was going to arrange for the affidavits to be put in the OPP's hands, a search warrant would uncover everything.

In another affidavit, I sketched out the details of the It Campaign and depicted how Grant Bristow had masterminded the whole thing as part of establishing a secretive Intelligence division of the Heritage Front.

Then there was my statement about Brad Coulbeck, a 24-year old young man I'd met by chance in a courthouse last summer. I had mingled in the crowd outside the courtroom just before the hearing was about to start. A tall, dark-haired guy came up to me. "Hi there," he said excitedly. "You're Elisse, right?" I shook hands with him. "I'm Brad," he had introduced himself. "I recognize you from a video of the HF rally last December. Really glad to meet you."

I'd chatted with him for a few minutes, enough to discover that the guy was an off-duty constable on the Toronto Police Services. Possibly in an effort to impress me, he bragged that he had just returned from a Ku Klux Klan rally up in Arkansas. I didn't say anything to his face, of course, but as I heard him talk about his collection of HF videos and Up Front magazines it struck me that if I were a cop, I wouldn't have gone around bragging to everybody about my profession, or boasting about how I got to carry a gun on the job. Nor would I have bought an HF membership. You wanted to keep that sort of thing private, least of all because you didn't want it to come back and bite you in the ass in the form of somebody's affidavit.

Still, I felt lousy. Brad's career was about to get flushed down the toilet. He would soon face charges under the Police Act. Hadn't he just been young and stupid, like me?

"Don't feel bad about it," said Martin, handing me the pen. "The guy's a loose cannon; we can't have him running around the city with a loaded weapon. Besides, word is he's already suspended because he and his fiancée were charged with assaulting each other."

Signing this particular affidavit was scary. No longer was the Heritage Front the only group after me – I had made enemies with city cops. It was time to get the hell out of Toronto.

Now was the time to move forward with the next phase of our plan – getting this wealth of information into the right hands. We had to do it as soon as possible, before anybody from the Front got wind that someone on the inside was spying on them. Besides, the clock was counting down to my trial – sooner or later, my case would wind its way through the courts and the story of what had really happened the night I gave Edan and Shannon the flyer at Brockton High School would come out. Once the Front discovered that I had meant to warn the target, they'd put two and two together.

Martin pulled a lot of strings to arrange a meeting with the Ontario Provincial Police at a hotel downtown. He had attempted, in vain, to contact reps from the Royal Canadian Mounted Police, the national body that superseded provincial law enforcement, but no one was available on short notice.

One drizzly morning I met Martin in the west end and we made our way to the Delta Chelsea hotel on Gerrard Street, where we were met outside the glass revolving doors by two officers in plain clothes – a stocky, middle-aged man and a petite brown-haired woman whom I will call Robert and Marianne respectively. Together, we traveled up to a high-floor business suite where the officers had already set up a tape recorder on the conference table, next to a plate of muffins.

Martin and I sat on one side of the table, the OPP people on the other side. Martin unzipped his black attaché case and presented the officers with copies of the affidavits I'd signed earlier. We had a single request: provide me with an alternate identity, as well as relocation outside the province of Ontario. Afterwards we sat back, confident that the officers would be so impressed with the specifics of the crimes and the illegal weapons stash that this deal would be a no-brainer.

To my surprise, Robert started shaking his head. "We need more than that," he said. "If we're going to go after the Heritage Front, we'll need much more specific info."

His lukewarm reaction left me bewildered. "But I've just given you names and addresses where arms are stored," I said. "I've described the weapons to the best of my ability – I've even recounted how Peter smuggled a gun over the border. There's ammunition, rifles, guns. What more do you need? Can't you guys just get warrants and seize the stuff? They're already stalking and harassing people. What if they go further?"

"In order to get a judge to sign off on the warrants, we'll need more evidence," he repeated as though we were retarded. "Direct proof."

"Like what? Isn't my eyewitness testimony proof enough? All you have to do is get a search warrant. Peter's place is packed with guns. He gets them at Klan rallies down south. Wouldn't that be enough to just get in the door? Once you're there, you'll find everything."

He shook his head again. "Hearsay. Your word against his. We don't have it on tape."

Marianne broke in, an apologetic expression on her face. "I understand that you fear for your safety, Miss Hategan. Unfortunately, we, as part of the Ontario police, have nothing to do with the Witness Protection Program. That falls under the jurisdiction of the RCMP. They're the ones who make the final decision about who is admitted into the program."

Martin frowned and leaned forward, pointing to the documents spread out on the conference table. "Let me get this right. We are presenting you with details of names, places and times where illegal activity was planned. There are dozens of witnesses in the community who can attest to the harassment and death threats they have received. We have answering machine recordings with Grant Bristow's voice on them. There is also a hit list in Bristow's handwriting where he directs Elisse to target innocent people for assault. I don't understand what the problem is. Surely there is enough to bring these guys up on *some* sort of charges?"

Robert stood up stiffly in his seat, looking as though his feathers had been ruffled. He cleared his throat indignantly. "Well, there's another matter. I wasn't supposed to mention this, but when we informed Head Office that we were meeting with a potential informant I was directed by my superiors to let you know that we can approve nothing and give no deals until we discuss this matter internally. We'll have to get back to the office and contact you later. I assume I can reach you through your organization, Mr. Theriault? Since Elisse is going to be in hiding?"

"Yes, that's right," Martin said. "We very much appreciate this opportunity to meet with you. I hope we'll speak again as soon as possible. As you can imagine, the situation is very delicate. The moment Elisse disappears, it'll raise a red flag. We need the raids on those residences to happen *before* she leaves."

"We'll see what we can do," the officer said. "Like I already said, I am mandated to discuss all this with my superior but I'm committed to getting back to you right away."

"You're a brave girl," said Marianne, touching my hand. "Everything's going to be all right. You hang in there."

After two hours of discussions, there was nothing more we could say to make them budge. Martin got up to leave, and I took my cue to do the same. We shook hands with the OPP officers and left the room before they could follow us. As we walked to the elevators, Martin seemed troubled.

"I wasn't anticipating this reaction," he said, scratching the side of his face. "Interesting. It's almost as though they have been told *not* to get involved by someone above them. I would have thought that, given all the disruption going on in this city, they would leap at the chance to shut down the Front. Instead, they're dilly-dallying." He paused. "They *could* be trying to protect Constable Coulbeck from Metro Police; he's one of their own."

"They *will* make a deal though, won't they?" I asked, feeling uneasy. "They said they'll have to contact the RCMP, so maybe if we meet with *them*…."

"Don't worry," Martin said, nudging me into the elevator. "No sense panicking until there's a tangible problem. As far as we're concerned, there's still an opportunity to make this happen. But this is definitely not the reception I expected."

We rode the elevator down to the lobby and burst out into a sopping afternoon. Martin didn't seem in the mood to talk so I wisely held off asking any more questions. He hailed us a cab, climbed beside me and wearily put his head back against the headrest. I was about to open my mouth and ask what we were going to do next when he smacked his fist against his knee. "Fuck this. We're not done yet."

"What are you thinking?" I asked.

"If the OPP don't want your testimony, the Human Rights Commission will," he replied. "They've been trying to go after the Front since Rodney Bobiwash lodged a complaint last year about the hate-line. They'll want to hear what you have to say."

TWENTY-SEVEN

DEFECTION

Martin's insistence that we had to go after the instigator of the It Campaign made Grant Bristow a forefront target in our minds: we had to take *him* down, perhaps more than anyone else. Every time I spoke with Grant over the phone and laughed along at his racist, lurid and homophobic jokes, I recorded his exact words, what he was planning to do next. But there was one thing I'd forgotten to do – look into his background.

On that particular morning, I waited until my mother left for work before jumping out of bed and looking up InterTec in the phone book. "Just calling to verify that you have an employee by the name of Grant Bristow," I said perfunctorily, recalling a trick he'd taught me about impersonating resume-checkers.

I could hear the secretary clicking on a computer, presumably looking at personnel files. "Bristow? I'm sorry, nobody by that name is employed here."

I swallowed. "You sure? Maybe he doesn't work there now, but in the past?"

"Nope. Nobody like that," she repeated.

I sat in my chair by the window for a long time, clicking the button on my ballpoint pen on and off. What the hell was going on?

I was still trying to process what all this meant when the phone rang a few days later. I gave no second thought to answering. On the other line, Grant' voice was steely, seething.

"I know what you've been up to."

A cold rush of fear spread through me. "I don't know what you're talking about."

"Let's not play this game, okay? I want to know the names of all the little conspirators who've been playing Private Eye behind my back."

My stomach sank at the prospect of Grant's awareness of my investigations into his background. At this point, trying to figure out how he found out about my digging really didn't matter. I could have handled a confrontation with anybody but him. He was scary as hell.

"I thought you were better than this," Grant said with disappointment.

As of this moment, my work with him was over and we both knew it. He was furious at my betrayal and I had to make a split-second decision – deny the accusation, or let the cat out of the bag. "The fact of the matter is, you're not really a private investigator, Grant. Nobody at InterTec has heard of you," I said. Of course I knew that he had done investigative work *somewhere*; he was too well-trained. But I no longer bought the story he told everyone, that he'd been fired after his photo came out in the Toronto Sun.

Silence. His breathing was laboured over the line. For a moment I thought he might hang up. Then he really lost it.

"*You little bitch*," he began. I closed my eyes and ignored the string of obscenities that spilled out of his mouth. After he calmed down a bit, he sputtered, "You've got *nothing* on me."

"But I've got enough ABOUT you," I replied.

He had to be taping our conversation, just as he had done with countless other people he'd harassed and he couldn't get over the fact that he'd been had. That I'd turned the tables on him without him knowing it. The snot-nosed kid he'd mentored had challenged the master at his own game.

Grant continued to breathe heavily. I could feel the wheels turning in his head. He was trying to figure out how much I knew, and I had to pretend it was more. Everything depended on it.

"Are you a cop?" I asked him, point blank.

He skipped a beat, then rasped, "Be serious."

"Are you working for the authorities?"

"Be serious," he said again.

"Is Grant Bristow even your real name?"

That made him really mad. "Well, I must've fallen off a truck and hit my head so's I got amnesia if I don't know what my real name is. So YOU tell me what my name is, eh?"

It was my turn to stay silent.

"Do you honestly believe I'm a cop, Elisse?"

"I think you're *something* like that. Maybe you work with them," I said.

"Where the fuck are you getting all this?" he exploded. "Who's been putting this shit into your head? Nicola and Marque? Those bitches? Who's talking behind my back? And what makes you think I can't send out a white van to pick you up tomorrow and take you on a little ride?"

A white van like the one that was involved in the kidnapping and torture of Tyrone Mason? Or a white van that had stalked the youth counselor at the Runnymede home for days before she was brutally raped? What kind of white van did Grant plan to send for me?

"You can't touch me," I said. "Don't you even think about it. In fact, you'd better make sure nothing happens to me, or else."

"*What the FUCK*? What do you mean by that? Have you been following me?"

I refused to go on his little fishing expedition. I thought of what he had done to Ruth and steeled myself. "I've done my research on you. I have information that you wouldn't like to get out."

"And where are you keeping this information? You think I don't have a way to get it if I want to?"

I laughed. "You think I'd tell you? It's in a safety deposit box. You can't get to it, I made copies. But if something happens to me, you won't like it."

I could hear him on the other side, breathing heavily. Finally he sputtered, "You've been watching too many spy movies, little girl. The whole safety deposit box thing is a fucking cliché. What do you think this is, Hollywood?"

"I wouldn't try to see if I'm bluffing, Grant." As he panted, I went in for the kill. "People who live in glass houses shouldn't throw stones."

He hung up on me.

I exhaled shakily, put down the notepad in which I had logged this conversation verbatim, and braced myself for Round Two.

It was Wolfgang's turn to call me the next morning. The sky was densely overcast, the autumn clouds packed together into an ominous shade of charcoal. A fine drizzle had started pitter-pattering against the window. I stood there, holding the phone against my ear, watching the rivulets stream down. Steadying myself for what was to come.

"Can you drop by my place this afternoon?" he asked casually. "I need to get all the mail-outs off this weekend. We're already behind."

Both of us knew I didn't have a choice. If I didn't show, they would come after me.

I was at his door by one PM. He offered me a coke as I walked in, making no mention that he knew of what had gone down between me and Grant. I took that as a cue to remain calm. Maybe everything had gone back to normal. I plopped on the sofa in front of his television and flipped the pop lid, scrutinizing it first to ensure it hadn't already been opened.

"Check out these nutcases," he laughed, pointing to the letters on his coffee table. "There's a rant by some unhinged guy who wants to avenge the white race by slaying all the Jews in Hollywood."

I sorted through the mail for a few minutes, trashing all the obvious psychos. When I was done, I started stuffing envelopes and stamping the PO box address in the top corners. When that too was done, I got up to leave.

Wolfgang put up his hand in protest. "Why don't you stay a bit longer? Peter's coming by later to hang out. You can watch HBO while I slip in the shower."

"Okay," I shrugged. I picked up the remote control and sifted through the channels. I was just settling on a movie when Peter walked through the unlocked front door.

"Hey-ya," he said. He sat on the sofa across from me, looking at me oddly. Something about his expression made me uncomfortable. I glanced toward the bathroom door. How much longer was Wolfgang planning to take?

"How's it going?" I asked.

"Not much. Was out today shopping for recorders."

"Oh, yeah?"

"Uh-huh. Always gotta stay a step ahead of the cops. Speaking of that, did you know that Wolf has a sensor right here in his apartment that can detect bugs?"

"Really?"

Wolfgang came out of the bathroom wearing only a towel around his waist. "It's true," he said, smiling, then slipped into his bedroom.

Peter leaned back and nodded smugly. "Do you have a recorder on you?"

My eyes narrowed in disbelief. "Are you for real?"

He didn't answer. Just tapped his foot and waited.

"No, of course I don't. Why would I?"

I frowned, feeling the tension rise up between us like a column of smoke. I wanted to leave. As I got up, Wolfgang re-emerged from the bedroom. A Cheshire smile lingered upon his lips, twisting them with malice. He looked at Peter and motioned toward me with his head.

"What's going on?" I asked.

Without warning, Peter flashed across the room and pinned me back in the loveseat, twisting my wrists down. I struggled to get him off me but his weight made it impossible. He straddled me, digging his knees into my thighs. I'd wrestled with him before, but this was the real thing. He was impossibly strong.

"Wolf, tell him to get off me," I yelled.

To my horror, Wolfgang sat down on the sofa across from us and said nothing.

Peter grasped my wrists harder, making me wince. "Are you wired?"

"What?"

"So you're deaf now? I said, are you wired? Don't play games with me."

"*NO!*"

"We know you've been talking to the cops."

"You're out of your mind. I've never talked to anybody."

"We have proof that you've turned informer."

"You're crazy. Now get the fuck off of me."

"Liar."

I looked past Peter's shoulder to Wolfgang and realized he was grinning. I'd never seen such a cold look on his face. The glassy, icy look of a reptile in a pet store window. I struggled to keep my voice steady. "Come on, stop this."

He crossed his arms and looked away. A wave of shock spread over me. Did Grant put them up to this? It was obvious that Wolfgang wanted a confrontation with me but had resorted to calling Peter to do his dirty work.

The thought of biting Peter crossed my mind. But if I escalated the situation by fighting back, they'd see it as proof that I'd done something wrong. With great effort I managed to keep myself calm. I looked into Peter Mitrevski's black eyes, which glared at me like hot coals and made my skin crawl.

I asked, "Why are you acting like this? Is it really necessary?"

He twisted my arm until I thought it would snap. He was enjoying this too much. "Just answer my questions," he said mockingly. "Talking back will get you hurt. Do you know what that means?"

"Yes," I said quietly.

"I don't think you know."

He reached inside his belt and pulled out the switchblade I'd seen him carry so many times before. Never did I think that one day it would be pointed at my throat. "Say you're sorry."

"No."

He pressed the tip against my skin until I thought it was going to draw blood.

"Ok, ok," I gasped. "I'm sorry."

He pushed me back against the cushions. While holding the blade steady against my neck, he brushed his left hand summarily over me, probing my shoulders, breasts, wandering down to my waist. Then he pulled me forward and reached under my shirt all the way up my back.

"Nothing." He backed off me slowly, all the while keeping his eyes fixed on mine. He closed his switchblade but didn't put it away. He kept holding it and passing it from one hand to another as he went to sit next to Wolfgang.

"I know you want out," Peter said. "I taped a conversation between Nicola and Marque last week. Guess what they were saying? That it would be better for you to get out of the Front while you still can. Imagine that. *My own girlfriend* saying that."

He shook his head exaggeratedly, as if he wanted me to feel sorry for him.

"You shouldn't make assumptions about my loyalty based on some third-party conversation," I said, rubbing my wrists. "What those women talk about has nothing to do with me. You shouldn't judge me for that."

Peter snorted. "Please. If Nicola told you to jump, you'd ask how high. Ever since you've been hanging out with them, you've gone weak in the head. And guess what else they were saying?"

I took a deep breath, bracing myself for the worst. "What?"

"They said you had Grant's handwritten hit list, the one with all those antiracists' names on it."

I didn't say anything. It was true and we all knew it.

"Where is that piece of paper now?" Peter asked.

I refused to answer.

Wolfgang started to shake his head. "Grant wanted me to organize a skinhead party to break into your place this week, but I refused. In all the years I've known him I don't think I ever saw him so angry. I told him we'd take care of this internally. The truth is, Elisse, you don't have a choice but to stay in. You think you can stop hating, just like that?" he snapped his fingers to demonstrate. "Hatred is an instinct, a reflex action. Even if you wanted to get out, it's too late. Who's going to have you?"

"You're tainted, damaged goods," Peter scoffed. "Who's going to overlook your past? Who's going to forgive a person who wished Hitler won the war?"

I stared at my feet. The words stung, as did the knowledge that they were right. Everybody would hate me after this. I had nowhere to go.

"People don't change, just like that," Wolfgang said. "You belong to us. Nobody else wants you. We've always been there for you. Me, Ernst, the Front – *we* are your family. Your *only* family."

My eyes watered. He'd struck bone. My hands twisted on my lap. I kept my eyes down and wondered if they were going to rape me.

"Give us the key to your safety deposit box," Wolfgang said.

So Grant *had* put them up to this. Despite having just been on the sharp end of Peter's switchblade, I couldn't help but feel strangely elated at the thought that my bluff had likely kept Grant up at night.

My head snapped up. "What are you afraid of," I asked, "if I've got nothing on you?"

Peter's face darkened. He leaned forward, elbows on his knees, and shouted, "The Heritage Front isn't going to be brought down by a young girl. What can you tell them, anyway? That somebody's got a collection of guns?"

"There is no *them*, Peter. I haven't sold out."

"Riiight."

"And if you really thought I did, would you have waited until now to conduct your little interrogation? Wouldn't you have done something about me by now?"

I could tell my argument made sense to him. He pursed his lips and glanced over to Wolfgang. "What kind of damage can a teenage girl do, anyway?"

They snickered among themselves at the thought of me, a stupid kid who they'd bottle-fed propaganda for the last two years, as being any sort of a threat. The prospect of a woman – no, not even that, a *girl* – holding something over their heads was hysterical to them. A total riot. I kept as still as possible and waited until they were done.

"Can I go now?" I asked.

"Get the fuck out of here," Peter said dismissively, tucking his knife into his back pocket. "But just remember what happens to rats – rats end up in the sewers."

I rose to my feet, steadying my heartbeat as I moved slowly toward the front door. I glanced at Wolfgang for the last time, meeting his crystalline blue eyes as I reached for the doorknob. A waver of unease flickered through them briefly and passed, promptly replaced by the old, smug expression I would perpetually remember on his face: the self-righteousness that had always led to his downfall.

"Goodbye, Wolfgang," I said as I walked out of his apartment and out of the Heritage Front forever.

TWENTY-EIGHT

A DIFFERENT GIRL

I ran the whole way from the Queen streetcar stop and fumbled at the door with the keys. My heart raced. Blood was pounding in my ears. Finally I burst in, slid on the deadbolt and ran to the phone. I gripped the receiver so hard I thought it would shatter and dialled the Montreal-area number Martin had given me in case of an emergency.

"*Bonjour*," the woman on the other line answered.

"Yes, it's Roxanne. I need to speak with Martin."

"He'll call you within a half hour," she said. "Stay by the phone."

I hung up and closed my eyes tightly, willing the time to pass quicker. My fingers tapped nervously against my leg. A vein in my temple started to throb. I rubbed my forehead, amazed at how cold my skin felt to the touch. Was this really happening?

The phone rang fifteen minutes later. I told Martin what had happened at Wolfgang's place. He took a deep breath. Seconds lapsed. Then, as if he'd been preparing for the occasion, he spoke in a flat, unemotional tone. As though he'd been expecting this to happen. "We're pulling you out tonight. Are you ready?"

In the corner of my bedroom, buried under piles of laundry, my pre-packed bag had waited for more than a week. My comfiest pair of jeans, indispensable toiletries, socks, underwear and a spare toothbrush were already zipped inside. I raced around my room throwing some last-minute things into my backpack: the diary I wrote in daily, a childhood photo album. I didn't have any other valuables. The photos and a pair of small 9-carat gold earrings I'd always worn as a child were my only sentimental possessions.

With the backpack slung over my shoulder, it was time to make one last call.

I was relieved that my mother hadn't gone off on a break. "What do you want?" she asked, not one for small talk.

I braced myself for another argument. "Remember how I told you I'd be moving out? Some friends hooked me up with a place to stay. I'm catching a ride there tonight."

"So soon?" she faltered. "When are you coming back for your stuff?"

"I took what I needed," I said. "Some people might be dropping by the apartment looking for me. If they ask any questions, tell them you don't know where I went."

"If that's what you want," she said, sounding resigned. "Hope you're not expecting to get any money from me, I've got nothing."

"Don't worry, I've never expected anything from you," I said, hanging up.

I knew what to do next. I'd rehearsed it in my mind several times already. After darkness had descended over the grassy commons of the Shuter Street tenement buildings, I was to take with me only a backpack and nothing larger than a duffel bag, in the event I had to break into a run. I would make my way to the streetcar and take it west, toward the subway. *Don't ask questions of who might follow you*, I was instructed. *Just operate on the assumption that you're being tailed.*

Trying not to constantly look over my shoulder, I headed north to the Bloor central hub and transferred to the westbound line. It was just after seven but the train was still packed with backpack-totting college students going to their night classes and office workers heading home. Any of them could be a potential tail, I thought as I took a seat next to a heavyset black woman in a flowered dress and kept my eyes down, telling myself she couldn't hear my heart beating as loudly as I did.

When we were about four stops away from the end of the line, I waited until the doors had been open for twenty seconds and everyone who was getting out at that stop had already filtered out. Then, just as the doors were about to slide shut, I jumped out of my seat and raced out of the subway car like a madwoman. Turning around to watch the doors slide shut, I felt satisfied that anyone following me wouldn't have had enough reaction time to exit.

I went up the escalator, crossed over to the other line and waited for the next train heading back into town, only to repeat the process five stations later. Finally confident that I'd shaken any potential tail, I got out at the prearranged station and went through the north exit, my eyes hazy with tension and adrenaline. Everything had turned blurry. Outlines became multidimensional, the subway lights danced in my retinas like I was high on drugs.

I glimpsed a car circle around the station and pull to an abrupt stop in front of me. The driver stuck his head out and asked me for the time.

"I forgot my watch," I said, reciting my memorized code-line.

"Never mind," he said. "Twenty past midnight."

Even as I climbed in, knowing it was safe to trust this man, whose name I'd never be told, to whisk me to a safe-house at an unknown destination where I would remain no longer than three nights, after which time I would be taken out of province, I did not feel liberated of the darkness that both haunted and hunted me, and only afterwards, noticing the bleeding crescent moons along my palms, would I come to realize that I'd dug my fingernails into my flesh until I'd pierced the skin.

"Welcome to your new life," Ruth said when she opened the door, sweeping me into a tight embrace. We stood back to stare at each other in disbelief. It had really come to this – what we'd talked about for so long had materialized into a raw, unpredictable reality.

The people who owned my first safe-house, the first of countless to come, were a pair of young professionals in their thirties. They had made me a bed in their sunroom and departed just before I'd arrived. I had no clue what they'd been told – whether they knew the truth about the person they were harbouring, or whether lending us their house was part of fulfilling a favour called in by a mutual friend. And truthfully, I didn't care.

"Come on, let's get you settled," she said, waving me through an arched alcove toward the back of the house. "Annetta will be here any minute."

I dropped my knapsack and duffel bag in the foyer and followed her along the hall to a navy-coloured sofa in a sitting room next to a galley kitchen. I sat down while Ruth went to the side table and picked up the phone, dialled a number from memory and said only, "She's here", before placing the receiver back down. She glided over to the kitchen and put on the kettle, poured me a steaming cup of tea while running through the basic rules.

"I know it's obvious but I do have to go over this, just for the record," Ruth said, carrying the earthenware mugs on a tray she deposited on the coffee table. "Stay away from the telephone, don't go outside, keep clear of any windows. Use common sense. Some of the places you'll be staying at are remote and may not have Caller ID so when Martin calls you, he'll use a code – ring twice, hang up, count to twenty, ring again. Pick up on the second ring."

Everything in the house was as comfortable as could be expected, but I would barely sleep during the first two nights – the glass enclosure of the sunroom made me feel exposed, like anybody could jump over the back fence and break through the flimsy French doors that opened into the spot where my bed was. Ruth noticed my apprehension when I stepped into my new quarters. "Annetta thought you might be a bit freaked about the sunroom," she joked. "But it's only for a couple of days. Nobody will ever know you're here. You yourself don't even know where you are."

I was there three days before being moved. It wasn't safe for me to stay in the west end anymore. There would be an unavoidable fallout from my Heritage Front defection. With the contempt of court case against Wolfgang moving full steam ahead and my name about to be added to the disclosure and witness list, a move like this wouldn't be lost on the media. Martin had already warned me to be prepared for the storm that would follow. At the time, I'd hoped he was exaggerating and chose instead to fantasize about getting a new name and moving on to a new destination, wherever it might be. But now, that fuzzy-coloured vision had transformed into a brutal, inescapable reality and there was no turning back.

Unbeknownst to me, a lot of machinations were already in progress to pave the way toward my speedy exit from the Toronto area. An emergency hearing had to be called in order to change my bail conditions, which stipulated that until my trial I had to remain within city boundaries. A motion would be placed on my behalf informing the court and legal aid that I had changed lawyers. At the same time this motion went out, my new lawyer as of last week, prominent human rights attorney Paul Copeland, who had a long reputation of left-wing politics and had taken me on a one-dollar retainer until legal aid could be expensed, sought an emergency amendment to my conditions. When that happened, my cover would be up – to dump the pair of Heritage Front lawyers in favour of someone like Copeland, who had a mile-long history of defending left-leaning activists, was a red flag to the movement that I had defected.

Everybody was expecting a hate crimes trial to start in November. Little did they know that Paul Copeland was going to ask for an adjournment, which he was certain we'd get because I had just fired Harry Doan and he hadn't had sufficient time to review my case. "It's going to be an easy in and out," Paul said. "A five-minute proceeding. But unfortunately, you have to be there. There's no way around it."

A move like this wouldn't be lost on the media. Martin warned me to be prepared for the storm that would follow. A part of me hoped he was exaggerating. Either way, I wasn't concerned about that. Day and night, I let my thoughts drift to what my new future might be. I fantasized about having the charges dismissed, getting a new name, moving on to a new destination, wherever it might be.

"It's going to get ugly," Ruth cautioned me. "*Real* ugly. You staying with any activists would place all of us in unnecessary danger. You cannot remain in Toronto. It's HF territory, too easy for them to track you down. We already know there are Front members on the police force – remember our friend Brad? It's not a far stretch to consider the possibility that they may have infiltrated telephone companies. No, you'll have to be moved out of the province."

"So how will we stay in touch? Can I call you?"

She shook her head. "I'm afraid not. Not until we make sure it's safe."

Two days before my court appearance, Martin came to see me. I ran to the entrance to greet him, grinning like an idiot, full of excitement that turned to anxiety as soon as I looked at his face. His expression was darkened with worry. "Let's sit down," he said. We faced each other at the kitchen table. He took a big sigh and started talking. What he said left me in utter shock. Everything was coming off the rails.

"I've just heard back from those OPP cops we met with at the Delta Chelsea," he said. "Something's wrong. Marianne is very worried about you. She told me privately that she'd wanted to do something, to provide you with protection, but her superiors have informed them that they shouldn't deal with us. The order came from above their heads. Someone upstairs has decided that your information is unreliable."

"What? You mean, they're not even going to get warrants for a raid on Peter Mitrevski's house? They're not going to do a search and seizure of Drew's rifles?"

He shook his head. No, no weapons were going to be recovered. It was over.

Shock replaced the elation I'd experienced a moment earlier. "But don't they know that once it gets out that I was an informer, the guys will move all their stuff, right? The time to go and pick them up is *now*," I insisted, on the verge of crying.

Martin pursed his lips. "*Mais oui*, I know. Everybody knows that. But somebody higher up pulled the plug. There's no point wondering about the What Ifs – the only thing you need to know is that, realistically, we do *not* have a deal with the police."

"But they know I was willing to testify, right? What about the It Campaign? Why don't they go and arrest Grant and Wolfgang? I gave them everything I had. What *more* do they want?"

He shook his head again. Stared at me with large, dark eyes.

"So...," I started. "There is no protection for me?"

"No."

"No witness protection program, no new identity...*nothing*?"

"Nope. You're on your own."

The world began to spin. "But they're going to come after me."

"There's only one thing left for us to do," Martin said, touching my arm sympathetically. "We have to use the media to tell our story. There are people in high places who want us to shut up and just go away —"

I stiffened. "Why would they do that?"

He held up his hand. "That's all I've been able to discern so far. But know this – powerful people have directed the provincial police and the RCMP to refuse you protection. They want us to get so scared we'll give up on this, but we're not going to. We're going public."

This meant everything would have to change drastically – our tactic of how we were going to go after the Heritage Front, how we were going to fight and shut them down without any police backup. Everything had to be rethought a hundred times over.

How were we going to keep me in hiding and on the move? Could we actually devise our *own* witness protection program? Could we keep me unharmed long enough to strike back?

For my court appearance on November 24, we had to devise a strategy to make up for my lack of police protection. Huge crowds were expected outside the courthouse, composed of both HF supporters and a large assemblage of ARA activists who were planning to demonstrate against me as well as Wolfgang, Ken Barker and Gary Schipper – as luck would have it, they were due in court on the same day on contempt charges. It was a nightmare waiting to happen.

After coordinating with Rodney Bobiwash, it was decided that the prudent thing to do was place my safety in the hands of a contingent of American Indian Movement (AIM) braves. They were terrifying, fierce, and utterly fearless. The sight of them would be enough to keep any Heritage Front members from getting too close. I would walk inside the cadre: two braves would be in front, two would flank me at left and right, and two would follow behind us, ready for any confrontation.

To make coordinating the whole thing easier, I was going to be moved the night before my court appearance. Promptly at six, Martin arrived to collect and deliver me to my next safe-house. "You'll be staying at John's place a couple of nights," he announced.

Martin and Ruth exchanged glances. "Big John? Now that'll be fun," she said.

"What do you mean by that?"

"Oh, you'll see," Martin snickered. "You'll have a good time. You're in good hands."

Big John was a strapping Native guy with jet-black waist-long hair. He towered over six feet and looked like he could single-handedly sweep Wolfgang up and snap him in half like a twig. He lived in a rooming house close to downtown which he shared with several other men who never seemed to be around. Martin dropped me on his doorstep. "Try to get some sleep tonight," he said, just before taking off. "All hell's going to break loose tomorrow."

"Hey there," Big John said with a smile. "Come on in."

The half dozen hulking braves who were going to be my bodyguards had gathered in the living room to coordinate the security arrangements for tomorrow. They sat around a small coffee table, chain-smoking and talking over beers. Nuzzled between two of them, a large, blue-eyed Husky stared at me suspiciously.

"Step right in," one of the guys waved to me. "Don't be afraid."

No sooner did I take a step forward, that the dog rose as high as he could, growling. I froze. The guys started laughing uncontrollably.

"See, I told ya," one of them said, wiping the corner of his eye. "He don't like white people." He looked at me and gestured, "Come on in, he ain't gonna bite you. I got him." He gripped the dog's collar firmly, forcing it to lay back down.

I sat stiffly on the edge of the sofa. The husky glared at me non-stop. I tried to avert my gaze. The guys watched the exchange with amusement. I wondered if I was supposed to be the evening's entertainment. Finally, the dog's owner let out a great sigh. "Oh, all right, I'll put him in the bedroom. Sheesh."

The braves were a rowdy bunch. It turned out there wasn't that much planning to do – they were just going to show up at eight in the morning, and we'd head over to the courthouse. But by the sounds of it, they were looking forward to a confrontation. "Oh, man, if Droege or that little twit Schipper even comes close…" they broke out in laughter. "I wish," said another guy, also named John. "Damn, just give me an excuse."

I couldn't imagine a better group with whom to show up at the courthouse.

What had started on a hot summer weekend ended four months later, on Nov. 24, 1993. On a cold, cloudy morning, six AIM warriors and me made our way toward the courthouse through Nathan Phillips Square. It was safer to walk through the back alley connecting the square to University Avenue than pull up in front of the actual building, where reporters and Front members would be waiting.

Martin met us at the far end of the street. "How you holding up?" he asked. I nodded to him that everything was fine and saw him smile. "Brace yourself, it's gonna be a bumpy ride."

The entrance to 361 University was a zoo. Every media outlet in town had sent somebody to cover the proceedings. After all, a hate trial was about to start, the fourth time ever in this country. Dozens of reporters and cameramen accosted us. Flash bulbs were going off, microphones were thrust in my face, questions exploded from all directions – *Miss Hategan, would you care to make a comment? This is So-and-So from CityTV, can we have a moment of your time?*

The CBC's rep ran around like a chicken with its head cut off, struggling to grasp the situation. "What's going on? What's going on?" he kept yelling, even as Big John shoved his hand in the cameraman's face. He stood in front of Martin and the AIM braves and gasped.

"My God," he said. "Have you guys gone over to the Heritage Front's side?"

While Martin was busy spelling it out to the media, I spotted Marque, Nicola and a bunch of Front people standing next to the cigarette pit outside the front doors. My supporters today, I thought sardonically. Were they in for a surprise.

Nicola beckoned me over. "Elisse, where've you been this week? What's going on?" she started to say. Then, as her eyes scanned the solemn faces of the Natives around me, her voice trailed off. Both she and Marque stood frozen in place, aghast. I was a rat, a race traitor. Who would've thought?

The OPP officers jostled us through the press crowd and the assemblage of furious neo-Nazis and anti-racist activists. Finally we were inside the lobby. From the corner of my eye, I spotted Bill Dunphy. His mouth was slightly open; I could see the wheels spinning in his head. Suddenly, an odd little smile broke on his face. He looked at Martin and shook his index finger, as if to say, '*You little bugger….*'

For his part, Martin kept a straight face when Dunphy approached him. "You knew this all along…" Dunphy began. Martin took him off to the side and they started to chat. I didn't have time to observe their exchange because all of a sudden my lawyer Paul Copeland was by my side.

Paul put his arm around my shoulder. "Ready for this?" he asked. I smiled back, feeling a hundred pairs of eyes at the back of my head. All the HF and ARA members who had managed to get past security were motionless in the pews, shoulder to shoulder, slack-jawed, paralyzed inside a collective *What the Fuck* moment.

It was time for the proceedings to commence. Visibly shocked, the crown prosecutor didn't argue over the motion for continuation and the trial was postponed until the new year. Paul then asked for an amendment of my bail conditions, specifically the one that pertained to me having to report every week at the downtown police division. It was too risky to have me go there, where someone could lay in wait for me. With that condition struck off, I would be able to go into hiding outside Toronto, where it was safer.

And then, nearly as soon as it had started, it was all over.

No sooner were we out of the building than a dozen camera flashes went off, blinding me. Big John grabbed my arm and pulled me forward through the swarm of reporters, toward the designated spot around the corner where a car would pick us up. Paul was right behind us. He was going to stand on the courtroom steps and speak to the media on my behalf, delaying them until we were gone. We would head back to Big John's place for the afternoon, where we'd lay low until my next move would be decided.

The first thing I did was change my appearance. Martin was right; we had to make the best of what we had – our brains. I didn't need the government to protect me. Would I really be safer enrolled in the RCMP's witness protection program, whose files could be accessed by any rookie agent with basic clearance? The reality was stark and completely inescapable: I had to make my own protection. Transform into another person. Someone so completely different that, had I brushed past Wolfgang downtown, he wouldn't recognize me.

Yes, I could dye my hair, gain or lose weight. Wear heels to alter my height. Wear contacts to change the colour of my eyes. I could go by any name I pleased, and none would be the wiser. But why not go beyond that? Why not embrace a completely different ethnicity? The men trying to hunt me down were looking for a white girl. What if I ceased to be one?

We spent my last night in Toronto at the first safe house. Martin left shortly after ten p.m., going back to the apartment of an old friend he was staying with in town. There was only one thing left to do. I perched on a stool in the middle of the bathroom while Annetta took a pair of scissors and started hacking at my hair. We laughed until we cried, pretending it was all a silly game. Curiously, I didn't feel any regrets at the sight of the long, auburn strands descending to the tiled floor like fall leaves giving way to an oncoming winter.

After my hair had been trimmed, I slipped on the plastic gloves that came with the Clairol box, leaned over the sink and dyed my hair black. While I waited the requisite forty-minutes, I used a cotton ball to apply tanning lotion to my pale skin. By midnight, I had transformed into a different girl.

The next morning Ruth, Annetta and I rushed around to have breakfast, not saying much as we ate. By eight we had gathered my belongings and exited the house by the back door, traversing a narrow alleyway to get to the garage out back. My heart pounded so hard it felt like it would burst. Could I say goodbye to them? Was it really over?

We pulled into the parking lot of a four-story building. Annetta carried my knapsack up the stairs to the third floor, with me and Ruth following behind. She rang the buzzer and Pat answered. She was a petite, dark-haired police officer in her forties who gave me a sympathetic smile while ushering us inside. I didn't know how she came to become involved, only that nobody in her police circles knew she had undertaken the task of offering me temporary shelter.

She proceeded to walk across the living room to the window and inspect the parking lot while Ruth, Annetta and I turned to one another.

"I guess this is it," Ruth started to say.

That's when it finally hit me: I was about to leave town without any promise of when I would see either of them again. Yes, we were supposed to reunite sometime in the next year, after they moved to Nova Scotia to start fresh. But with the way things were, anything could happen. I struggled not to throw my arms desperately around their necks and beg them not to leave. Why couldn't I go back with them and pretend none of this had happened?

Annetta squeezed me hard and kissed me on the cheek. "Don't cry," she whispered in my ear. "We'll see each other again. Be brave. Remember what we're all fighting for."

"I don't care," I wept. "I don't want to say goodbye."

"Stay strong," Ruth said before she turned and walked off quickly, never looking back. She didn't want me to see her getting teary-eyed. This was an end we had all foreseen, but never imagined would feel so traumatic.

Annetta swept me into a last hug, stared at me sadly and then followed Ruth. The echo of their footsteps continued to linger in my ears minutes after they had disappeared from sight. I wanted to run down the staircase after them, catch them into the parking lot and plead with them to let me stay just one more night, but my legs wouldn't carry me.

I shook with grief, tears streaming down my face, completely out of breath. My chest ached as though my lungs would collapse.

It couldn't end like this. And yet it did.

Pat came around and locked the door, shaking her head. I stood there, rooted to the same spot in the foyer, quivering. Me – the streetwise teen, the hardcore revolutionary recruited by some of the most influential men of the neo-Nazi movement since the Second World War – bawling like a little kid on her first day of school.

"Come, it's going to be all right," Pat said. "Nobody can get you here. I'm armed."

She didn't understand. With Ruth gone, I didn't care who got me. It was all about being left behind.

TWENTY-NINE

THE UNDERGROUND

I wept for two hours straight and spent the rest of the day moping at the window in the unrealistic hope that Ruth or Annetta might return. Pat pretended she didn't see any of it. I was secretly grateful to her for not saying a word and leaving me with a shred of dignity intact. Despite my misery, I couldn't deny that I felt safe in her two-bedroom apartment. It was roomy and comfortable, and I had the run of the house when she was on duty. Later that evening I slipped into her tub and washed my hair, running my hands through the tangles to massage my scalp. After I got out, I wrapped up in a white robe she'd lent me and brushed my black hair.

"Your friends did a good job," Pat remarked when I went back in the living room. "All that red hair – that's the first thing they'd look for."

Who was she kidding? There were enough photos and videos of me floating around that a simple haircut wasn't going to be much of a disguise. But it was a start.

Pat had cable and a stocked fridge, and I didn't have to look far to find a diversion. One of her guilty pleasures had to be her secret stash of lurid true-crime paperbacks. As I curled up on the guest room bed with a stack of books detailing murders and organized crime, it occurred to me that they didn't necessarily make good bedtime reading material.

After four days, Pat drove me to my next safe-house. Just before I got out of the car, she turned to me and said, "You shouldn't be afraid of police officers. There may be a few rotten apples in TPS but not all cops are Nazis, you know."

I thought back to the scariness of my own arrest and interrogation. To the squads of drug enforcers who regularly carried out raids in the inner city. Cops in bullet-proof jackets hovering outside my housing project as I walked to and from school, just waiting for an excuse to use their clubs on someone. I thought about the brutality of cops in Romania, who made a habit out of shaking people down for bribes. I thought of the fact that the head of Toronto's Hate Crimes Unit had gone to Wolfgang's apartment and asked him to ID photos of Anti-Racist Action activists so that the cops would focus on prosecuting them instead.

And then I looked at Pat, who was watching me expectantly. "I know that," I said. "Sometimes they start out idealistic."

She let out a laugh. "Good luck, Nina," she said to me pointedly, eluding to my temporary new name, before she took off.

Mary was a sweet Scottish grandmother in her late sixties. She looked just like Betty White from the Golden Girls. She'd emigrated in her youth but still retained her accent, and her place was full of little old lady things: frilly doilies and porcelain tea sets hand-painted with burgeoning pink and red roses, all sorts of Royal Dolton knickknacks in her china cabinet. *From England*, she said. Mary liked my company and chattered about her daughters who had all moved away to university, gotten married and had children, and how she couldn't wait for more grandkids to come along.

"You don't mind sleeping in the den?" she asked. "It's not really a proper bed, just a daybed that pulls out. But you're a wee thing, you'll fit right in there, won't you, dearie?"

"It'll be absolutely fine," I said. "Thanks for letting me stay over."

"Are you doing anything tomorrow?" she asked. "There's a Swiss Chalet right across from us. I always take the grand-kiddies there. Those booths are so comfy."

I felt embarrassed to refuse her invitation, but I had no cash on me whatsoever.

"My treat," she said. "It's an excuse to go out for lunch."

I beamed at her. "Sure, I'd love to come."

We had our quarter chicken meals on an exceptionally sunny afternoon, in a booth as wide and comfortable as Mary had described. I had been in Canada for nearly eight years but it was my first time in a Swiss Chalet. I probably should have followed Martin's instructions to stay indoors, but I would always be thankful to Mary for making me feel normal that day. *If I was one of her daughters I'd visit far more often*, I thought. *And I would bring her roses.*

My grassroots Witness Protection Program, orchestrated by Martin Theriault as my handler, had been financed by activists and everyday Canadians who wanted to make a difference, rather than by a government that had denied me any sort of assistance or defence against the men who had called in death threats to Martin and myself. Every new location filled me with more gratitude and admiration of the generosity of those who so readily took in a transient kid and asked no questions. Like a tulip bulb buried in snow at the beginning of spring, my faith in humanity, in the goodness of people, slowly began to thaw again.

The first six months of hiding were unbelievably hectic. I never spent more than a week in any one place. My sleeping arrangements consisted of a revolving array of houses, apartments, empty offices, student dorms, roadside motels and people's floors. Every time I was moved, I used a different name. But the rules stayed the same – I couldn't answer the phone or go to the window unless they lived in a high-rise. I had to stay put and not answer any questions until Martin or somebody he sent along in his place came to fetch me. I traveled throughout Ontario to Quebec and back; often I had no clue what municipality I was in, and after a while I stopped trying to keep track.

Now and then, while passing through Ottawa, Rodney Bobiwash invited me to crash on the sofa in his den. At first I couldn't help being nervous and tongue-tied around him, certain that he hated me. He'd occupied a top spot on the Heritage Front's hit list and had endured several death threats while director of the Native Canadian Centre in Toronto because he had lodged the first complaint against them with the Human Rights Commission. Knowing what the HF had done to Rodney, the campaign of dirty tricks and death threats, I was moved by the fact that he had so completely forgiven me my past that he would let down his guard and bring me into his home. But Rodney was the type of person who didn't fall back on his accomplishments and refused to be broken by the hatred that had been hurled at him. Through the worst of it, even as he was forced to wear a bulletproof vest and have bodyguards while in Toronto, his resilience had shined through. My heart ached for all that had been done to him.

Rodney's place was decorated with intricately-carved aboriginal masks from all his travels. They hung from the whitewashed walls, perched from the tops of his bookshelves – hovered, watching everything with frozen, painted eyes of wood. As soon as you stepped into his apartment, you could feel the energy of those artifacts. I admired the beauty of some of the masks, while others were so ugly and ferocious that they frightened me. I supposed that must have been their intention – to scare away outsiders while protecting the warriors and medicine men who wore them.

Rodney spotted me staring at them and chuckled. "You're spooked, eh?" I refused to admit it, but it was true. Rodney knew I had seen the energy in them. It was almost as if the spirits inside those masks came alive in the night, after the lights in the apartment were turned off. They morphed into elongated shapes, twitched their beaks and ruffled their feathers. I buried my head in my pillow so they wouldn't notice I had seen them. My nights were filled with strange dreams that reverberate with tribal drumming. *I am lost inside an Amazonian Rainforest crawling with scary carnivorous plants that reach toward me, trying to bite. I stare up toward the tall green canopy of gigantic trees above. The striped colours of a toucan flash across the sky as he lifts up in flight. The air is dripping with humidity. It envelops me in its stillness, it cocoons my movements. Everything around pulsates and drips with green goo. When I breathe, I can feel the heavy, moist respiration of the jungle in my lungs.*

There was talk that Rodney might call upon his American Indian Movement contacts and hide me on a reserve somewhere in the wilderness that stretched between the US and Canadian border. No one could find me in the remoteness of the Akwesasne reservation, where white man's law was inapplicable and scoffed at.

Lots of the braves were involved with smuggling cigarette cartons and various other goodies from the US to Canada through the reserve lands, which weren't patrolled by border police, and selling them on the cheap to whites who wanted to avoid the extra taxes on tobacco and alcohol imposed upon them by provincial governments. Aside from operating casinos on native land, the smuggling of illicit contraband was a very profitable enterprise for the people involved.

On a reservation, living among people who didn't recognize the authority of what they called an occupying government upon their affairs, I'd be as remote from the white man's world as could be.

Anybody trying to track me down was sure to lose my scent. The problem was, I'd also stick out; if as much as a neighbour complained or started asking about the white teenager who'd moved in next door, those who'd provide me shelter might incur the wrath of tribal elders, so that plan was scrapped.

Instead, I spent some time moving around Quebec. In the Montreal area, I stayed with preppy college students in various flats. Some were frat houses – sinks full of dirty dishes congealed with spaghetti sauce, empty beer bottles on every surface. Some places were cleaner, usually the ones with female residents – the need to scrub a toilet clean must have been just one of those things us girls took for granted. Typically Martin pulled me out just before I'd overstay my welcome, before people started to ask questions.

At least, that's how it was at first. As the weeks rolled on and we started running out of safe-houses, the situation became more dire. Martin got sloppy, promising he'd leave me somewhere for a couple of days only to resurface after a week. His drinking grew heavier and I feared for his liver but there was no way I could talk him out of it, especially at night. His stress levels were so high that alcohol was the only thing that could make him sleep. But no matter how often I asked him, he refused to share the things that troubled him, the rumours he'd heard about the Heritage Front. He didn't want to burden me with the weight of the stresses he carried alone on his shoulders. He also refused to tell me about a nasty computer video game some skinheads had developed where I was the central focus. "Can't I see it?" I asked.

"Absolutely not."

"What are they doing to me?" I joked. "Target-practicing?"

"It's ugly. Really vicious. You don't want to know," he replied, not budging when I pressed for more.

Knowing we both needed a break from being on the move, Martin arranged for me to have an extended stay in Ottawa at the flat of one of his acquaintances. Mike was a radical environmentalist who, within a week's time, had me scared silly that by the end of the decade we would live in a desert-like climate with barely any sources of potable water. He was a big, sturdy man with a scraggly beard that came halfway down his chest; the type of guy who would be equally comfortable building a bomb shelter in the backwoods of British

Columbia or being chained to a tree at an anti-logging demonstration. Peaceful resistance was his motto, Gandhi his ultimate hero, and he was full of pride at having chained himself to scores of trees and gates in his day. He operated a volunteer-run environmental resource centre around the corner from where he lived, a two-bedroom flat in the Glebe.

Mike shared his flat with his earthy roommates: a huge barrel-come-worm-compost that came up to your waist. He'd placed it right in middle of his kitchen, at arm's length from the stove, and he was quite proud of it. There was something both fascinating and grotesque about seeing the brown worms squiggling through the moist black earth that swallowed egg shells and vegetable peels. They could eat through anything, I thought with a shiver. I wouldn't be surprised if they'd outlive us all.

Mike had human friends as well – ardent environmentalists who wore the obligatory beatnik uniform: colourful, fair-trade sweaters woven by rural Guatemalan peasants, reed sandals from the remote villages of the Himalayas, tie-dyc skirts fringed with beads sown by Nepalese workers and army-green knapsacks made out of hemp, decorated with political buttons. They took very seriously the distinctions between being vegan and vegetarian, while I secretly found it mind-blowing that they could spend hours discussing all the things you could cook up with a sack of lentils.

Despite his quirky ways Mike was a really cool guy, a walking encyclopedia on climate change and non-violent activism. We spent hours at his kitchen table, where he'd frighten me with tales of horrific climate change. "Ten years from now, we'll be killing each other for clean water," he said with a freaky smile. I thought he was trying to get a rise out of me; he was funny that way. At Mike's place I was left to my own devices, not that there was much to do. He didn't have a television, only a staticky radio in the kitchen and a bookshelf jam-packed with clandestine, small-press books, the kind that were shipped in plain brown envelopes.

In the afternoons I hang out with Lestat, a former street kid in his early twenties whom Mike had taken under his wing. Lestat worshipped Anne Rice, dressed in black velvet, had straggly blue-black hair and was heavily into the Goth scene. I suspected his growing infatuation with me may have had a little something to do with his discovering that my family hailed from Transylvania.

"Did you know you look quite a bit like Wynona Ryder in Dracula?" he asked as we were eating Big Macs and knocking back glasses of cheap Manischewitz wine. "You know, being so pale and having all that black hair? And those dark circles under your eyes, they're sexy."

This was the first time someone had complemented me on my anemic look. Lestat didn't question me about my past; the mystery that surrounded me intrigued rather than bothered him. "So your problem is you can't use any of your ID, huh?" he asked. "I guess welfare's out of the question."

He decided to take it upon himself to teach me the ropes of surviving without money. I couldn't just drop in on an Evergreen-type youth centre or a church basement for a meal as I did in Toronto; those places were teeming with skinheads and street youth who'd undoubtedly recognize me from the press.

My first lesson came as he set the coffee to brew and sat me down in Mike's kitchen. The ornate silver rings he wore on his fingers tinkled against the handle of the mug as he handed it to me. "First thing you have to do, my dear girl, is get to know the best dumpsters downtown grocery stores have to offer. Go there around five o'clock, after shift change but before the sun goes down."

Lestat was particularly fond of the dumpster behind the Hartmann store on Bank street. It was the least smelly in town, he said when he took me there one afternoon. He leaned over the edge as far as he could and tried to reach down. "Damn," he groaned. "Gotta go in."

As he lowered himself among the crates and the garbage, I marveled at how his skinny body was able to twist itself through the tightest corners. He maneuvered himself between stale cabbages and cardboard boxes sopping with soured milk, spoiled yoghurts and god knows what else. I wrinkled my nose. Glancing up, he laughed at me. "You just wait," he said, fishing around in the slop. When he came back up for air he was holding a perfectly ripe, juicy pear. I snapped the cover off my backpack and began to stuff it with whatever Lestat plucked from the depths of the dumpster.

"You're lucky if you find something from the bakery," he said, prodding with his boot. "Other than bread and stale bagels, there's not much in here. The workers put aside the pies and cakes that don't sell and take them home at the end of the night. Still, we might get lucky and come across a pack of danishes. But stay away from the meat. You can eat pretty much anything out of here and not get sick, but if it's from the meat department check the expiry date first."

He scurried about, lifting the wet cardboard and quickly tossing to me anything he pronounced consumable. With his wiry frame and two-tailed black overcoat, he looked like a clever rat. I could almost see a pair of invisible whiskers sprout out of his gaunt cheeks and twitch every time he saw something we could use for tonight's dinner.

We walked back giddy with excitement, moldy legumes rolling inside my backpack. We peeked into the alleyway behind every store. Lestat chuckled, "See, I knew you'd get hooked. Why pay for something you can find for free?"

Back at Mike's flat, we emptied the backpack on the kitchen table, sending the turnips, carrots and bagels rolling. Lestat went to the counter to peel potatoes for the stew. His head jerked up again and he peered at me through clumpy strands of jet-black hair. "So you're absolutely sure you like girls?" he asked. "Because if you ever wanted to experiment with someone…"

I punched him in the arm. "Sure, right after *you* try being with a guy to figure out if you like it."

"Whoa, wait a minute. How do you know I haven't? As a matter of fact, I've made out with a couple of guys in my day, thank you very much. I just like girls better. Especially ones who look like a vamp."

"Oh, shut up!" I said, throwing a potato peel at him. He ducked, laughing.

One month before the contempt of court trial was to start, Paul Copeland arranged for us to meet at the offices of the Human Rights Commission so I could speak with Eddie Taylor, one of the two Commission attorneys. "When Mr. Theriault showed me your affidavits, we were thrilled about the possibility of your testimony," Taylor said. "The Heritage Front always seems to elude authorities. Proving that they broke the law when they set up their alternate hotline is one way to shut them down. Your information is the break we needed. But…"

His voice trailed off. He ran a hand through his wild red hair. "It would be unfair not to warn you about the mud-slinging that will come from the defense. They will make you out to be a confused girl who didn't really know anything about the Heritage Front and is just doing this for attention. Can you handle that?"

I nodded. "I can do this. I *want* to do it."

He put his elbows on the desk and leaned forward. "Why?"

"I want to tell the truth of what I saw. And I want to make up for my involvement."

"But can you handle the cross-examination? If there's anything that can be constituted as a veiled threat or a fishing expedition, you can be sure I will jump up and object vehemently. At the same time, are you prepared to be called a liar on the stand without losing your cool?"

"I know I am."

"It is imperative that the judge sees you as calm and sincere. The defense will try to shake you up and break you down. Don't allow them to get inside your head. It's all a game of strategy where they'll do their best to discredit you because their clients' freedom hangs in the balance. They *need* you to falter. It's what they're counting on. They might try to throw your words back at you. They may ask if myself, Paul, your counsel, Mr. Theriault or any of our staff have coached you. Just tell the truth. That's the only thing I ask."

I tried to imagine Wolfgang staring at me from the defence bench. Would he be poker-faced and unperturbed? Or would his face divulge the hatred he held for me?

"You'll have to prepare yourself for the media circus that will follow. Everything in this trial will be picked up by the press."

As the days drew closer to the beginning of the trial, Martin grew nervous and decided to pull me out of Ottawa. Too sprawling, too urban. Too many possibilities to be spotted. All that was left was Gilles's farm, and I hated every moment that I spent there.

Gilles' farm was a remote place somewhere in rural Quebec. It was, quite literally, in the middle of nowhere. To get there you'd have to imagine turning off the main highway, going down a dirt road until you hit a dead end and then flipping a coin. I could never tell where I was since *everything* from cornfields to rooftops and timeworn mom-and-pop diners, was coated in a suffocating, heavy deposit of snow.

You didn't need to be blindfolded on the way to keep this place a secret; it embodied the definition of anonymity. If you've ever wondered what it would be like to live inside a snow globe that's just been shaken, this was it. Only unlike the globe, the snow here never settled; it kept coming down persistently, and the winds howled in despair and rattled the frame of the century-old farmhouse and I kept thinking, *This is it*. This is how I'm gonna go: not blissfully, asleep in my bed like my 89-year old grandmother, but crushed to death under some beam or splintered roof where nobody would find me until spring thaw.

Gilles himself worked in town and was gone for days on end – torturously long days that I spent with absolutely nothing to do. There was no cable reception and the radio was shot. There were no books, newspapers, not even a trashy Enquirer lying around. I couldn't cook because the kitchen cupboards were empty, holding only a package of Lipton's chicken noodle soup and a pack of crackers.

My stomach growled inconsolably, but how could I ask Gilles, a francophone who didn't speak a lick of English, for food? He obviously had his meals at the local diner before coming home late at night and I couldn't ask him to bring me back some dinner because I felt so guilty about imposing to begin with. I wasn't his responsibility. I had to be thankful that he even had that package of noodle soup around.

So much for emergency supplies, I thought. Gilles would have been royally screwed if he'd been snowed in. There was no convenience store around the corner where I could go to buy a can of beans even if I'd had the money (which I didn't), and besides, I wasn't allowed to leave the property, which sprawled out over what seemed like acres upon acres.

Whenever he wanted to get a rise out of me, Martin liked to joke about me staying at the farm again. He knew how much I hated it. It wasn't because Gilles himself wasn't a nice guy, but his place was remote and badly-insulated. With wind sneaking through fissures in the windowsills, it was mind-numbingly cold all day and night. There was so little for me to do, I felt like I would go stark-raving mad. And I was always hungry. Always so hungry.

Day melted into another day, and I could tell by the questioning glances that Gilles threw my way that he himself was wondering how much longer I was going to be staying but was too polite to ask. Not that he cared terribly much since he was gone during daylight hours. I divided my time between roving around the farm until my feet turned into blocks of ice.

In those desolate flatlands, I came down with a mild case paranoia; I'd cross through the frozen field, swirling around at the slightest movement. One time I nearly had a panic attack when one of the neighbours' cows somehow got free and coursed through the fields onto Gilles's property, coming up behind me. She stared at me blankly, chewing on some dried crud, smoke bellowing from her wide nostrils while I doubled over laughing.

Finally, at the end of February, there was a break in the snow. The sky was clear and altogether peaceful. As the receding clouds gave way to sunshine, I decided to chase after the cats who roamed the property. Unlike the kittens on my grandmother's farm, these feral cats would have none of it. They growled and hissed when I stepped too close, lifting their noses high into the air to sniff me. Once they determined I hadn't poured any fresh milk into the metal pail Gilles always left for them outside the front step, they lost any interest in hanging around and vanished into the blistery air.

I was left squinting in the bright winter sun, trying to figure out where they went. I shivered, turned up the collar of my ratty winter coat and stomped in place, trying to stir up some warmth. I squeezed my hands into small balls and made up my mind to do some investigating of my own. My breath spilled from my mouth like a foaming cloud, evolving higher and higher until it dissolved into air. Even my nose seemed to let out smoke; I must have looked like an enraged bull in a kids' cartoon, scratching at the ground with his hoof.

I decided to follow the cats' small paw prints across the field to the back of the property. I had to walk some ways before I reached the slightly parted door of a barn. The inside of it was musty and dark. It looked just like the ones I remembered visiting when we'd gone on a school trip to the Black Creek Pioneer Village to see what life was like for settlers of the New World.

Slivers of light came in through the narrow gaps and warping in the planks and beams that formed the structure, and also through the spaces under the eaves. In some parts, hay was piled up to the second-level loft area, which could only be reached via a long, rickety ladder. Strange instruments forged out of iron and copper hung from hooks attached to one of the main supporting joists, which traversed from one end of the barn to the other. There was a small orange-red tractor

246

retired in a corner, next to several shovels and a rusty plow. The whole place smelled like horses: I could pick up the whiff of sopping wet coats and manes, muck under hooves, freshly-shoveled manure. But there were no horses here, not anymore. Given how rarely he was home, Gilles wouldn't have had time to look after anything.

A scurrying noise made me glance up, startled. There, glowing from the hayloft, a pair of golden eyes was attempting to stare me down. So that's where the cats hung out. They must have loved to huddle in the warmth generated by the decomposing hay. Judging by the annoyed manner in which the one-eared creature was staring at me, tilting its head sideways as though trying to size up which way he could spring on me to claw my eyes out, I got the impression he definitely didn't want me here. I understood him perfectly; I didn't want me here either.

I turned around and walked out of the barn into a flash of blinding light. The sun had come out in its full splendour. The moment its rays hit the snow, they shattered into a million reflections. The brilliance was startling; it overwhelmed the senses. Everywhere I looked, the earth glowed a complete, radiant whiteness, starkly contrasted against the bluest of skies. A current of electricity ran through me. Soon I'd be on the move, and I was ready for whatever came next.

THIRTY

TRIAL AND RETRIBUTION
March, 1994

The Canadian Human Rights Commission trial against the Heritage Front began on March 15th, 1994. As the Human Rights Commission's star witness against the Heritage Front I had been cleared for airfare money back to Toronto and promised protection to, from, and within the courthouse, as well as lodgings at a safe-house if my testimony dragged on for more than a day. For his part, Martin was to accompany me from Ruth's place to the lobby of the hotel where we would meet up with the OPP officers first thing the morning of the trial. Since an actual hotel wasn't in the budget and nobody could be trusted to safe-house us, I slept on a thin mat on the floor of Ruth's house for four nights. The only spare bedroom would go to Martin because he wasn't feeling well.

"I need to tell you something," Ruth said after we had finished eating dinner.

I followed her to the living room as Martin went upstairs to catch up on his CCRP calls. Ruth sat beside me on the couch while Annetta went into the kitchen and fetched a couple of beers. She handed one to Ruth and then stood propped against the doorframe, staring at me silently.

Ruth hesitated. "Annetta and I debated long and hard about sharing this with you. I'm still not sure whether we should."

Her hands wrung on her lap. I realized that she had been unusually quiet since I'd arrived. Her eyes were rimmed with red. A closer inspection of her face told me she had spent some time crying. Glancing back at Annetta, I saw that she looked visibly shaken as well.

A sense of foreboding crept up in my throat. "What is it? What's going on?"

"It started last year, with an activist who was targeted as *It*. Him and his girlfriend are good friends of mine," Ruth said. "M. had been so badly terrorized by the It Campaign in Toronto that they both decided to move across the country."

I nodded. "I remember. One of the first three-way calls I was ever listened in on was to this guy. His name was on everybody's *It* list."

"They couldn't take it anymore," Ruth continued. "M's life had been destroyed by the harassment. They figured that if they got away from Toronto, they could make a fresh start."

The night he arrived in Vancouver, M made a crucial mistake: he called a friend in Toronto and left his new contact information on their answering machine. Someone in the Heritage Front broke into that answering machine before the message was intercepted. The next morning, the activist received a frightening call: "This is your Ku Klux Klan welcome wagon. Welcome to Vancouver!"

It didn't stop there.

Shortly after settling in Vancouver, M's girlfriend was kidnapped by two men who crossed the border from Seattle to do the deed. She was taken to a motel where she was tied up, beaten and raped for hours. She was told that they were Klansmen and they were doing it because she had anti-racist friends back in Toronto.

The final act of degradation was when they inserted a gun into her vagina and threatened to pull the trigger. "Tell your friends that they're next," she was told.

The very next morning, a Heritage Front individual called up the Toronto-area phone number whose answering machine had initially been hacked and left a smug, cryptic message: "*Some people get what they don't deserve.*"

It was the same voice that had made several ARA activists' ears prick up when they heard it on Heritage Front rally tapes. The same voice that had called people 20-30 times a day, all day and night.

"He's harassed me for a year," Ruth said, breaking into tears. "I know that voice. I hear it in my sleep. It's why I had to take stress leave from work last year."

Minutes before we were to leave for court, I padded to the bathroom to fix my wig for the last time. I glanced at myself in the mirror, smoothed the fabric of the royal blue velvet dress I was wearing, a Laura Ashley piece I'd retrieved from the donation bin of a homeless women's shelter, and fought back the cold wave of anxiety that had begun to travel up my spine. I clenched my fists. *I can do this. They're not going to get away with this.*

The low temperatures of the previous night remained. As Martin and I crossed the street I shuddered involuntarily, even as I saw the sun beginning to crown through the overcast sky. Out of nowhere, a fast northerly wind started to disperse the clouds and more sunshine flooded the street, making me squint. It would be a hazy, brilliant day after all.

By eight a.m. we were in the lobby of the Delta Chelsea again, just to the left of the revolving doors. Martin had decided this was the best spot for the OPP to meet us. He instructed me not to mention anything about where I was staying; after the fiasco with the affidavits they wanted to bury, he was convinced the OPP weren't on our side. He refused to tell me what fueled his suspicions, but was adamant that I should be careful about what I said in the company of any OPP or RCMP officers.

"Why?" I asked him. "Do you think it would get leaked? To who?"

He gave me that funny look that made me wonder how he knew the things he did; just how high up did his sources actually go?

"I can't tell you," he finally answered. Same old song and dance routine: there was so much I didn't know and it was better that I didn't so I wouldn't get rattled before the trial started. But no, the OPP could not be trusted; they were good only for physical protection but I shouldn't say anything to them regarding my whereabouts. At the end of the day we'd "lose" them by asking to be dropped off at the same hotel, from where we'd take a cab to another location. Only on the way there could I take off my wig.

My first day in court went exactly as I'd expected: reporters ambushing us outside the courthouse, flash bulbs going off in my eyes, a long line of people outside the courtroom getting frisked by police and having to go through metal detectors for the privilege of being witness to the proceedings. There were journalists from all the media outlets, HF supporters and skinheads, ARA activists, reps from the Native Canadian centre, the Canadian Jewish Congress, and the list went on. Although recording the proceedings was supposed to be a big no-no, many of them had tape-recorders. It was strange to see so many activists crammed elbow-to-elbow in the pews and I briefly wondered how they managed not to bash each other's heads in.

The OPP cops ushered me in through a side door, and all eyes turned to me. I felt glares pinprick the back of my neck as the court clerk directed me to step up on the stand. *Would I swear on the Bible or choose to Affirm*, he asked. After everything that had happened, believing in a benevolent god would have been a joke. Never mind the fact that I didn't identify as Christian. I held up my right hand to make the oath, affirming that everything coming out of my mouth was the truth and nothing but the truth.

Then my testimony before the female judge began (the Front had decided to go with a judge rather than a jury trial, on the supposition that the average jury member might be more likely to be biased due to the defendants' controversial views.) Eddie Taylor, the counsel for the Human Rights Commission, started by asking me the basic questions that would prove their case: How did I know the defendants? What did I see and hear when I was in their company? How do I know they conspired to breach the order to shut down the hotline? It was all stuff I expected to answer, but being up there, in front of so many people, seated to the left of a judge in a black robe who watched me closely as I spoke, was nerve-raking.

"The Front leaders chose Ken Barker to set up the new hotline after theirs was ordered to be shut down," I said. "The way they were going to get around the court order itself was by forging a back-dated resignation letter that Ken was supposed to sign to say he was no longer a member of the Front. They could then show it to anybody who accused him of violating the court order as an official HF member. I was there when they discussed this and they were all in on it. I remember Wolfgang actually saying '*They'll never shut us down.*'"

During the examination, my hands felt clammy on my lap. Absentmindedly, I wrung my fingers together in the lap of my blue velvet dress. Like Paul had instructed me, I tried to look only at the judge and the lawyer questioning me and at nobody else. A hard thing to do, when the courtroom has more than a hundred people present and all eyes are trained on you. I tried to ignore Wolfgang and Ken's unblinking, smug attempts to stare me down: Ken with a grim, lock-jawed face, Wolfgang sitting back, his arms crossed, his lips twisted in his usual smirk. They were sending me a non-verbal, visceral message: *You fucking race-traitor, who do you think you are? You think you can rat us out without consequences? We know you, we can get you. You don't actually have the guts to do this to us. Just watch, you'll crumple on the stand.*

The first thing Harry Doan did was jump up and request that Martin be excluded from the hearing on the pretext that he might coach me from the bench. They probably thought that by depriving me of Martin's emotional support during the trial, I'd fall apart on the stand.

They thought wrong.

I reflected back to Gary Schipper's CTV interview right after it had been announced that I was a key witness. "She doesn't know nothing," he'd boasted. "Can't wait until she gets on the stand. We're gonna have a lot of fun with her."

How could they lie so blatantly, I'd thought. How could they think they could get away with it? Stealing a glance at Gary, who was squirming in his oversize suit, I doubted he was having that much fun right now.

During the first break in what would turn out to be three full days of unrelenting cross-examination on the part of the defense team, I realized that going to the washroom was going to be a chore in itself. The OPP female officer assigned to accompany me had to go inside first, hand on her gun, and do a visual sweep of the place to make sure nobody was lurking there, waiting to murder me or something. She opened every stall and checked behind each door while I shifted from foot to foot, willing the process to go faster. Finally, she waved to me: I was okay to pee.

"Could I have some privacy?" I asked.

No, she said, this was what she was being paid to do. If I valued my life, I had to give up the idea of privacy. I supposed that being under police protection was, in its own right, kind of like being in jail. I had to flush just to make some noise because the idea of someone listening to me urinate was unnerving.

As we were walking out of the washroom, a familiar sight greeted me. Coming from the other end of the corridor, there was Gary Schipper with the Elliotts and Harry Doan on his side.

I froze in place. Gary gave a contemptuous stare to the ear-length brown wig on my head and sneered, "Look who it is. Feel good to betray your own race?"

My mind went blank. Suddenly, an iron grip locked onto my arm. "Come on, keep moving," the cop hissed in my ear. She forcefully dragged me past the group. "Just put one foot ahead of another."

Unsteadily, I did as she said. Seeing Gary's face so close up left me shaken. Once we reentered the courtroom, the bright lights and throng of people all staring at me snapped me out of my stupor. *Stay focused*, I told myself. *Take a deep breath. You can do this.*

During a break on the second day I was approached by a woman who had volunteered to let me stay at her home while in hiding. "I wanted to pass on a message from someone who wants to thank you," she said. "The staff worker from the Runnymede group home who was arrested by police after she was raped? She wanted to express her gratitude, because it's only after you offered to testify in her defense at her trial that the prosecutor dropped the charges. They withdrew the charge just minutes before her trial was to start. They were afraid your testimony would corroborate her account and make the cops look bad."

How could I respond to this? No words could convey the injustice that had been perpetrated upon WM, the group home youth counsellor who was raped and then charged with mischief for purportedly lying about the incident. Yes, I had signed an affidavit citing what Dave had told me about skinheads planning an attack on someone working at that home. But WM shouldn't have had to thank ME, a former Front member, for confirming that I'd heard someone at the group home was marked as a target. She should have been treated with respect and empathy by a system that had, in the end, utterly failed her.

But they had broken her. They had not only raped this 29-year old woman by putting her through 11 months of hell, but broken her trust in the powers that were supposed to protect her. Her high-profile lawyer Clayton Ruby had called it "the police turning on the victim." White cops working for a Police Department with confirmed Heritage Front members on its force had arrested *her*, two days after she called them for help, for telling the truth about her attack.

She shouldn't have felt the need to thank me for validating that what had happened to her was REAL. Imagine, to actually feel so relieved about your charges being dropped that the horrific violation you suffered pales in comparison to the violation you incurred at the hands of a police department that is supposed to protect you. Add to it the violation she would experience less than a year from now, when she learned that the group these skinheads belonged to was created by a man on the payroll of her own country's intelligence service.

Harry Doan, my old lawyer who was now representing the Heritage Front in nearly all their cases, didn't want to cross-examine me directly, saying something about it being improper because he had represented me before. So the unpleasant task fell to his attractive and very Aryan-looking co-counsel, Ms. Owen. She looked to be in her late twenties and fresh out of law school. She wore high-heels, a smartly-tailored skirt suit, and liked to whip around her long blonde ponytail as she trotted from the defendants' side of the room to the witness stand and back again.

"But you were a neo-Nazi, weren't you?" she kept asking me.

I wondered why she thought she could discredit me as a witness by calling me a racist. Did she think I was going to deny it? If I hadn't been a racist, I wouldn't have come to be in the defendants' company. I wouldn't have heard their plans for the future. If anything, admitting my racist past and history with Wolfgang, Zundel and the lot of them was a way to fortify the validity of my incriminating evidence against them, not diminish it.

"Yes, I was. That's how come they trusted me and allowed me in their circle."

"You were a racist. You hated people of colour, correct?"

"If I didn't share their beliefs, they never would have let me overhear their meetings."

"Aha! So you do admit you were an ardent, hardcore Heritage Front supporter?"

Oh, God. How thick could she be? The recounting of my progression into the racist movement and the repetitive cross-examination left me more drained than I could've predicted. But just to make sure everybody got to see how much of a racist I was, Ms. Owen wheeled in a TV and played videos of my speeches at Heritage Front rallies.

"That was you, wasn't it? Giving the Sieg Heil salute?"

254

I could have saved her the trouble. There was nothing about my past that I would hide or deny. Yes, I was a hateful teenage Nazi. But those rallies were organized by the defendants.

At one point during Day Two, I leaned my elbows on the ledge in front of me and clutched my forehead. "Yes," I sighed, closing my eyes. "I've already told you—"

By then, the judge had had enough. "Enough already," she interrupted, snapping at Ms. Owen. "What is the point of you asking the same thing, over and over? She has said yes to your questions, again and again, why is it necessary to keep repeating this line of questioning? I think the witness needs a break. Let's take an hour for lunch, shall we?"

At the adjournment of each day of testifying I retreated back to Ruth's place. With my nerves frayed, I ran upstairs to be alone. I sat in the second floor window and squinted, trying to make out the approximate direction of Regent Park. Somewhere in that multitude of millions of people flittering about like ants was my mother, friendless, alone and pitiable in the confines of her shitty apartment. There was Grant, no doubt strategizing a way to discredit me. And, if I strained my eyes hard enough, I might even catch a glimpse of the courthouse, where Wolfgang, Gary and Ken would soon be led out the back way and loaded into a paddy wagon that would take them to a jail cell which was all my doing. I was racked with guilt for testifying against Ken Barker – he might have been a rabid racist who had already been arrested in connection with the armed robbery of a coffee shop and found in possession of scores of illegal weapons, but he was also a devoted single father of two daughters. I had been friends with his eldest daughter: T.B. was only a year younger than me and already on her way to becoming a Chelsea who shared her dad's values. What would happen to them if Ken went to jail? Would they ever leave the movement?

Before I went to sleep each night, all I could see was Wolfgang's piercing blue gaze as it bore into me unwaveringly. The smirk on his face. The way he silently communicated the fact that I was a filthy rat, a defector from a world that no longer existed for me.

A race traitor.

What did the OPP officers think of me? Were they repulsed to protect someone who sold out her own family? Who got other police officers investigated and kicked off the force? I speculated about what it would be like to have their job, defending the lives of scumbags with rap sheets a mile-long who sold out their compatriots. How could they do it, spend the better part of their days surrounded by such moral ambiguity? Surely they looked down on people like myself, people whom they had been sworn to protect. How could they hide their derision, if I myself was so torn over it?

Did they think I was weak for betraying those who once cared for me in order to protect men and women I'd never met face to face, activists who probably hated me anyway and would remain unforgiving of my involvement in the neo-fascist movement?

Or was I completely mistaken? Maybe I was projecting, maybe it wasn't the cops who hated me but me, myself and I.

I hated myself for betraying the loyalty of the only family I'd ever had. What did that make me? The newspapers called me a hero, a brave young girl, but what did any of that matter if every time I looked in the mirror, I saw a coward? If, underneath it all, I was still the same scared girl who froze in place when my friend Pereta was attacked back in Bucharest?

Maybe my so-called bravery was a front for an insidious weakness of character, a wobbly-kneed reluctance to fight. Maybe the defense lawyers were right when they accused me of testifying against the Front as a pathetic attempt to save my own hide, to jump off the sinking ship before it sailed out of the harbour.

I wanted to believe that I had betrayed the Heritage Front because of the sickening things they had done – the escalation of their attacks against innocent people, the great deal of pity I felt for the victims of the It Campaign, for that poor woman whose name I didn't know but whose assault had shaken me up so viscerally.

But what if all of it was true – that my testimony had been hurled against the Front vengefully, like a grenade, and my act of avenging their victims was intertwined with my desperation to escape? Were the two mutually-exclusive? Or was it possible that my decision to end the violence of the It Campaign was a subconscious way for me to save myself?

I fell to my knees on the floor and started sobbing. A bright, searing pain engulfed my chest, like something had ripped its way inside me and was tearing me apart. I was going to die, right then and there, and I welcomed it. That's when I heard a voice in my mind, *Pull yourself together. They're messing with your head. These games are meant to trip you up. Be strong.*

On the third day on the stand, I heard one of the activists sitting in the front row, a young man wearing a tee-shirt with the tagline Ganja Power written above the image of a lushly-green marijuana plant, mutter, "Fucking hell. One and a half hours of testimony, and three days of cross-examination. What do they think this is, a murder trial? All at the tax-payers money, too. This is bullshit."

Then court resumed and Ms. Owen pressed on.

"So can you tell me again why you decided to leave the Heritage Front?"

"I became concerned with the direction of the group after they started a terror campaign targeting innocent people for harassment. And I didn't want to just leave – I wanted to stop what was going on before it escalated."

"And who specifically directed this so-called terror campaign?"

"The head of Heritage Front Intelligence and co-founder of our group, Grant Bristow."

"Isn't it true you made a deal with the police to testify here so you could have your own charges of hate propaganda dropped?"

"No, it's not true. There is no deal."

"So why would you want to testify against your old friends? To rat them out, as you would put it?"

"Because it's the truth."

"And you didn't make a deal? Aren't those OPP officers in the room with you?"

"They're only offering me protection for the duration of this trial. But no, I have not been offered any deals."

"But you are in hiding?"

"Yes."

"And not in the Witness Protection Program?"

"No. I wish."

"And where is it that you are living now?"

This is where pandemonium broke. *Objection*, said the Human Rights Commission lawyers, jumping to their feet. The judge – yet again – directed the defense counsel to refrain from such obvious fishing expeditions. The exact coordinates of my location have no bearing on the facts at hand, she told them.

When I was finally excused I could barely walk away of the courtroom, my legs were so shaky. *Is this it?* I wondered. *Is it really over? What's going to happen next?*

"Did I do okay?" I asked Martin after we met next door, in a small, enclosed room with an opaque glass door where the OPP had designated for us to wait before, during the trial and just before we were to be escorted out of the building. Even when there were just the two of us in there, we were careful not to say anything important, on Martin's suspicion that it was bugged. But I couldn't resist asking for reassurance.

"You did a great job, Elisse. A fantastic job. Don't beat yourself up," he said.

"But do you think it'll be enough?"

He patted my back. "You've done everything you could. You told the truth. You lasted through three days of cross-examination without backing down. What else could anybody ask for? The defense team pulled out every stunt in the book trying to discredit your testimony, but it didn't work. You should be very proud of yourself. Everyone's predicting a conviction."

Rodney Bobiwash came over to join us. He beamed at me. "Your testimony was fine. But you know, where you *really* shined was during your cross-examination. You made them look even worse, if that's at all possible. Every question that woman asked, it was like she was putting her foot in her mouth, because your answer made things even worse for them. She should've stopped while she was ahead."

The defense team's strategy had backfired. The story of how Wolfgang had recruited a naïve sixteen-year old into his extremist organization and gave her the materials to compose those hotline messages did not serve to discredit me as much as their own humanity.

Right after court adjourned, Martin and Rodney took me out to dinner in Chinatown. When we were standing up to leave, Martin put his arms around me. I pressed my head tight against his chest and listened to his heartbeat. The desperation I felt every time I had to say goodbye washed over me again, and I promptly burst into tears.

"Don't worry. We'll see each other again in three months, when your trial's scheduled to start," he said, as if reading my mind. He held me a long time, until the weeping had subsided.

"I'm very proud of you, you know that," he added as I clutched his jacket, unwilling to let go, afraid to melt away into the darkening sky only to wake up tomorrow on the other side of the country.

Alone.

THIRTY-ONE

A NEW LIFE

The drive to Halifax took nearly three days. Martin drove ten hours a day, until the daylight had vanished and his body couldn't take it anymore. We slept at obscure roadside inns and truck-stop motels that had an attached diner where we could grab a bite before going to sleep. Our rooms had double beds covered with hideous floral bedspreads – explosions of Hawaiian orchids and tuberoses met with the regurgitated contents of a cabana party – and banana-yellow striped wallpaper, even in the outdated bathroom where the starchy towels had the texture of sandpaper.

Stress coursed through us like an electrical charge. Dark circles pooled under my eyes, making my face gaunt and restless. One night, as we were about to sit down for a meal, Martin took a long look at me and started laughing. "What is it?" I asked, indignant.

"You look like you just came out of a concentration camp," he said, wiping his eyes. "I don't know if I should laugh or cry. Are you sure you're not Jewish?"

I marched into the washroom and took an honest look at myself. I was down to almost a hundred pounds. My dark hair was shorn close to my scalp. The old winter coat I got from Ruth was about six sizes too big, hanging off my near-skeletal frame. The blackness in my eyes reminded me of an old photograph of my grandmother, taken after WW1. The same haunted black eyes, the same secret heritage she had run from all of her life. The same blood that ran in my father's veins.

Every night I crashed into my bed, utterly exhausted, after begging Martin to get some rest. But he continued to sit in front of the television for another couple of hours, ashen and silent. Blue hues threw electric shadows over his face as he drank beer after beer in an attempt to numb himself enough to fall asleep.

Our journey northeast was dark and dreary; every single day, ominous clouds loomed overhead. But it gave us the precious time we needed to be together and discuss our next strategic move against the Heritage Front.

Once we got past Montreal, the highway was empty save for the massive logging trucks. I put my feet up on the dashboard and chewed on my fingernails, speculating what the future would bring. I was contented to finally be on the way to my brand new life, but a part of me was terrified. Nova Scotia was a thousand miles north-east of Toronto. I'd never been so far away before.

Calm down, relax, I told myself. This is everything you've been waiting for – a chance to settle down somewhere and stop living out of a suitcase.

Martin had arranged for me to stay in Dartmouth, Halifax's twin city, which was just across the harbour and could be reached via any of three massive bridges that tied both naval ports together. I would stay at the townhouse of a black Baptist reverend who preached to an all-black congregation. He watched for my reaction.

"Do I have to go to church with them?" I asked.

Martin laughed. "I'd imagine you'll go wherever they take you. But they won't kick you out if you don't cross yourself, if that's what worries you."

"How long did you tell him I was staying? Does he know anything?"

"He has a general idea of what's going on but his girlfriend doesn't, so be careful of what you say around her. She's got a couple of kids living there and we don't want her panicking." We drove some more before he asked, "Have you decided on a new name?"

"Mhh-mm."

He cocked an eyebrow. "So what's it gonna be?"

"Emma. Emma Donovan."

"Not Goldman?" he laughed. "Emma," he said again, mouthing the word. " I like it."

We pulled into Dartmouth late in the evening, and we were so exhausted there was barely any time for introductions before Martin went off to his guest room, I took the cot in the basement, and we slept the sleep of the dead.

In the morning we sat down with the Reverend and his common-law wife Joyce for breakfast. They seemed like nice, welcoming people. Joyce had a teenage daughter named Stacy and an eight-year old son, Anthony, and she made both of them say hello to us before they gobbled their cereal and scurried away.

Joyce, who was under the impression that Martin was a long-time friend of the Reverend's and had been asked to guest me temporarily as a personal favour, stood at the stove and made us scrambled eggs and fried sausage. As she put out the plates, asked Martin how long he was going to be in Halifax.

"I'm heading back tomorrow," he answered.

I nearly dropped my fork. "So soon?"

"I'm sitting on a lot of stuff," he said. "Can't be away for too long."

I spent my last day with Martin down by the Halifax harbour. We went to an Irish pub close to the pier where all the booths were padded with dark green velvet and the coasters printed with four-leaf clovers. He ordered a tall glass of beer while I leaned on an elbow and watched him closely, wondering when I'd see him again. The reality of his impending departure was starting to sink in. I was a three-day drive away from anyplace I knew, in a part of the country that didn't even seem like what I'd imagined Canada to be. Somehow, we had beamed ourselves to a rainy, mist-wrapped corner of Ireland or the Scottish highlands.

"You'll be all right," Martin said, as though he could sense my trepidation. "You know how to get a hold of me if anything comes up."

"What if you get sick again?" It was a valid question, one I hated having to ask. "What's our backup?"

He shrugged. "I think you'll be fine here. Just focus on starting again – this is your new life. It's what you've always wanted, isn't it? Settle in and make friends. You're tough, you'll make it work."

I was suddenly aware of a headache building at the top of my head. "I'm sick and tired of people who think I'm so tough," I exploded. "I've never had the luxury to fall apart. It's not like I could turn to alcohol or antidepressants since I can't even afford groceries. And since I can't use my ID, hospitalization due to nervous breakdown is out of the question."

Martin giggled softly. He knocked down the rest of his beer and gestured to the waitress to bring him another.

"It's not funny, you know," I said indignantly. "I'm nowhere near the fucking pillar of strength everybody thinks I am."

"Honestly, just put one foot in front of another," he said. "As soon as I get back home, I'm faxing the rest of the affidavits to the press. We're going after Grant and the rest of the gang next so there's a good chance we may need you to fly in and testify in another proceeding."

True to his word, Martin left first thing Monday morning. I stood in the threshold of Joyce's townhouse and watched him drive off, struggling not to break down; I'd always been horrible with goodbyes. But the part of me that was Emma took over. She was like a little kid at Halloween, so excited to put on a mask and begin her new life that she wouldn't let me wallow in more heartbreak.

The first half of the week, the Reverend took me along to his office in East Preston, an area historically-known as having been a destination point on the underground railroad back in the 1800s. Many descendants of runaway American slaves still lived there, but the community was poor and in desperate need of revitalization. The Reverend, who had moved here from Montreal a few years ago, hoped that spirituality was the key to renewing the region.

While he went off to his meetings, he left me in charge of the office. "Just answer the phone if it rings and take a message," he said. "Turn on the computer, maybe you'll find something fun to do." Unfortunately the only 'fun' program was a game called Bible Quiz, so I decided to sweep the place instead and sorted the Reverend's papers into manageable folders.

On Sundays we stayed in Dartmouth and attended church. The Reverend's main parish was located within a short walking distance of the pier. It was so close to the water you could practically smell the mussels being grilled along the restaurants on the other side of the harbour. The smell weaved itself in the tang of floating algae lattices and the formations of limestone that coated the shore. They said that just before dawn, the ghosts of drowned sailors would walk the scraggly rocks alongside the water in search of their loved ones. On days like these, I tended to believe it.

My second Sunday was drizzly and overcast. Joyce told me to wear my finest outfit because there was a special ceremony taking place today. "What's going on?" I asked Stacy, who was a year younger than me and had already dragged me tooth-and-nail to the first meeting of her Bible Study group. She was standing in the bathroom of our shared basement, curling her bangs with pomade and a hot iron that sizzled each time it touched her hair.

"We're making a purity pledge," she said. "All the teenagers who do it receive a ring to symbolize their commitment to remaining virgins until marriage. Wanna do it too?"

"Um, I don't think so." This was the first time I'd ever heard of such a thing. It seemed a little sick, going up in front of a whole group of people that included your step-dad and talking about how you were going to abstain from sex. I mean, it was nobody's business.

"You can pledge anytime, even as a born-again virgin," she said, looking at me dubiously but being too polite to ask. "It's just that today a whole bunch of us are going up to pledge our purity before God and the congregation."

"Wow," I said. Wow was my favourite non-committal word. The best thing about it was that it didn't imply either a positive or a negative; it just bridged the silence that came after I was expected to say something.

The worshippers were there in droves. Many of the women wore fancy hats and dresses bordered with white lace. Some of the older ones even wore gloves. The children were all dolled up as well: little boys in dark suits, little girls whose hair was braided neatly and tied up with bows. Wearing vibrant robes, the Gospel choir were clapping and singing of Jesus' glories. I sat among the middle pews and watched Stacy as she walked up to the pulpit, so pretty in her crisp white dress, and received her purity ring. A dozen other youngsters followed suit.

Their life was so simple. You just obey some divine governance until the day you die. You don't have to think for yourself. You don't move in with someone before marriage, or try out sex to see if you're compatible with your lover. No, there's no complexity in being evangelical – you just let the rules take you to your destination. You don't have ownership over your life; some invisible deity up in the sky determines what you can or cannot do. Some book written thousands of years ago gets to dictate how many times a day you pray and on which days of the week you can eat meat. *I don't think I could be an evangelical*, I thought. As comforting as it would be to have all

264

the rules spelled out for me, I was done with organizations that told me what to think or do.

I watched the happy people around me sing and praise the lord above and thought, *There is no god*. His inexistence was proven to me back when, locked outside our apartment by my father and his mistress, my childhood self had crouched on Bucharest's streets in the darkness. All the times I was groped by strangers, when I went hungry and unloved, there was no god beside me. There was only a deep aloneness and a sadness that crushed my ribs and choked my voice until it grew thin and wispy, and went unheard by the world. And the only way I could make myself heard, then, was through the explosive power of my hateful words – through the fiery speeches where hundreds of skinheads cheered and fed, like sin-eaters, on the palpable expulsion of my pain.

THIRTY-TWO

THE ATLANTIC COAST

As much as I helped Joyce in the kitchen and with the laundry, I could tell she was getting frustrated. "So what do you think you want to do?" she asked me as we were loading dishes into the sink. "Get a job or something?"

Martin had specifically forbidden me from using my ID. "Uh, I have to wait for Martin to arrange where I'm moving next," I stammered.

"You know, Emma," she started to say, hand on her hip. "I don't want you to take this the wrong way, but when I was told you were going to stay here with us, I was under the impression it wasn't going to be for more than two weeks."

I bit my lip. It was a classic move on Martin's part – he convinced someone to let me stay at their place for a few days and it turned into a week. But I thought he'd arranged everything with the Reverend up front, and up until today I hadn't realized that Joyce had been quoted a specific timeline which obviously had expired. Now she was on my case, demanding when I was going to move out or start paying rent.

"You understand it's not personal," she continued. "But you eat with us every day, you use up extra hydro, and costs are adding up. So I need you to start looking into finding another place to live, or at the very least contribute financially until you find a room in town."

I was mortified. My search for under-the-table jobs in Halifax had gone nowhere; tons of students were looking for the same thing and in a small university town like this jobs that didn't demand a whole lot of previous experience were slow to come by; when they did, they got snatched up right away.

"I'll get right on top of it," I managed to say, then went into the bedroom and tried unsuccessfully to get a hold of Martin. I left a message and willed that he get back to me before Joyce really freaked out.

Later that night, Joyce and the Reverend began to quarrel again. They didn't have that great of a relationship to begin with, but no doubt my being there added to the hostility brewing between them. My cot in the basement was directly underneath the kitchen and when they argued and stomped around, I could hear absolutely everything reverberating through the ceramic tiles. "This isn't what you told me," Joyce yelled. "I pay all the bills around here!"

Just when I thought it couldn't get any worse, the phone rang early the next morning, and I thought nothing of picking it up. There was total silence from the other line. "Hello?" I tried again.

A male voice rasped, "We know where you are."

Instinctively I hung up. A sensation of terror paralyzed me into place. Several minutes later, the phone rang again. "We saw you," the man said. A woman's voice tittered in the background.

"Go to hell!" I slammed the receiver down, but it rang again. Over and over. I heard Joyce cursing in the other room. I had no choice but to pick up. "Listen to me and stop hanging up!" the man said. "Don't be stupid."

"Who are you?" I asked, reaching for a notepad on the kitchen table to note the exact time and the words being said. It was a habit I'd developed while recording Grant's calls.

"You know who we are," he growled. "You may think you're safe but you're not. If we don't get you tonight, we will tomorrow. We know where you are!"

I steeled myself. "What do you want?"

"Meet us tonight. If you're not there, the people you're with are going to get hurt. Don't be selfish. Do you want something bad to happen to them? We know what you look like. Don't fuck around."

"Oh, yeah? What do I look like?"

"You have short hair."

"I had short hair in court. Tell me something else."

The man sighed. "This isn't a game. You betrayed us. Don't just think about yourself, think about those you're living with. Do you really want them to get hurt because of you? Meet us tonight."

"Where?"

"By the ferry terminal, at 5:30. Don't fuck around."

I lost it. I clutched the phone and yelled into the receiver. "Listen, I know the games you're playing. Grant trained me, I've done it myself. You'll have to give me something more substantial, or I'm not buying it."

The man hesitated. For a moment, I thought I'd won. Then he spoke again. "We've seen you. You're wearing a beige jacket."

"Fuck off!" I screamed into the mouthpiece.

No sooner had I hang up than Joyce darted into the kitchen and snapped. "What is going on with these weird calls?"

It was time to get the fuck out of there. I couldn't have anyone placed at risk because of me. Without bothering to answer Joyce, who continued to yell at my back, I ran to the basement and dashed around, plucking clothes from drawers and stuffing them into my suitcase. I crammed all essentials into a backpack I'd take with me and prayed that Joyce wasn't going to put my suitcase out on the curb until I came back for it. I slid the backpack straps over my shoulders and went back upstairs.

Joyce glared at me. Before she could open her mouth, I said, "I'm going into Halifax to see about a room. I promise I'll get all my stuff out of here within a couple of days, okay?"

She shook her head. Although she couldn't make out the connection between the phone calls and me, she suspected I had something to do with it. As she was getting ready to tell me so, the phone rang again. We stared at one another like deer caught in headlights. "I'll be back," I breathed. "And I'll get the rest of my things, I swear."

I sprinted out of the house and didn't stop running until I reached the bus stop. Panting, I bent over to catch my breath. Where the hell was I going to go? My heart pounded so loudly I thought it was going to burst. A gust of Acadian wind swept over me, cooling off my forehead. I straightened again and fished around in my pocket for the bus fare. I had no idea where I was going or where I would sleep tonight, but that seemed like the least of my concerns.

Located at 2421 Brunswick Road, right in the heart of Halifax, stands a tall Victorian house. Its exterior brick is painted a deep forest green, and the trim along the door and front cathedral windows is a creamy white. I'd read about it in the community brochures I'd scoured when I was looking for work; logically, it was the first and only place I could think of.

I went to the front door and rang the doorbell. A young woman with a buzz-cut answered. "May I help you?" she asked.

"I don't really know if I should be here."

She motioned for me to come in. "Let's go into my office and talk," she said.

I crumpled a Kleenex from the box she offered me and spun a tale about being stalked by an abusive ex-boyfriend. I was counting on this being a story she heard often, and it was. I didn't have to say much before her face turned white. "Of course you can stay here," she said. "We'll do all we can to help you. But you will have to apply for welfare."

The welfare thing was a deal-breaker – it would involve having a social worker and presenting my ID. I delayed the appointment with the social worker for as long as I could, and in the meantime arranged to have a staff member fetch my suitcase from Joyce's place. I was assigned a cot in a bedroom on the second floor that was supposed to hold a dozen women but had only two occupants, one of whom snored like there were eleven more of her. But it didn't matter. I took advantage of all the amenities: did laundry, showered daily, ate well and slept like a baby.

On my second day at Adsum House, I walked into town and began to dig through the library archives, pulling up obituaries from newspaper microfiches until I found what I was looking for – four little girls who had died as infants circa my birth year. If I could summon the nerve to apply for their birth certificates, I'd be all set with several new identities. I was scared of being caught, but I'd ran out of choices.

By the following month I was on welfare under an assumed name and subletting an apartment from a couple of university students who were backpacking in Australia for the summer. I also had a new crowd to hang with: the kids who attended the Gay Youth drop-in meetings at the Planned Parenthood office on Quinpool Road. There were about fifteen of us crammed elbow-to-elbow in a narrow room full of Safe Sex posters and jars of multi-coloured condoms. The meetings were chaperoned by a native of Maine, a twenty-seven year old social worker named Moira. Barely older than the teens she counseled, Moira was all business, taking us under her wing like a mother hen.

There was a fairly even split of guys and girls who gathered on Thursday afternoons. Some of them had purple hair and a ring through their eyebrow; others were more subdued and shyer because they still lived at home and were in the closet. Among them I always felt like an impostor, expecting that at any moment somebody was going to recognize me from the news and kick me out. When they asked what my story was, I told them my family had thrown me out when they discovered I was gay. It was a convenient explanation; people didn't question it because it had happened to them. I wished it had happened to me also, because the reality was far worse. I hadn't just been thrown out by my family – I was on the run from them, and I feared for my life.

Martin called the first week of June. "I wanted to call and tell you the good news myself," he said. "Are you ready?"

"Tell me!" I demanded, nearly bursting with excitement.

"Well, we've done it. They were found guilty. All three of them. The judge wrote in sentencing that she was impressed with how believable and candid you were during that intensive cross-examination. She said there was no doubt in her mind at all that you were credible."

Happiness overwhelmed me. "We did it, Martin! Have you told Ruth?"

"Yes, everybody in Toronto knows. The Heritage Front is officially dead in the water. Most of its leadership are going to jail this summer. Bristow excepted, of course. We did it, Elisse. We shut them down."

How badly that I could have been in Toronto that day! I'd be dancing with joy in the middle of Ruth and Annetta's living room, surrounded by Martin and Rodney and all those who had made this day a reality.

Martin read me the judgment, in which Madame Tremblay-Lamer did not mince her words:

"Freedom of expression in a democratic society includes the right to criticize government as well as the right to be politically incorrect. However, it does not include the right to deliberately disobey a valid order of the Court which is not under attack. In my

270

opinion, to tolerate such action jeopardizes the very integrity of our Canadian judicial system upon which all citizens depend and to which all have a right. It is the duty of the courts to ensure that deference to their process is not undermined in any way. The rule of law must be maintained; in order to do so it is essential that respect for the authority of the courts is enforced. I have no sympathy for unscrupulous fanatics who deliberately attempt to subvert that authority.

After careful consideration of the testimony of witnesses as well as the documents submitted, I conclude that the evidence is beyond a reasonable doubt that the respondents, the Heritage Front and Wolfgang Droege, deliberately disobeyed the order of Joyal J. dated October 8, 1993 and are thus in contempt of this Court pursuant to Rule 355 of the Federal Court Rules."

When it came to my testimony, she had this to say:

"I found Ms. Hategan very credible, candid, calm and patient during an intensive cross-examination. She has never contradicted herself, and her forthright demeanour and manner of expression left no doubt in my mind that she was credible. Such was the strength of her oral and affidavit evidence, that neither Mr. Droege's testimony nor that of any other witness could refute or even seriously challenge it. Based on the evidence of Ms. Hategan alone, I am satisfied beyond a reasonable doubt that the defendants are guilty."

Less than two weeks later, I flew back to Toronto for the start of my own trial. But there would never be a trial. On June 24, 1994, after reviewing two affidavits sworn by Edan and Shannon, the two Anti-Racist Action activists I had given the Animal Life II flyer to at Brockton High School, the Crown prosecution admitted defeat.

There was no *Mens Rea* here, no intent to do harm. I had done nothing wrong. A judicial precedent had already been established in Canadian law that if an action was performed as a warning to others, to deflect potential danger, the action in question cannot be illegal. And the affidavits stated that when I handed the flyer over to them and asked them to pass it on to Celeste, the HF's intended target, I'd said, 'This is what the Heritage Front is doing now.'

I stood next to my attorney Paul Copeland and watched numbly as the Crown Prosecutor addressed the judge and made the formal request that my charges be withdrawn. I struggled to stir up some sort of emotion, but drew a blank. I felt so empty. After yearning for this day of vindication for so long, I wasn't happy or sad. Just relieved.

What would be the point of describing the media circus that followed? Countless people accused me of making deals with the police in order to have my charged dropped. There was no convincing them otherwise, because in so many minds it was inconceivable that guilt, remorse and transformation could provoke someone like me to genuinely want to shut down the organization that had terrorized so many others.

Even in months to come, after being invited as a guest speaker at rallies organized by community organizations and ARA groups, there were still those who screamed out, "Once a Nazi, always a Nazi!", jeered at me, and in a couple of cases literally spat on me.

But the affidavits are part of the court system, and there is no reason to elaborate further on a matter of public record. Suffice it to say, once the libel and hate propaganda charges were dismissed, I was free to travel as far away from my past as Canada is big.

THIRTY-THREE

PLAYING NORMAL

One Saturday morning Moira organized a carpool to the beach of one of the national parks that surrounded Halifax and faced the Atlantic ocean. The ten of us who showed up scampered around the beach, barefoot, screaming like seagulls when the cold waves immersed our feet. Cory, the would-be drag queen of our bunch, screeched louder than anybody else. He whipped off his top and ran in the water, waving his arms in the air like a madman. I tossed my towel on the sand, wiggled out of my sundress and ran toward the ocean, trying to catch up with him. Leighann followed us and then the three of us doggy-paddled in place, freezing our asses off but trying to look brave, waving at everybody else to come and join us.

Out of the blue, a massive wave crashed over my head. Saltwater went everywhere: in my throat, in my eyes, half-blinding me. I ran out of the ocean and shook my head like a dog, trying to get the water out of my ears. I didn't even realize until seconds later that I was being watched by a light-haired girl called Pamela who was sitting on the sand, puffing on a cigarette.

Embarrassed, I grabbed my towel and wiped my face. "Shit, did I splash you?"

She grinned. "Nah, don't worry about it."

"You don't want to come swimming with us?"

"Nah, not today. But I love being near the ocean," she said, glancing over my shoulder. "The smell, the seaweed, all of it. It's in my blood. My grandparents came from Ireland, you know." She tilted her head sideways. "Hey, what are you doing later? There's a bunch of us having a bonfire and clam bake at sunset."

I brushed the sand off my bare legs and started toweling my hair. "I've never been to one of those before."

"Then you'll have to come and see what it's like."

Our first kiss came two days later, when we sat on the grassy north slope of Citadel Hill, baking in the afternoon heat. We had been watching the ships come and leave the harbour, while others were being packed with cargo for their lengthy trans-Atlantic voyages. Against the horizon, the bluer than blue ocean waves glittered in the sun. As they neared the shore they gathered in strength and smashed against the boardwalk planks, only to go crashing backwards in ripples of white froth. The acrid smells of fishnets and algae and steamed mussels from the boardwalk vendors tangled in the air.

Without warning, Pamela leaned in and planted a peck on my left ear. I turned to face her and wordlessly allowed myself to be drawn into the heat of a kiss. We made out right in the open, not giving a damn who might be watching us. Then we got up from the grass, brushed off the dirt from out clothes and, hand-in-hand, walked over to a donair stand where we bought two delicious pita wraps, my favourite thing to eat in Halifax. Later on, we headed over to a local lesbian watering hole where we danced the night away.

We stumbled back into my apartment around three in the morning, locked in a fierce embrace. Somehow we managed to tumble into the bedroom and fell back onto the futon, struggling out of our clothes. She buried her face in my chest, reached behind to unhook my bra, slipped it off my shoulders in one fast sweep. Then she moved down to my hips, aiming to slide my underwear off.

I pulled back slightly. "Let's turn the light off," I suggested.

"I didn't know you were this shy," she said, bemused.

I turned red, and she let out a sigh. "Okay, fine," she said and went to the wall to snap off the overhead light switch. We groped in the dark for a minute, trying to kiss again, but smashed our foreheads together. "Ouch," she giggled. "I'm not sure this is going to work. Let's try the lamp, okay?"

She reached for the lamp on the nightstand and turned it back on, aiming the bulb away from us. "Let me see you," she whispered, reaching to pull down the blanket I'd scrambled under. "That's what drew me to you the most. Your curves."

I tilted my head. "Are you calling me fat?"

She laughed. "When I saw you at the beach for the first time, I could barely keep myself from running to you right there, in the waves." She traced the outline of my hips and thighs." I can't believe you're here now."

When we were finished, I clung to her for a long time, willing time to stand still. I didn't want to feel the air rushing between our bodies, to be alone again.

She sat up on an elbow and nudged me. "You know, it strikes me that we've just slept together and I know nothing about you. Seriously, I want you to tell me everything about yourself. And I mean, *absolutely everything*. Like, where'd you go to school and what's your mother's maiden name."

I shook my head. The room grew colder around me and I pulled the blanket higher. I knew I shouldn't have, that it was wrong and I'd very likely regret it. That it might forever change the way she looked at me. But I found myself weakening. For a split second, with Pamela sitting there so lovely and earnest, I allowed myself to succumb to the magic of happy endings. *Perhaps she'd understand*, I thought. I wanted to believe it. I really did.

Pamela listened aptly and didn't interrupt once. I told her everything – about the men I'd betrayed, about being on the run. If she was shocked by what I had to say, she was careful not to show it. She held me in her arms until I was finished.

A distinct chill had come over us. "Do you think we're safe now?" she finally asked.

"Yeah, I think so. I sublet this place under a fake name; not even Martin knows the number. If I need to get in touch with him, I use the phone booths at the downtown library."

We lay back on our pillows. She stared at the ceiling, shell-shocked.

I turned to face her. "I had to tell you. So that if I suddenly have to take off without notice, you'd know why." Her silence felt ominous. "*Say* something," I insisted.

"I don't really know what to say, to be honest," she said quietly. "It's a lot to take in. We've had a very long day – maybe we should just go to sleep."

She wrapped her arms around me and we lay like that for what seemed like hours, before sleep finally overtook us. In the morning, Pamela dressed hastily and gave me a peck on the cheek. "I have to go," she said. "I'll come by later this afternoon and we can talk then. I promised to meet Ian for brunch."

I silently noted that she didn't ask me to come along. I slipped my tee-shirt over my head and remained in bed, staring up at her. "I freaked you out last night, didn't I?" It was more of a statement than a question. "I'm sorry. I wanted so badly to tell someone. To be called by my real name. But I made a mistake. I shouldn't have told you."

"It's okay," she said, inching toward the door. "I'm glad you told me. I'll see you later, okay?"

"Do you still want to go out with me?" I asked, point-blank.

She chewed her lip. I'd taken her by surprise. She thought about it, sighed and decided to tell me the truth. "I think we should just be friends."

And that was it – the infamous kiss of death. She let herself out of the apartment, insisting I remain in bed. I buried my face in the pillows. What was I thinking, to pour my heart out like that to a girl I barely knew? *Of course* my guilt and confession had frightened her. She was an average, innocent eighteen-year old. She didn't know anything about men with guns and neo-Nazis. What made me think she'd have any sympathy for me when I couldn't forgive my own past?

I'd wrecked everything.

THIRTY-FOUR

A SPY UNMASKED

I had put my grocery bags down on the porch and started fishing for my keys when I found the note lodged in the front door of the yellow clapboard house on Artz street where I'd been staying for about a month. The note was folded in half, tucked between the frame and the lock. Across its back, a message is scrawled out: *"To Elisse, all the best. Love, Ruth."*

It wasn't Ruth's handwriting. My heart stopped. I unfolded the note slowly, looking to the left and right of me. The street was empty of parked cars. It was silent, too silent, and it smelled like the puckered green buds that had been swept across the sidewalk by the splash of an overnight rainfall.

My eyes fell back to the note. It looked like a photocopied religious pamphlet and carried an ominous message:

Free from fear, free from pain, free yourself of your fear of death.

They'd found me.

This was part of the game: let the hunted feel safe for a while; allow her a brief taste of imaginary freedom, then pounce again just when she finally breathes out in relief.

"It's more effective," Grant used to say, "than terrorizing someone night after night. After a couple weeks of peace and quiet, you go after them again. You know what that does to a person's head? It fucks with their mind. It's more terrifying than if they'd already gotten used to the fear."

My heartbeat pounded like a drum inside my skull. I rushed into my room, reached beneath the bed to pull out my backpack and unzipped the main compartment, sweeping all the toiletries on my nightstand into it. Then I stopped abruptly. If they wanted to, they could easily have taken me out by now; I couldn't fool myself to believe otherwise.

This is about intimidation, I thought as I put the note down, careful not to smudge any fingerprints. When you really want to go after someone, you don't leave them a warning note.

The phone calls started within 24 hours. A girl I had gone out with only once suddenly called to say someone had left her a message at work to call me back. The phone line started cutting in and out, becoming staticky. The same typical shit that I had encountered at Joyce's place – whoever was trying to scare me had access to telephone lines.

What neo-Nazi can get their shit together enough to manipulate phone lines, to create havoc and terrorize people? These psychological games of intimidation had Grant Bristow's signature all over them. But nobody in the Heritage Front could have the technical know-how to do this. To scramble telephone lines at the push of a button, to know all my friends' phone numbers at home and work, to ensure that my number would show up on their call display screens night and day, even when I'd never telephoned them. Even when *I didn't even know* their workplace numbers.

But how could Grant have tracked me down? How did the people who called me at the Reverend's place know I had short hair and a beige jacket? Who had me under surveillance?

In the nine months I lived in Halifax, I had used only my Social Insurance Number to get social assistance. Whoever knew I was in Halifax had the ability to tap into my SIN card data. There was no other way they could have tracked me through multiple addresses.

How could an unemployed private investigator orchestrate all this?

August 13, 1994

Bill Dunphy called in the evening, having received my phone number from Martin. From the sound of his voice, which reverberated deep in his throat, I knew that whatever he had to say wasn't going to leave me unscathed.

"I have something to tell you, Elisse. Something bad. I wanted you to hear it from me first. It involves Grant Bristow. I want you to brace yourself."

I closed the door to my room and sat on the edge of my bed. I took a deep breath. "Did he kill someone?"

"It's worse than that." Dunphy hesitated. "He's a CSIS agent."

Dunphy proceeded to inform me that the Toronto Sun was going to press with an exposé that would change everything that we thought we knew about the Heritage Front. "By tomorrow morning, the entire country will know that the Heritage Front was a CSIS operation. Wait until the public finds out that Grant Bristow, co-founder of the Heritage Front, chief of HF intelligence, head of security, is an agent provocateur paid by CSIS to stir shit up. He was on their payroll for almost a year before the group was founded. And do you know what, Elisse? When I confronted him about your allegations, he as much as admitted it.

He told me, "*You know what we did with the numbers from their hotline, you know what the game was... Call and say we were from The Third Reich Welcome Wagon and when they asked where you'd got their number you'd say Rodney sold it for $2. Nothing illegal about that. No threats and if they hang up you don't call back. We called it 'Stirring it up.'*"

In retrospect, I can't describe what emotions coursed through me when Dunphy broke the news to me that night. I'd like to imagine that I got angry, that I cursed our government and all its minions. I might even have cried at the injustice of it. But, hard as I try to recall, all that comes back is the brusque flash of white that shook my consciousness. The cold feeling that ran through my body. And both those things turned, faster than I'd have imagined, into numbness. Every nerve in me went motionless, flat like the surface of a stagnant pool of water.

"Why didn't you tell me?" I demanded to know when I called Martin later that night.

He took a deep breath. "Rodney and I knew about this for a while. I was tempted to tell you so many times, but we wanted to protect you. Sometimes ignorance lets you sleep at night. But if you must know, this is how it went down.

Rodney had spotted Bristow by the payphones outside the courtroom that day you were testifying in front of the Human Rights Commission. He walked up to him and said: '*What's up, Bristow? Calling Ottawa?*'

Grant freaked out, turned completely white. He slammed down the phone and took off. Rodney tracked me down inside the courthouse and whispered, 'All hell's gonna break loose. They'll be pulling Bristow out now. He's just learned we know *who* and *what* he is.'"

"I can't believe you knew this all along and didn't tell me," I said flatly.

"It's not personal. I didn't want you to panic."

"On the contrary, it would have helped me fill in the blanks."

"Well, I think you *would* have freaked out. With all due respect, you have no idea what we've gone through over the last year to protect you, knowing what we knew. We weren't hiding you from the Front as much as from his handlers and *their* people."

My mind raced; everything was starting to make sense. The hijinks with telephone lines, the ability to track me based on SIN number alone. "Oh, God," I breathed.

"Did you know CSIS had instructed everyone to disregard any evidence in order to protect their rogue agent, whose name was prominent in your affidavits? That was the factor that led to the dismissal of your statements. But it didn't stop there, Elisse. Even while you were testifying against the Front, CSIS was there, in charge of your cross-examination. They didn't want their operation to be compromised by anybody going to jail, much less Wolfgang. This was their chance to completely obliterate your credibility. To 'tear you to shreds' on the stand so you wouldn't be judged a good witness in any future proceedings against Grant.

CSIS fed Bristow questions which he, in turn, fed to Doan and the Heritage Front defence. One could say that CSIS itself was cross-examining you. But you didn't back down. You should always be proud of that. Always."

As shocked as I felt, I couldn't imagine what a blow this had served to the Front. *Wolfgang must be going out of his mind*, I thought. The idea made me smile; he deserved this.

"It gets worse," Martin cautioned me. "SIRC is going to start an investigation soon, and you can bet it will find that Bristow acted in good faith. CSIS will try to whitewash the whole thing. Bristow is already going around telling everybody you were a bicycle for the Front."

"What does that mean?"

Martin paused to exhale. "You know, a bicycle – everyone's had a ride on you."

"I've never slept with a man in my life. I'll take a polygraph any day to back up every word I've said."

"Do you think they'd care? They're taking everything he says at face value. You want to know where Grant got his flair for drama? He was a comedian in his previous incarnation. Before he got hooked up with CSIS, he worked in a strip joint. The girls were uncomfortable around him. The way he looked at them, the jokes he made, creeped people out."

I flashed back to the sleazy quips he'd made about Ruth, the sexual perversions he had accused so many others of. His penchant for sleaze, his attraction to seedy nightclubs where he interacted with strippers like the exotic dancer he was known to have dated. It sickened me. He was the same comedian he'd always been, using shock value for kicks; only his stage and audience had changed.

"And another thing," Martin continued. "Remember last summer, when he found out you were checking up on him? Did you know that Bristow approached Wolfgang and asked him to organize a break-in at your mother's apartment? That's how scared he was. Wolfgang told him no, and that made him furious. They had an argument about it, actually. The most heated argument they'd ever had. Apparently Wolfgang couldn't understand why Bristow was so adamant to get into your place. The idea of doing the break & enter made him uncomfortable."

I fell silent. I'd had no idea how close I came to the white van ride that Grant had threatened me with in the last conversation we had before I defected.

The revelation that CSIS had a vested interest in protecting both Grant (who walked around with a Get-Out-Of-Jail-Free card in his back-pocket) and their Heritage Front operation also helped answer one of the biggest questions on everyone's mind: why did the Attorney General never go after Wolfgang Droege with hate propaganda for the production of the Animal Life Series flyer that I had been charged with? Throughout 1995 my attorney, Paul Copeland, would write repeatedly to Metro Police and the OPP requesting that Wolfgang be charged with promoting racial hatred.

They would refuse.

"But there's a silver lining to this whole mess," Martin continued. "Wolfgang has called off the hunt for you. He's told everybody they should lay low and not bother to track you down. He actually likes that your affidavits tell exactly what Bristow's role was. Right now he's trying to position himself as a completely innocent party here, insinuating that the Front was meant to be a non-violent political party all along. As of this moment, you don't have to worry about the HF anymore. It's the other guys we still have to watch out for.

You've already seen the arsenal of tricks Bristow had up his sleeve. You know what we're up against. We're not dealing with dim-witted skinheads but sophisticated agents. Look at what they did to Brian McInnis. He was a Tory aide who intercepted a secret CSIS report more than a year ago that warned of a potentially rogue agent in the field. Brian couldn't live with his conscience and leaked the report. The RCMP charged him under the Official Secrets Act, squashed the whole thing and CSIS's operation continued merrily on its way.

Right now they're in damage control mode, and they're dangerous as hell."

THIRTY-FIVE

BABUSHKA DOLL

I saw Ruth and Annetta one last time before I left Nova Scotia. I rode the bus up the coastline to the rural town where they had bought a pretty, yellow two-story house. I remember little of that visit because the pain that stemmed from seeing them for the last time and facing Ruth's anger again made me shut down inside. What I do remember is sitting in a chair in the middle of their living room and Ruth practically shaking the living lights out of me.

"What the hell are you doing?" she was asking. "Can you hear me? *Hello?...*"

I closed my eyes. Maybe if I crawled into a tiny space inside my mind and went to sleep, I would wake up tomorrow and find out that everything had been a horrible dream.

Ruth leaned over and grasped me by the shoulders. "Elisse, *listen*. Going back to Ontario is suicidal. You do realize how dangerous Ottawa is, how close it is to Toronto? It's CSIS headquarters. The Hartmanns live there. What if you ran into Eric or his mother on the street? Are you sure you want to take the risk?"

When I said nothing, she spat out viciously, "Nobody should have to put themselves on the line for you. You're on your own. If you get into trouble, don't expect that you can run back to us. We've put ourselves in danger, put lots of cash into coordinating your travel expenses, all those long-distance phone calls to arrange safe houses for you, and for *what*? You've got to stop playing these fucking games."

Numbness was spreading through my limbs like venom. Why didn't she understand that I couldn't make it work in Halifax? Why did she have to put that huge burden of guilt on me? I could try to explain to her how hard it was to remain strong, to be in my shoes, always scared, hungry and alone. But by then I'd ran out of words. *What did it matter anymore?* We were all traumatized by what had happened. We were both victims. Only Ruth didn't see it; she was looking to pick a fight, trying to seek some form of acknowledgement from me, and I couldn't be bothered to make her understand. I was too far gone.

Getting no response from me, Ruth raised her voice. "Doesn't *anything* I've just said mean anything to you? What do you care about? Just name one thing. *One* goddamn thing."

I stared into her dark, furious eyes, and said nothing. What could I say that she didn't already know?

I love you. I've always loved you. You know this already. Martin knows this. Annetta does too. I wanted so badly for Grant Bristow and the It Campaign to be shut down because they hurt the woman I fell in love with. The woman who made me confront, for the first time, the reality that I was gay.

I did all this to protect you and all those other women hurt by his actions. You were my role model, my deprogrammer. I worshipped you. And now you hate me. Because by trying to keep me safe, you had to give up your life as you knew it.

In the end, he made enemies of us both.

But I said nothing.

I was ebbing away, fading into the nothingness of the kitchen walls, no energy left to defend myself. One lone tear slid down my cheek. As if anaesthetized, I couldn't make my hand reach up to wipe it off. Ruth was invariably right. By endangering my life, I'd found a way to keep myself alive, just as I did whenever I cut myself: it wasn't because I want to die but to save myself, to unclog the chimney, to release the muffled smoke that was trapped inside.

Some days I would drop a plate or a glass, just to see if it would really shatter. I wondered, *Is this real*? Is it me who is disassociating or is the universe a figment of my imagination? I'd flex my arm and wiggle my fingers, and they seemed real enough. The danger likewise was real, more than ever, but I could not, for the life of me, bring myself to feel it.

"What's wrong with you?" I heard Ruth's voice in the distance. "Are you in total denial? In shock? What the fuck's going on with you?"

I heard myself answer in a flat voice, "I'm a fucking coward."

"Wait, let me get this straight. You actually *want* them to find you? Do you have any idea what they'll do to you?"

She paused for dramatic effect, no doubt intending to make me conjure up a slew of horrible possibilities, but my mind remained blissfully blank.

I didn't care anymore.

As the purple streaks of the burgeoning sunset flittered over the horizon, I stared at my likeness in the glass of her kitchen window, at a face that reflected back to me an expression I could no longer understand.

In that face I saw history repeating itself – a hundred sagging sofas, washing underwear in scummy sinks, a new name to answer to, a never-ending succession of boring conversations and introductions to new roommates – running the dishwasher on Fridays, Spaghetti night Monday; the girl on the amateur volleyball team, the boyfriend who sleeps over on the weekends. A daisy chain of universes to which I am both mute witness and illegal immigrant.

'You can't run away forever,' an internal voice said. 'There comes a time when everything has to make its way back to its source. Water to water, earth to earth, dust to dust. Everything about you is a lie. Without official ID, you don't exist.'

Was I a ghost? Everywhere I went, I left no mark – no strand of fallen hair, no shred of emotional DNA. And once I passed through, it was as if I hadn't been there to begin with. The voices continued to mock me: *'Could anything be worse than this? Never knowing if you'll sleep in a real bed tonight, where your next meal will come from? Could it be that the idea of having your teeth kicked in and your head slammed against the pavement has turned into a numbness that makes you take risks you shouldn't?'*

I was a nobody. I'd made a habit of going through life stealing little pieces of everyone else's stories, but *I* was no one. My own life had been reduced to a series of quick fixes and emotional one-night-stands along a journey not of self-discovery, but of self-forgetting.

"I'm dead already," I said out loud, listening to my voice bounce hollowly off those whitewashed walls. "What's the point of hiding anymore? It only prolongs the finality of what's going to happen anyway."

Paradoxically, death was the only way out – either by my own hand, or by turning myself in to those who were trying to find me. It wasn't suicide, not really; true suicide meant having a new name, a different haircut, a fresh identity every month. Suicide was the death of my *Self*.

The real me had died a long time ago, and somebody else stood in my place. The only time when *I* counted anymore, when I could answer to my real name, was in a courtroom, on the witness stand. When I signed affidavits that destroyed other people's lives. When I destroyed everybody else at the cost of saving myself.

I went to stand in front of the bathroom mirror and stared blankly at a pale young girl who stared back at me through thick-fringed, haunted eyes.

"Why bother? I asked her. "Everybody's after you. What makes you think a fucked-up teenage girl can take on CSIS?"

When you're in hiding, you become a Babushka doll – one of those Russian lacquered dolls that's nestled one inside another, getting smaller and smaller until an itty-bitty core is reached. The problem was, the Babushka doll that formed my identity was so large that no matter how many shells I would come to peel back over the year to come, there was always another figure underneath. Roxanne, Nina, Emma, Eileen, Kate…. another incarnation, another past to fabricate, another story to hide behind.

I had carried the past like a house of bricks on my back. I kept its door bolted at all times. Rain fell, grass grew, snow blanketed the roof and promptly melted with the spring, but all entrances and windows were shuttered so tight that nothing could enter or escape.

Those who had seen my invisible house crouched away from it like old babushkas who'd survived world wars: they crossed the road with wooden canes, hunched over and afraid to look it in the eye.

They said things like, *Forgive and forget them, dear. Let God take care of dispersing punishment. If you want to live for the future, forget the past.*

What do you hope to accomplish? Shame us all, and what's the use?

The past is better left forgotten. Are YOU not a traitor? You think that airing out their *secrets somehow absolves you of* your *guilt and complicity?*

I looked back at the girl in the mirror. "I live the traitor's life," she taunted me. "Unlisted numbers, untraceable memories. Only the mirror knows my nationality. But the more I hide, the more I seem to remember. And the more I feel the weight of that house digging into my back."

It would never be over. *Never*.

A great rage went off inside me, a chill like liquid mercury. If I gave in now, *they* would win. All the work that Martin, Ruth and countless activists unknown to me put into ending the horrors of the Heritage Front would come to nothing. If I gave myself the release I wanted to badly, Grant and Wolfgang would triumph. I owed it to their victims to stay alive. To remain enraged.

I sent my fist smashing through the face that stared back at me. The girl's reflection split into a thousand slivers that slid down to my feet like crystal plumage. In the explosion of pain that ensued, my mind howled: "*I want to live! To love without endangering anyone, to not be afraid anymore. I want to be alive again.*"

And in that moment, surrounded by the agony of broken glass, I picked up a shard, held it against my arm, and made myself *feel*.

THIRTY-SIX

HITTING RESET

The Greyhound bus pulled into Ottawa's Catherine Street station just after ten PM on a rainy, freezing night. I emerged oozy and bleary-eyed, clutching a scruffy backpack, a black garbage bag filled with some extra clothes, and the address of an elderly German woman who would put me up for a month as a personal favour to Annetta.

I only had ten dollars in my pocket and the cab ride had taken seven bucks of it. Shivering, I climbed the three short steps that led up to a the porch of a Victorian brownstone and rang the doorbell. My stomach clenched. Even Annetta's tenderness and dedication to keeping me safe hadn't managed to heal the kneejerk reflex of panic triggered in me whenever I heard a German accent. It would be years before I could shed the visceral memory of all those Nazi sympathizers in Zundel's basement; before I could convince myself, at least in theory, that not all Germans are fascists.

Ulla was tall and broad-shouldered, with graying mid-ear hair, and exceedingly fond of slippers and wool cardigans. Her living room was occupied with dark green bookcases bursting with volumes I devoured on rainy afternoons. Ulla did not believe in television. She was enamored with BBC radio and read her morning newspapers with a side cup of English tea. I liked to watch her over breakfast, sipping my tea and scooping out the half of a grapefruit she had placed in front of me.

The mother of four grown sons who now lived all over the world, Ulla seemed content to live alone in her century-old house. Its pride and joy was an enormous claw-foot bathtub in a sunny bathroom with a backsplash of daisy-yellow tiles and solid, maple wood floors. I soaked in it for hours on end, trying to forget the nightmares of Nova Scotia, savouring the pleasure of thinking about nothing at all.

The first thing Ulla did after getting up punctually at seven every morning was put the kettle on. Then she shuffled over to the front door to let the Patches, her one-eyed tomcat, out for his daybreak roaming. She scooped up the Citizen off the porch landing, brought it inside and unfurled it over breakfast, perusing everything from the front page to the obituaries. Following breakfast, she slipped into her overcoat and went out to the small grocery store on Bank Street. I washed the dishes, added another spoonful of honey to my tea and felt like a tiny mouse lost in her house, tiptoeing around armchairs, bookshelves and windowsills.

Most of my days were spent maneuvering through the snowy streets of Ottawa, going door to door in stores and restaurants to inquire about work. Nobody had any need for additional staff, and I wasn't enough of a flirt to chat up some restaurant manager into changing his mind. I was too deflated by the constant rejections to come across as anything beyond morose. In retrospect, how could I blame those business owners for not hiring me, when all I had on was a ratty winter coat and running shoes whose soles had been eroded by the coarse salt shopkeepers threw along the roads to keep them from icing? I looked like a bum and nobody wanted to have anything to do with me.

Unfortunately, I still had no means of making money under the table, and the whole ID issue was putting a major damper on any prospects of legal employment. A desperate call to Martin led to an emergency proposition.

"Remember Gilles' farm?" he asked. "You could stay there for a while."

"What is a *while*, Martin?" I asked, clutching the receiver in desperation. "Is he gonna kick me out after a week? What exactly are you going to tell him?"

"Don't worry," Martin said in his usual blasé way that drove me absolutely nuts. "I will take care of it. He's a good, dependable guy."

"Jesus," I sighed, slamming the phone down. At the back of my mind I knew I should be grateful for Martin's last-ditch efforts to keep a roof over my head, but by now I couldn't help being more angry than appreciative. I'd be damned before I allowed what happened in Halifax to repeat.

The silver lining was, I absolutely loved living with Ulla. I tried my best to hide my concerns, recognizing that she needed to supplement her income with a tenant. At the end of the month I couldn't bring myself to put her in the position where she'd have to decide whether to let me stay for free or ask me to move out. I respected her too much so I lied and told her I was leaving town again.

Martin redoubled his efforts and arranged for me to make a few hundred dollars here and there from interviews with CTV National News, for appearing in *Hearts of Hate*, as well as giving a number of racism-prevention talks in Ontario high schools. I also participated in a high-profile Toronto City Hall meeting ran by the Toronto Coalition on Race Relations called *They Don't All Wear Sheets*. It wasn't a lot of money, but it sustained me temporarily since I could no longer depend on social assistance. We all knew what had happened the last time I'd used my SIN card.

Because I was adamant to remain in Ottawa, Martin asked his environmental activist acquaintance Mike to let me stay at his place again. This time I insisted on paying him $50 a month for rent, on principle, and even though Mike refused it at first, my persistence eventually wore him out.

Getting free food from the dumpster was one thing, but to truly survive you had to make money. Other than selling your blood at the Red Cross blood bank (which I couldn't bring myself to do because the sight of needles freaked me out), Lestat knew a quick and painless way to do it: just as my old pals Holly and Dave had taught me back in Toronto, the fastest, most efficient way of getting twenty bucks was through panhandling.

"You'll get at least twenty in a couple of hours. Being a girl has its advantages. But we can speed up the process. Sit still and let me transform you into the ultimate street waif."

He took some black shoe polish and smudged my cheeks. Then he picked up a roll of silver duct tape and wrapped it around the edges of my running shoes. He straightened, stared at me and started laughing.

"I should've gone into theatre. It's minus ten degrees outside with the wind chill and you have holes in your shoes. That'll really get them."

Looking uncannily like little Cossette out of *Les Miserables*, I parked myself on the front step of an office building on Cooper street in the business district, one of the smaller ones that didn't have a doorman to shoo me away. It was next to a soup and sandwich place that was a hotspot for office workers going for lunch.

Middle-aged office ladies hummed and hawed over my destitute state and especially those miserable running shoes. "You poor thing, you must be freezing," they fretted as they dropped coins, even five-dollar bills into my shivering hands.

"Have you had something to eat today?" someone invariably asked. I always said no, prompting the asker to dig in her purse for another pocketful of change. Once in a while someone would go into the café next door and bring me a brown paper bag with a hot sandwich. I'd take a tiny bite out of it until they looked satisfied and went back to their offices, whereupon I'd stuff it deep into my coat pocket.

Guilt prevented me from keeping any food for myself without splitting it with Lestat, who came and checked on me every hour. When I was so frozen I couldn't feel my toes and fingers anymore, he decided I'd had enough. "Come on, let's get moving," he whispered, rubbing my shoulders to get my circulation going again. On the way back to Mike's place he begged me to buy him a pie and I wouldn't. To this day, I regret being so frugal that I didn't splurge and get him that $4 pumpkin pie he had been craving all week.

In the span of four days, I made two hundred dollars. And by the time Lestat got locked up in the mental unit of CHEO a couple of months later, for having drained a willing Goth girl of a pint of blood and drinking it, I was proficient in the art of living without a penny to my name.

As spring came, I felt increasingly frustrated. My search for an under-the-table job was a complete failure. I called Ruth in Nova Scotia collect to ask for advice. I had no idea she'd scare me half to death when she heard how I was making my money.

"*Panhandling?*" she exploded over the phone. "Have you completely lost your mind? In *Ottawa*, of all places? The headquarters of CSIS, the one city you can bet all the government functionaries read the morning paper cover to cover? It only takes one person to recognize your face from the newspaper photos, Elisse. From all those CTV National broadcasts. *One* person, and your cover's blown. You don't want to move again, do you? Not that living in Ontario isn't an idiotic thing to do!"

She had a point. Too bad she couldn't express it without becoming enraged. Our friendship had dissolved long before this conversation took place. In Toronto I had been like a child to her, eager to please; once in Halifax, I'd evolved into a rebellious teenager. She'd had enough of it and didn't hesitate to remind me of this every time we spoke.

But the harsh words and abrasive way in which she approached the topic left me crying. I felt broken up inside, knowing that Ruth couldn't stand me. She didn't consider me family anymore, even though she had promised that she'd always be in my life. But the stresses of the past year had traumatized both of us in different ways. I understood her position implicitly. At the same time, how could I explain to her that she wasn't there in my shoes, she didn't have to deal with the constant deprivation and the fear that had turned to numbness. As much as I hated being a total disappointment to her, I knew I had to be accountable to myself first.

"You don't know what it's like...." I tried to say. "Nobody will hire me...."

"Did you know that begging for money is technically *illegal*?" she yelled into the receiver, so loudly that I had to hold it away from my ear. "Any cop could pick you up and enter your name into the computer. Do you want to be arrested again? Do you have *anything* to say for yourself? How can you do this to us, after we've put so much money over the last year into keeping you underground and on the move? We don't have CSIS's witness protection budget, you know. Just who the hell do you think you are?"

That day in Mike's vegan kitchen was the last time I would speak with Ruth. I sobbed into the telephone, apologizing for having made yet another mistake. I promised to stop panhandling and I kept my word, but that left me in the same lurch as before – penniless and dependent on Mike, Lestat and the dumpster for my every meal.

At the environmental centre where Mike was director, I got a tip-off about a program run by the Youth Services Bureau on Rideau Street. It was a last-resort for youth who couldn't otherwise be hired due to their young age or lack of references. They paid kids $3 an hour to train them in 'job skills' for 2 weeks, then arranged 3-month job placements. Afterwards it was expected that we would have a good reference and might even be kept on by the employer.

292

Working for three bucks an hour seemed like modern-day sweatshop, but you do what you have to out of necessity. I had no choice but to use my ID – it was either that or panhandle for survival. Behind closed doors, I rattled off a brief description of my situation: "I've been a witness in a court case but the cops refused to give me witness protection and therefore I have no money and I'm supposed to be in hiding."

My assigned social worker promised that I could enter my job placement under an alias since their government-run youth employment agency was the only one cutting the cheques. I made up a fictitious address to put in their dossier and figured nobody could track me down unless they ambushed me going in or out of the centre on Rideau Street.

After two weeks of instructional classes on making resumes and the basics of labour laws, everyone was pumped with excitement. The adrenaline swelled as we began making phone calls and faxing our resumes. Most of the guys approached mechanic and auto-body shops; the girls were mostly keen on service and sales positions. I wanted to do something completely different.

Following an afternoon appointment with a Human Resources manager, I landed a position in the mailroom of a large downtown law firm, one with seven names to their title, like Smith & Wesson & Clarke & Gamble, Esquire, Attorneys at law. The whole time I worked there, I never got the hang of answering the phone and rattling off the name of the firm as smoothly as the girl who'd been there two years already. All of the lawyers' names started with the same letter, forming a veritable tongue-twister. Whenever the phone rang and I was alone in the backroom, I cheated. "Mailroom!" I'd answer perkily, crossing my fingers that nobody would call me on it.

The next month I bid Mike farewell and moved closer to the office. For the $3 per hour I was being paid I couldn't afford the bus fare from Mike's flat in the Glebe to work so I rented a room closer to downtown for $200 monthly from a university student doing her Master's degree at the University of Ottawa.

The move ended up being a good choice. Julie filled my evenings with stories of her crushes on professors and adventures at school. Her ultimate dream was to meet the man of her dreams and pop out a couple of kids – and the sooner these happened, the better.

"Do you ever want to have kids?" she asked me.

My answer was always, "No. I don't want to worry about a child."

"But risk is part of life. You have to risk getting hurt when you fall in love, don't you?"

"It's different."

I wanted to ask her, Do you *really* want the trepidation of watching the one you cradled in your arms and fed at your breast stumble away from you, falling and crying but always moving further out of range, propelled by an inexplicable ache for exploration that stabs you through the heart?

Julie pressed on. "Is it because you're afraid you'll end up like your mother?"

I wanted to tell her, I don't want to bear the weight of my grandmother's fears as she looked out the same window where so many other women stood before her, arms tucked like prayers in the hollows of elbows, holding themselves tightly as they fought against the cold that always finds a way to seep in – the cold of *What If? Will my boy come home tonight?*

No, I don't want to be like my mother, standing on that concrete balcony, her eyes piercing the back of my head, so heavy with regrets - regrets of abandonment, regrets of a wretched life that vibrates between us like a shout. Eyes that plead after me wordlessly until I am swallowed up by the urban greyness of the city.

I don't want to carry my worry inside me like a shadow infant. Everyone knows that after the actual birth a secret pregnancy continues, an afterbirth that you carry in your spirit forever. Even as your baby turns into a toddler, then youth and finally adult, your worry claws you through the heart, becoming the pulse in your veins and the throb in your gut.

I don't want that. I don't want to bear the pain of creating something as fragile as a human being only to watch her slip away. I don't want to tell her about my past hurts and all the hurts of her grandmothers and great-grandmothers before that. I don't want her to inherit the suffering of her forefathers, the ache of a wounded country, the flesh of generations of women bloodied by revolutions and wretched men, by abandonment and despair.

"No," I said instead. "I will never be like that, because I've never had a mother."

THIRTY-SEVEN

THE SHADOWS

Darkness. Streaks of gunfire against the backdrop of a bloody horizon. A tattered banner strung over the top of a rolled barbed-wire formation. Strips that looked as though they'd been sliced by a knife, wavering in the daybreak winds. A small group of survivalists huddled together inside a warehouse with ample wood slats hammered in places where once there had been windows. They kept their heads down, busily loading bullets into magazines, locking those magazines into place as the sound of explosions loomed in the near distance. I struggled to make out the people's features in the dimness. Nobody took any notice of me. They continued to labor over weapons silently, beads of sweat wetting the edges of bandannas that covered the lower part of their faces.

One man looked up, without warning. Our eyes met. A hideous glare of unadulterated hatred knocked my breath away. Then the man began to smile – I could see the formations of his lips twisting underneath the cloth mask, the crinkles along the sides of his eyes deepening as he now broke into laughter. I turned to run, but my feet were soldered into place.

My eyes snapped open. Cold sweat had dampened my hair along my brow ridge and behind my head, where the nape of my neck remained sticky against the pillow. I exhaled, relief spreading through me. *Only a dream.*

No matter how many nightmares I'd had over the last year, I could never get used to them. I was impressed by the ability of my subconscious mind to make up disturbing violence, each episode more gruesome than the last. People's limbs being torn clear off, decapitated heads rolling to my feet, bodies flapping around spurting blood like my grandmother's chickens after their heads had been severed with a hack of her butcher knife.

The nightmares had gotten so bad that, just like in Halifax, my social worker at the Youth Employment Services office referred me to a psychotherapist.

"Everyone finds it helpful to talk to someone," he told me. "Even people with a fraction of the things you've had to deal with. Just work on your PTSD so you can at least sleep at night."

Over a period of several months I met with a counsellor in the converted attic of an old Edwardian house off Bank Street. My therapist was fond of fruity teas, so every session I was offered a mug of strawberry-flavoured Lipton. I held the cup in my hands, stared at the swirling steam rising and allowed myself to unwind. "Is it possible to feel sorry for someone but not forgive them?" I asked her. "Is it possible to move forward without forgetting the past?"

"Sure it is. There is a great difference between forgiving and forgetting – when you forgive, you hang up your coat of anger. When you forget, you put aside all memories of bad things. Forgiving is implied since you can't be angry at someone when you forget what they've done."

She paused. "But there are things that cannot be forgotten. Some scars you can't wipe clean, so you do your best to forgive those who cut them into your heart. Even then, some people don't deserve that forgiveness."

I nodded. "I think that by forcing yourself to forgive, you do more harm than good – you harm the integrity of your own pain. You betray your own suffering." I contemplated the narrow walls, the way the roof sloped toward the corner. "I think there's such a thing as healthy anger. Letting go of pain and fear without necessarily forgiving someone. Why does everybody always think you can't heal unless you forgive a perpetrator?"

"Exactly," she said. "You can move on in life without having to give blessing to someone who harms you. You owe them nothing. Your experiences have made you who you are today. You're stronger because of everything you went through."

"I choose *not* to forget," I said. "Nor to forgive. I read somewhere that history which is forgotten is doomed to repeat itself."

"We all learn lessons from our own histories. Trying to excise the bad from the good only serves to deprive us of the strength we gained from those challenges."

Growing up, I'd heard people say that "time heals all wounds." Somehow this expression always seemed wrong to me. As if you're only entitled to a brief acceptable period in which to feel pain, and after that the expectation is that the pain will have lessened just because your memory has receded. But what if you simply let go of the pain – by making the commitment to yourself that you will *not* forget? Wouldn't this honour your history more, by not adding or subtracting anything from its pages?

After the session I went for a walk to my favourite spot in Ottawa, the peak of Major Hill's Park. From its summit, I could face the flowing Rideau River and the Parliament buildings and listen to the churn of boat engines and the screaming of seagulls in the air. I'd eat a deep-fried Beaver Tail pastry I bought from the Market, sprinkled with sugar and lemon juice, and watch the water splash white spume against the rocks below.

That's where I invariably asked myself how long this moment would last. Before I'd have to move again. Before I'd be tempted to reach over that balustrade and hurl myself into the waves.

I reflected on the fact that we live in a world where right and left are mirror images of each other. They march along the rivers of Belief toward the Utopia of the Revolution. They pray to red flags and place manifestos under pillows. And each soldier has become blinded to the fact that, at first, everyone carries the same dreams, the same hopes, the same faces of youth toward the fervent zealotry that fuels the flames of radicalism.

In every city that became my home I was a prisoner to freedom, to the infinity of the roads I could take. There were so many possibilities to choose from that I couldn't budge from the crossroads. *Who am I? Who do I want to be?* What part of my fake identities has been discarded, what has remained? Where is my essence? Am I Elisse, the teenage revolutionary, or little Eliza running through the streets of Bucharest in her tattered dress? Which fragments of my splintered self do I still keep, which do I throw away?

THIRTY-EIGHT

BROKEN SUNLIGHT

In April 1995, Dale Brazao of the Toronto Star blew the cover on Grant Bristow's new name and whereabouts. He was now in St. Albert, a suburb of Edmonton, Alberta, where he was enjoying a 2000 square foot, four-bedroom, three-car garage home worth at the time about $200K in an exclusive neighbourhood. Both him and his wife had two new cars – a minivan and a Ford sedan – and drawing a $3,000-a-month government allowance. According to Brazao, Bristow's wife had apparently negotiated unlimited long-distance calling privileges and several all-expense-paid trips each year to visit family in Mississauga.

It was sickening.

After my initial shock wore off, something inside me snapped. I woke up one morning and realized that I didn't give a shit anymore. Why spend the spend the rest of my life angry about the generosity this government showered upon the man who had founded the Heritage Front and organized a campaign of terror and abuse against innocent people? What was the point? If the Canadian public didn't feel outraged enough to put an end to this miscarriage of justice, why should I care?

Many would say I was rightfully entitled to hate Grant and the organization that had covered up for him. The thing is, I didn't hate the fact that he hit the CSIS jackpot just by being, in my mind, a remorseless asshole who had followed his sadistic nature and got away with it – I hated him because he hurt people I loved. Because I saw the subtle changes in their eyes – the loss of innocence, the hardness caused by being fearful and mistrusting. The emotional scars that had transformed Ruth imperceptibly, even if she herself didn't know it.

But in the end, holding on to resentments would mean I allowed them to win. Not just Grant himself, but his despicable handler Al

Treddenick and all those without a conscience in CSIS and SIRC who had already accomplished their objective when they whitewashed the truth and promoted their revisionist version of what actually took place. When SIRC acted, as former Tory ministerial aide Brian McInnis put it, "more as a lapdog than a watchdog" by conceding that while 'The Source' may have been just a tad 'overzealous' in his work, he had done so in the best interest of society.

They could rewrite history all they wanted, but I wasn't going to let them destroy my future. Unlike Grant, I didn't need CSIS or their blood money to make a new life – I would earn my keep by my own hand.

Sharing the flat with Julie was a lot of fun. We went to the movies together and chatted about cinema, sex and philosophy, the latter of which was her field of study. Her family owned a moving company that was regularly contracted to pack up the contents of vacant houses and clear storage spaces. As a result they often came into possession of discarded furniture and books that ended up in Julie's collection. We spent hours talking about literature on our daily walks. Julie weighed over two hundred lbs. and was determined to get in shape by embarking on a regimen of brisk walks through the neighboring streets. Not having much else to do, I tagged along and we became fast friends.

Two months after living together, I told her my story. I didn't really have a choice since a documentary I had participated in, *Hearts of Hate*, was airing on all the networks and she was bound to see it.

Her first reaction was, "No shit. You're like, a spy. How cool is that?"

It felt like she'd just slapped me, but I kept my mouth shut. How could I hold it against her, this Hollywood-fed incomprehension of how fortunate she was to have a family? To belong to a circle of friends, to love someone without fearing that any day now the phone will ring and she'd have to pack her entire life into a carry-on suitcase and run out the back door. How could she *ever* understand that in order to live out this kind of existence, the real you must *die*. There's no excitement in that - there's no love or tenderness there, no security whatsoever.

One afternoon in early spring, while marking papers for a first-year class, Julie paused to take a drag of her cigarette. She looked sideways at me and blurted out, "You know, I meet such idiots every day. I mark essays written so badly they make me want to puke. I don't see why *they're* in school and not you. You write better than that. You're so bright. Why don't you apply for September?"

Her question took me by surprise. "Do you really think I could do it?"

She snickered. "If you only knew some of the people enrolled in higher education… it's all a scam, a class-based misconception, the whole idea that people in university are so much smarter than everybody else. All you need to succeed are two things – be able to write well and have the ability to memorize. With either one of these you can make it through school. If you have both, sky's the limit. I don't think you'd have *any* problems."

Later that evening I gave it more thought. I stretched out on my lumpy futon, unable to sleep. Indeed, why not? Provided that I hadn't attended school for two years, all I needed to apply as a Mature Student was a high school diploma, an essay and two reference letters. I wondered what it would be like to be part of a grand institution with ivy-covered walls and teachers who inspire and shape the best in the generations of tomorrow. Maybe I romanticized something that didn't exist anymore. Still, could I *really* do it? There was no one to call for advice or support. Who would care if I succeeded? Who would I celebrate my victories with?

Back in Halifax, I'd taken the High School equivalency exam. My social worker had asked if I wanted to enroll in evening classes, but I'd declined. "Let me just take the test," I said. "If I pass it, I don't have to go to night school."

She looked at me dubiously. "You haven't had any schooling since ninth grade. Do you really think you can just show up at the testing centre one day and pass every subject?"

"We won't know until I try," I told her.

The standardized GED exam took two full days to complete. I was the youngest person in a room of close to two hundred people. Balling my hands into fists, I picked up my pencil and battled the questions in front of me with the same earnest, idealistic desperation that had propelled me through the last year.

Six weeks later, a large envelope arrived in the mail from the Nova Scotia Board of Education. Inside was my diploma – my real-life, high school diploma! Scanning the transcript of results, I saw that my English essay had scored in the 99th percentile. I sank down on the edge of my bed and wept. How odd, to feel both so empowered and sad at how long it had taken for me to get here.

The week Julie mentioned I should go to university, I decided to stroll through Ottawa U.'s grounds in Sandy Hill. The campus was crawling with sheltered kids who were going home for the summer. Staring at them, I knew that in order to succeed I had to accept the fact that I was alone. Truly alone. This realization haunted me as I walked through the parks and back streets of the campus watching scores of cars pull up to dorm buildings. Parents would walk up the path, embrace their offspring, go inside and then reemerge with roll-on suitcases and laundry hampers full of their kids' belongings.

Strength is a choice. Whether I do this or not, no one will care. I matter to nobody. This is a hard truth for a nineteen-year old girl to admit, but nonetheless it had to be done in order to move into the next stage of my life.

I'm a weed growing through cracked cement. I am my only source of water.

With nobody to impress, can I motivate myself to thrive?

I couldn't move forward until I sorted this stuff out in my head and toughened up. *I won't back down,* I told myself. Just like when I was a little kid in Bucharest, using anger as a propelling force to show that I mattered too. If I could be that strong at nine years old, why couldn't I do it at nineteen?

It seemed like everywhere I went, at the Youth Employment Services meetings, at the free women's counseling drop-ins, I was surrounded by others who embraced their failures; who relived, over and over, sad stories of alcohol and drug abuse. So rampant were people's tales of how their lives had been so completely fucked up by neglecting and alcoholic parents that it all turned into a mantra in my head, a mantra that justified an abandonment of control over one's own reality.

Pain was their comfort zone. The only thing they found familiar. They couldn't see that owning their lives wasn't about topping each other's sob story to catch the attention of a counselor who really didn't give a shit because he or she was paid by the hour.

As I sat in circle after circle of people recounting their pain, I started getting angry, not just at the abusers but at the ones who were so readily embracing their fates as victims. Ultimately, isn't there always someone with a worse story? There are kids in this world who have been raped every day, who've been beaten so badly their bones are a heap of fracture upon fracture, who were locked in rooms for years with no stimulation until they turned feral. And if you aren't one of them, if somehow you made it out of your childhood more or less in one piece, you should be *proud* to have survived.

I refused to give my "parents" that much power. I didn't owe them anything. I hadn't asked to be born. I didn't do anything to deserve being hurt and neglected. At this crossroads where adolescence merged into adulthood, I had to be more resilient than ever before. I had to choose whether I'd allow myself to fall apart and blame my current situation, along with my fluctuating states of depression, on everyone else or take charge of my own life.

This is about defiance, I thought. An unadulterated, ferocious defiance – defying the lousy cards you were dealt, defying the beatings, the bad words, the labels that have been affixed upon you. Getting past the fact that nobody has ever recognized your potential or your basic worth as a human being. That someone who, with full legal impunity, terrorized others to the brink of mental breakdown and suicide was handed a happy ending by a government that couldn't care less about your harsh beginning.

So fucking what?

So what if everybody's always looked at you with a mixture of pity and revulsion in their eyes, laughed at your dreams, bashed your future goals and said you couldn't do it – you're too damaged, too broken to get anywhere in life?

Only *you*, deep within your own heart, know what you are capable of. Nobody else can determine that for you. This is about defying the rest of the world who goes to sleep at night and doesn't have to encounter the nightmares that lurk there.

It's about transforming the rage that burns inside you into a propelling force that pushes you forward.

It's about looking straight into the eyes of the children whose middle-class parents footed their university fees and saying silently: *I will do better than you.* When you're out partying and getting wasted during frosh week like a spoiled kid away from home for the first time, I will beat you.

I will get a 90% grade point average in my first year.

I will get into that sought-after Honours Criminology program that lets in only twenty people every year, and then into Psychology too because hey, two majors are better than one.

I'll be accepted into that coveted writing class and I will beat you to the varsity team.

I will be on the Dean's Honour List for four years in a row while you have to explain to your mommy and daddy why you're failing first year English.

And finally, I will graduate Magna cum Laude (in 1999, as it turned out) while you barely screech past the finish line, all the while bitching that your professors are elitist and unfair.

But before all this would come to pass, on that first night after Julie had planted the thought in my mind, I couldn't fall asleep. I twisted around in bed, trying to push away the crazy idea that I – a ninth grade dropout nobody thought would amount to anything – could actually do it. But the thought had taken root already. Like a fast-growing beanstalk, it sprouted all sorts of possibilities within me.

So what was stopping me?

"I have no money," I said out loud.

Julie offered to lend me a hundred dollars for the application fee. She went over all the ins and outs of student loans. As long as I have no family to support me, I shouldn't have any problems qualifying. She herself had left home a year earlier in order to qualify for OSAP without a co-signer. She was a veteran now, well into her fifth year of borrowing.

On Monday she walked me over to the Office of the Registrar and we picked up an application. Back at home, she wrote me a cheque. The following week, after I'd my received my recommendation letters, I dropped off the application in the mail. The waiting had begun.

The day I received the letter of acceptance from the University of Ottawa, I was sitting on the front steps of my boarding house. I tore open the envelope eagerly, a stream of sunlight making me squint just as I read the words "We are pleased to extend our acceptance…".

I started laughing and crying at the same time. It was surreal to know that after everything that happened, I had a chance to start again. At nineteen, I was only one year older than most other freshmen but it felt like I had lived a lifetime. I had skipped high school and gone directly into the study of human nature and its incredible range of expression: I had learned about brutality, deceit and intolerance from Grant Bristow, Wolfgang Droege and Ernst Zundel, and I had experienced compassion, love and tenderness from people I'd thought were my enemies.

The following Wednesday I dropped by the Youth Services Bureau to share the good news with my caseworker. He didn't believe me. In fact, until I produced two letters of acceptance bearing the crests of both Carleton and the University of Ottawa, everyone in the office thought I was kidding. After some whispering, one of the social workers finally decided to take it upon himself to pull me into his office. He closed the door and gestured for me to take a seat. He leaned against the edge of his desk.

"I heard you're applying to university, Kat."

"Yes," I beamed. "I got my acceptance letters this week from both of the universities where I applied. Can you believe it? *Both* of them."

"Right, yes," he said, his chin nearly falling into his chest. "I wanted to speak with you about that." He finally met my gaze. "You *do* know university is very, very difficult, don't you? It's extremely hard to keep your grades straight and keep up with the academic demand. Not a lot of people make it."

"I don't think I'll have any problems," I said.

He frowned. "Yes, well, the thing is, I would hate to see you fail after a semester. You *do* know a lot of first-years drop out after six months, right? It's a very rigorous, demanding commitment and I'd hate to have you lose your place in our program, only to start from scratch in a few months…"

"I won't be back here," I said, looking him right in the eye. "Do you think I *want* to be in a program that pays me three bucks an hour to do menial work? You're a social worker – aren't you supposed to encourage me? Why are you sitting here trying to talk me out of pursuing higher education? *I know* I can do this. I don't need you to tell me what *you* think is good for me. You know absolutely *nothing* about my potential!"

With that, I leapt out of the chair, slammed the door to his office behind me and walked out of the Youth Services office into the gusty Ottawa Market. I was done with people judging my worth. I was done being afraid of powerful men in influential positions who used the scars of my childhood and the turbulence of my teenage years as a pretext to condescend, manipulate and intimidate.

A brilliant sunlight greeted me when I was back on the street. I paused, all too aware that I had no money in my pockets and no guarantees in my empty hands. I carried within me only a lifetime's worth of dreams that probably would never come true and yet, somehow, I felt freer than I'd ever felt before. As if to punctuate that moment, the warm breeze on my face felt like a caress and tasted like freedom.

THIRTY-NINE

DENOUEMENT

It didn't come as a surprise to anybody that the first investigation into The Grant Bristow Affair, fast-tracked by the Security Intelligence Review Committee (SIRC), would clear the man identified only as The Source of any specific wrongdoing. Three factors in particular set off everybody' bullshit detector:

1) SIRC was not especially interested in interviewing victims of the terror campaign, nor were they willing to pay for my flight back to Toronto to testify, even though I had witnessed Bristow in action. Being that at the time of their investigation I was stuck in Halifax with no money to buy a winter coat and dumpster-diving for survival, I'm pretty sure that – with some serious budget-crunching, no doubt – CSIS' coffers could have withstood the enormous blow of paying for a flight that, in 1994, cost $200 return. Especially as it involved the most serious allegations against a Canadian spy since CSIS' inception.

2) The hearings would be held behind closed doors, in total secrecy. There was absolutely nothing to guarantee that a witness or victim's statements wouldn't be altered in any way. They denied everyone who requested it the presence of a lawyer during the questioning. After what Grant Bristow and his handlers had done already, could anyone be blamed for being nervous about secret hearings and a lack of transparency?

3) The extent of fabrications in the whitewashed report, spurred on by boldfaced lies from CSIS, was disturbing. Coupled with the omission of victim testimonies, the findings generated enough public outrage and ridicule to provoke a brand new investigation. From far left to conservative right, all were united in their anger. Preston Manning, whose Reform Party's reputation was significantly damaged by the

Heritage Front infiltration, called SIRC's report "a whitewash, a cover-up and a disgrace".

The new investigation would not to be conducted by CSIS. Testimony would be presented in the House of Commons in Ottawa, in front of a newly-established panel of cabinet ministers in charge of assessing the questionable actions of 'The Source'.

Martin and I didn't really expect that any government committee, as impartial as they might be, would find CSIS guilty of bankrolling a white supremacist organization. A scandal like that could shake up a government to its foundations. But, judging by the fact that they were at least willing to accommodate travel expenses for me and Paul Copeland, my legal counsel, to attend the hearing in order to be interviewed, they were noticeably more open to the truth than the previous investigative panel had been.

And what did we have to lose, anyway, that we hadn't lost already? I was willing to tell everybody what I had seen. I wanted to scream it from the rooftops, to shake the reality into ordinary Canadians who were more preoccupied with Hockey Night in Canada than with the actions of their own government.

To add insult to injury, SIRC's findings stated that although Bristow was involved in *some* harassment campaigns against anti-racist activists (*Some*? He was involved in *all* of them. He gave out the target names!), they were "at the limit of the tolerable."

Did the "limit of tolerable" include bringing together disagreeing racists who'd seldom worked together effectively and teaching them how to provide security, how to infiltrate political parties, how to use private investigation skills, tactical deception and high-end gadgetry to hone in on an unsuspecting target? Was it *tolerable* for CSIS to use taxpayers' money to routinely (1988-1994) cover the cost of white supremacists' meals, office supplies, gifts (such as the gold jewelry and dress I received), meeting hall costs, gas and car rentals, plus throwing cash into the potty as needed?

Did the "limit of tolerable" involve The Source getting up one morning and deciding, *This isn't fun enough. Let me start my own spy group* within *the movement, just for kicks?* Was it within "the limit of tolerable" to distribute lists of target names whom Heritage Front members had never heard before? To give out home/work addresses and phone numbers and instruct skinheads he knew were armed and dangerous to go after these activists 24 hours a day – to stalk, harass, telephone, play dirty tricks upon, follow along on the street (while teaching us how to cover our tracks) until our victims, to put it in Grant Bristow's exact words, "shit their pants, have a total breakdown and self-destruct"?

Was it tolerable for Grant to call me one afternoon, full of glee, and tell me that Ruth finally "had a breakdown" and took "a leave of absence"? To laugh to the point of tears when he said, "She's tried very hard to hold unto sanity and not given any names as of yet, but I'm confident she'll break soon. She's even had people move in with her because she's so scared" (an admission that he had people watching her house). And because of that, that we needed to target her more than ever, until she became completely suicidal? Until she "ended up in a mental hospital, being spoon-fed and unable to control her bowel movements". Was it tolerable for him to tell an impressionable Heritage Front member, "I want to pound Ruth's head in. I want to give her a facial massage with a sledgehammer."

Was it within the *"limits of tolerable"* for CSIS that dozens of activists were terrorized, some driven to psychological breakdowns or contemplated suicide? Was it *tolerable* for Rodney Bobiwash to wear a bulletproof vest 24 hours a day? Was it *tolerable* for Bristow to privately assist White Aryan Resistance leaders Tom and John Metzger to enter Canada illegally, and then, just for shows, have them nabbed in a major immigration sting/aka photo-op for CSIS?

Was it *tolerable* for Bristow to circulate rumours that I was an unbalanced whore who had slept with every guy in the group? Was it *tolerable* for his handlers /superiors to send out specific directives to every police force from OPP to RCMP to disregard my affidavits? Was it *tolerable* for them to made sure none of the white supremacists in Grant's circle would ever be charged or convicted with weapons possession or any other criminal activity? There is no doubt in my mind that thanks to CSIS' interference, most of the AK47s, M16s and .45s I provided information about are still on the street today, and likely in the hands of extremists.

The night before my testimony, Martin and I met at an undisclosed location where he proceeded to fill me in on the ugly details of what had transpired over the last year. While I had attempted to pull my life together, CSIS had fought to salvage their reputation and had succeeded for the most part.

"Always remember that these guys started out as RCMP," he told me. "Before CSIS was born in the 1980s, RCMP officers were breaking into offices, bugging telephones, burning down barns and blaming that on the FLQ. Why do you think that intelligence squad was disbanded and CSIS was born?"

Martin laughed hollowly. "It was the same men, Elisse. They were just transferred from one organization to the next. Bristow's handler Al Treddenick used to be with the RCMP before *that* intelligence service was discredited and CSIS was created. CSIS's regional director in Quebec was part of dirty tricks carried out by the RCMP in the 1970s. His second-in-command was the handler of Marc Boivin, who was involved in dirty tricks in the labour movement in Quebec in the 1980s. The same guys who provoked criminal activity and blamed it on Quebecois separatists, now spearhead our nation's intelligence agency. It's the same old boys club."

After the Bristow fallout, CSIS went into damage-control mode by showing a united front. In the meanwhile, an internal clean-up investigation commenced in order to rid their ranks of rotten apples. Although no one wanted to go on record to confirm this, word along the grapevine was, Grant' handler was either demoted or removed from his post.

But not Grant.

Martin shook his head. "The SIRC Report states The Source acted in good faith. We know that's bullshit. We know how interested they were in the truth when they refused to fly you down from Halifax. How were you supposed to go meet them, with no money? And why did they only want to interview you in a clandestine proceeding, without Paul Copeland present. *Why* is that? What were they trying to hide?" He paused. "And not all the victims have come forward. They're too frightened."

"So we did all this for nothing."

"No. We dismantled the Heritage Front. And we put an end to Operation Governor – you, me, Rodney, Ruth, Annetta, Brian McInnis, Bill Dunphy….just the few of us. We all played our part. You know how bad this looks for them, don't you? That a handful of civilians single-handedly destroyed something that had taken them years to build? And we didn't even know what we were doing, not at first."

Martin stifled a laugh. He got up and went to the coffee-maker to pour himself a cup of coffee. His hand shook involuntarily as he walked back to the table, nearly spilling the liquid.

A public commendation, a fast handshake, was the only way for the Canada's Security Intelligence Service to scrub-clean its name. By clearing Grant Bristow of all his dues, they themselves evaded scrutiny. Otherwise, how could they justify sucking funds from Canadian taxpayers if they had to be accountable for protecting a criminal? They wanted him to fade into the shadows, someplace far up north, and never take the stand against them because who knew what kind of information might be revealed if *he* opened his mouth?

I was seized by an impulse to stomp my feet, to scream out loud: THIS ISN'T FAIR! But my pragmatic, disillusioned side kicked in. Nothing that had happened was fair. CSIS would never be accountable for their actions in Operation Governor. In fact, with SIRC as their overseer, they would most likely continue to be above reproach.

They would destroy wiretapping evidence on suspects in the 1985 Air India bombing as part of a "default" policy that included *erasing hundreds of hours* of phone calls by Talwinder Singh Parmar, a well-known Sikh extremist and prime suspect in the Air India bombing. Why would an intelligence agency erase *anything*, one wonders, if there wasn't anything to hide?

Along with the RCMP, they would pay informers millions of dollars to testify against alleged terrorists without addressing the obvious question of conflict of interest.

They would be used on behalf of the Harper government to spy on critics of oil pipeline projects that include the Sierra Club, the Council of Canadians, and even Green Party Leader Elizabeth May. Even as I write this segment now, in 2014, documents obtained through Access of Information requests show that CSIS and the RCMP took direction from the National Energy Board to monitor and report on "threats" to the project's federal review panel by pipeline opponents – including advocacy groups Idle No More and ForestEthics.

Although this is only a perfunctory shortlist, such behaviour on the part of a taxpayer-funded agency that is supposed to guard the rights of its nation's citizens underscores a decades-long pattern of abuse, deception, secrecy and lack of accountability, as well as an ingrained, endemic mentality that its agents are above the law.

And indeed, they are. When is the last time CSIS admitted wrongdoing and issued an official apology? When has a CSIS officer ever been prosecuted under the same laws that we are all supposed to abide by?

The official cover-up of Grant Bristow's misconduct was only the tip of the iceberg. The It Campaign's list of victims was long, and the criminals were going to get away scot-free. Maybe even get a plaque of commendation.

The system of checks and balances that should have been in place had failed spectacularly. Grant and his superiors had become locked in a puppeteer's fantasy of omnipotence from where they could play one human being against the other with impunity. They had turned the entire city into a playground where they pitched people against each other in a disturbing spy-against-spy scenario of psychological warfare. Even the remote possibility of an internal demotion or clean-up job would do nothing to make up for what had taken place.

"It's a pity that your affidavits were never followed up on," Martin said, a heart-wrenching smile playing on his face. He lit up another cigarette, and the blue haze that was swirling between us accentuated the equally-blue spidery veins in his pallid face, the deep hollows ever-present beneath his dark eyes.

"If the public ever realized how many convictions we could have gotten, how many illegal weapons could have been taken off the streets....All that evidence flushed down the toilet, just to protect *one* rogue agent. And the sick thing is, Grant Bristow wasn't somebody who was recruited out of the Heritage Front – he was recruited by CSIS nearly a year *BEFORE* the founding of the Heritage Front." He exhaled. "Without Bristow, the Front would not have come to be the group it became."

I started to shake my head. "But what about us? Do *we* get a new identity? Are *we* being publicly hailed as heroes?"

Martin smiled again. "You can't stop the average Joe from believing what's spoon-fed to him on the evening news. You can't stop the Canadian Jewish Congress from inviting Grant to be their guest speaker. They cannot face the truth of how insidious this operation was, how they themselves were targets. That reality is too painful for most people to bear. It's easier to give him a standing ovation than accept that your own government set up the extremist group that spray-painted three synagogues in Toronto last year."

"But people have a right to know what really happened. If we don't do something about it, decades from now their version will be accepted as the official story. I refuse to let them get away with it!"

"You may not have a choice in the matter, Elisse."

I placed my hand over his long, ashen fingers, and looked him right in the eye. My heart was breaking for him. After all he had done to shut down the Heritage Front, he was likely blackballed for government positions, the government funding to the Canadian Centre on Racism and Prejudice had been revoked without explanation, and the only comfort he could find was at the bottom of a bottle.

"Of course I have a choice," I said. "*You*, of all people, have taught me this. If it's the last thing I do, I'm not going to let them rewrite history. I'm not afraid anymore."

FORTY

TESTAMENT
Ottawa, Tuesday, June 13, 1995

Today I testified in front of the House of Commons Sub-Committee on National Security about the criminal activities of an agent on the payroll of our country's Intelligence agency. My testimony and subsequent question period lasted just over two hours. When I was excused, my legs quivered badly. I couldn't tell if it was due to elation or just being drained.

Then it was Martin's turn in front of the panel.

What I can tell you about as a researcher - because I also work for the English magazine Searchlight *- is that I had a contract in February 1993 with the Office of the Solicitor General of Canada to do a study of racist groups in Canada and their potential danger to national security. In the course of this study, I met members of the OPP, of various police forces, and so forth. I also met Crown prosecutors in Ontario and Quebec. I noticed that when Elisse's affidavits were handed over to the OPP, it was a new officer who was looking after these issues and he was not at all familiar with the neo-Nazi movement in Canada. So, obviously, I thought he was going to consult with other people to find out what this was all about. He even asked Ms. Hategan what Grant's last name was, so he really knew nothing about the case.*

So when the request for protection was turned down - and logically, this officer must have asked other people for advice - it became obvious to us that Mr. Bristow and certain other individuals - there was a whole list of names in the affidavits - enjoyed some kind of protection. I must admit that initially, we thought that it was because the affidavits included the names of certain officers in Toronto's Metro police force that the request was denied.

In any case, we gave the OPP three weeks to conduct this investigation before Ms. Hategan publicly broke with the Heritage

Front. At the time, Ms. Hategan was still living with her mother. Since Bristow thought she was passing out information to us or to others, he started threatening her. We had no way to protect her, but we kept her there to maintain her credibility and to give the police time to finish their investigation and proceed with the arrests.

When on November 24 we had to go to court with Mr. Copeland, it was already public knowledge that Ms. Hategan was working for anti-racist groups, so the specific information we had given concerning the presence of firearms in certain residences was no longer relevant.

After Ms. Hategan testified in March against Wolfgang Droege, Gary Shipper and Ken Barker, the OPP sent a letter saying: ``She's not our witness. She's not our responsibility".

I shook hands with Paul Copeland outside the doors of the Parliament of Canada, and Martin gave me a hug. Whether, in the years to come, history would show that CSIS had managed to sweep the whole thing under the rug, no longer mattered. Whether there would come a day when Grant Bristow would speak at a Jewish community centre and get a standing ovation for being "a hero who had done his duty", or get a James Bond-style write-up in a prominent magazine, was irrelevant. Only those of us who were there would know the truth: the Canadian government had used taxpayers' money to develop a terrorist group on its own shores.

We were standing on the steps of the Canadian Parliament building, Martin and I, having come to the end of such a long road. I looked up at him with tears in my eyes. How could I ever repay what he had done for me? The way he'd backed me up and mobilized a whole underground network of supporters – our own grassroots witness protection program. Not one made up of Royal Canadian Mounted Police officers but average Canadian citizens of every race and background – farmers, activists, university students, white-haired grandmothers, regular cops – who all opened their doors unquestioningly to hide me.

We weren't a secret network of superheroes or a mysterious army made up of masked crusaders. We were ordinary people – activists, journalists, researchers, street kids, cabinet aides and professors. Our source of pride rests in the fact that we were not bystanders. We fought back against a government that would stand by and allow its own citizens to be terrorized by the state.

It was the last time I would see Martin. I told him that after I testified about the Bristow affair, I was out of politics forever. Once I started school in September, I had to get on with my life. As uncertain as my future might be, I had to cut off ties with everyone in order to have a new beginning.

He understood completely.

As we held each other tightly, we knew that our roads would diverge from this point forward. We had done our best to make a difference. We risked our lives, our livelihoods, our well-being. We risked everything to speak the truth.

And what *is* that truth?

No matter how many years have passed since these events transpired, these are the facts that have shaped my life:

I was sixteen years old when I was recruited by a domestic terrorist group later revealed to have been founded by the Canadian Security Intelligence Service.

I was eighteen years old when I turned against this group, testified in court about its leadership, and contributed to an agent provocateur's cover being blown.

In the last twenty years I've often wanted the profound sense of betrayal inside me to take the form of a voice that would speak on behalf of all of us who were there, who saw things that others would rather deny because the truth is too horrific.

It's not that people in this day and age don't care about their own personal liberties. I think they allow themselves to be manipulated, inadvertently becoming co-conspirators in their own delusion, because it's the only option that lets them sleep at night. Self-imposed blindfolds are more the result of feeling utterly terrified to face that your own governments may have financed arms deals and terrorist organizations, both homegrown and international. Your own governments may have baited, incited, fabricated and staged criminal activities in order to justify new, increasingly restrictive laws superimposed upon innocent human beings.

As time went on and I had more to lose, I grew convinced that if I talked about what I witnessed in my teens my life as I know it might change, and not for the better. To this day, my heart stops when *Blocked Caller* appears on my phone. When I see a car parked for too long outside my house. I know there are other people out there similarly scarred by CSIS' terror campaign, who share my kneejerk reaction and probably will for the rest of their lives. Who suffer from a collective sense of betrayal stemming from the realization that in our government's eyes, we were expandable.

And yet the older I get, the more I realize that I *have* to tell this. I have a responsibility to everyone who fought so hard to shut down the Heritage Front and saved my life, quite literally, that I honour them by doing my best to ensure that the redacted version of Operation Governor does not wipe away what really happened in Canada in the 1990s.

I may be broken inside, but I must set the record straight. As Spanish philosopher George Santayana wrote, *Those who cannot remember the past are condemned to repeat it.* After having my affidavits ignored, my offers to take polygraphs summarily dismissed and my requests for justice go unanswered, I have only one tool left.

My voice.

If I was brave enough, as a young girl, to take on white supremacists and speak for what is right, I owe it to her and to all the people who were there to leave this testament.

Most of the victims of the It Campaign have gone on with their lives, yet questions remain: Why did an internal report circulate inside CSIS for a whole year earlier, going all the way up to the Attorney General and warning of the possibility of unlawful activities on the part of an undercover source, but nobody did anything to stop it?

Nobody took action, not even after the cabinet minister's own aide, Brian McInnis, decided to leak the report because he felt so disgusted that the government was paying an informer to build a neo-Nazi organization. Instead of being commended, the aide got arrested for Treason under the Official Secrets Act, his career permanently ruined.

McInnis leaked that report before it was cool to be a Julian Assange. There were no Edward Snowdens to serve as inspiration, no Bradley Mannings, no multitudes of Anonymous hackers to break into an intelligence database and shine a light on corruption.

Brian McInnis was an ordinary man with a conscience, who did what he felt was right. One of my regrets is that I never met him in person – he died of cancer in 2010.

In Canada, most of us believe that we live in a free and democratic country where telephones don't beep every thirty seconds, where there is no secret agent following you in an unmarked car. Gross injustices that infringe on people's fundamental human rights only happen someplace else, in some terrible war-torn zone we see on the evening news. Things like that just don't exist *here*. Canada doesn't have agent provocateurs inciting fringe extremists into stalking, threatening and assaulting innocent people, destroying careers and reputations, driving them to suicide. That's the stuff of action movies where the bad guys have Russian accents. Where an agent who goes rogue is hunted down by the agency who employs him rather than get cleared, paid off, and publicly commended for his actions.

And yet how do we explain why Canada lacked an effective system of checks and balances to weed out potentially-unbalanced individuals with delusions of grandeur from turning an entire province into a playground for their secret double-agent fantasies? What kind of handler would go along with this? How many people would have to be targeted, how much property damaged, before someone at CSIS headquarters would pull the plug on something like Operation Governor?

The answer to that is, nobody knows. Nobody can predict how long Grant Bristow would have stayed inside the Heritage Front, and how much destruction or violence his covert activities would have resulted in.

Only one thing is clear: it was NOT as a consequence of an internal clean-up, nor a system of accountability on the part of the Canadian Security Intelligence Service that Operation Governor was shut down, but as a result of the actions of an eighteen-year-old girl, an investigative journalist, and the brave activists who would risk their lives to put a stop to it.

Hundreds of thousands of dollars were paid to Bristow, consisting not only of a salary for his agent provocateur role (media reports list it as up to $60,000 annually, which around 1988-1994 was quite the income), but also the four-bedroom suburban house, two new minivans and generous $3000 monthly stipend he would receive *for years* after he was placed into witness protection.

And for all that money, what did our country get from Grant Bristow? Not ONE conviction, not a single statement that lead to any Heritage Front member's arrest and prosecution. Not one gun recovered from a skinhead's home, not one individual convicted of mischief, arson, rape or criminal harassment.

In contrast, I possessed enough information to send at least ten Heritage Front and Northern Hammerskins individuals to jail. Probably more, but it hurts too much to start thinking about all the *What Ifs*. Aside from learning how to hack into telephone systems and how to push people to the brink of suicide, I was taught another important lesson by CSIS – that *the weight of truth depends on the perceived worth of those who speak it.*

To the OPP and RCMP officers who had been advised by CSIS to disregard my statements, the intrinsic value of my evidence was judged by my worth as a human being – and as an abused, impoverished teenage girl with no education, family or powerful clique of good old CSIS boys to back me up, what I had to say meant absolutely nothing.

Thanks to Canada's Security and Intelligence Service, millions of dollars were sank into ugly, bottomless pit that was Operation Governor. Falsehoods were spun to assert that Bristow had somehow "prevented" crime from happening, though the fabrications included in the SIRC Report tell us just how much their words are worth. And when Martin Theriault and I brought *real, concrete evidence* forth to prosecute dangerous individuals, they buried it.

Just as the Heritage Front could never have become the strategic, well-mobilized group that it was without CSIS's direction, CSIS couldn't have built up a domestic terrorist organization without a few already-rotten apples in existence. We cannot dismiss the fact that so many members of the Heritage Front already had criminal records, often for violent assault. They might have been a disorganized bunch of misfits, but theirs was a violent ideology that required only a spark to set it off.

But this is perhaps the biggest reason why CSIS should have been even *MORE* careful in monitoring their agent's behaviour and ensuring that he did not push dangerous, potentially-unbalanced people, to commit crimes against innocent civilians.

Instead, what CSIS did was go through a forest, gather up kindling and bring it all together in a nice stack. And then they took a match and struck that first spark.

It wasn't CSIS' mandate to sit back and watch the fire that build, but this is precisely what Grant Bristow and his CSIS handlers did. Nor was it to sit back and laugh at the casualties, secure in the knowledge that if their actions should ever be exposed, the only punishment anyone would face is being whisked to another province and given half a million dollars in cash and prizes.

For all my efforts to expose the corruption of the Heritage Front and its founding parent, CSIS, I was given no deals, no new name, no witness protection and certainly not a dime's worth of largesse from the government of my adopted country. But when I go to sleep at night, I know I've done the right thing – I was instrumental in helping to dismantle a vicious organization that recruited, brainwashed and used kids like myself to create terror and hate in the world.

Unlike the men who tried to bury the reality of what took place, I can go to my grave with the knowledge that my conscience will always be clean. And do you know that feeling you get from knowing that you made a difference?

I wouldn't trade it for anything.

EXCERPT from *"Fighting racism going out of fashion for Harris team Hatred"*
By Clayton Ruby. Toronto Star, Dec 13, 1995.

[...]

On Jan. 18, 1995, Paul Copeland, Hategan's lawyer and a bencher of the Law Society of Upper Canada, wrote to Metro Police asking that Droege be charged with promoting racial hatred based on Hategan's testimony. He invited the OPP to pursue the matter as well.

At the same time Copeland wrote and asked Attorney General Charles Harnick to consent to the prosecution.

On Feb. 13, Staff Inspector Terry Knox, commander of intelligence services of Metro police, indicated the police were indeed interested in prosecuting those responsible for the publication and distribution of hate propaganda. But, ah, despite Hategan's evidence under oath, he thought there was "insufficient evidence to form the requisite reasonable and probable grounds" to charge Wolfgang Droege.

What is Elisse Hategan? Chopped liver?

Hategan is credible. She testified before Madame Justice Daniele Tremblay-Lamer in the Federal Court of Canada in the course of a contempt hearing against Wolfgang Droege and Gary Schipper. Justice Tremblay-Lamer explicitly accepted her evidence as credible and ultimately sent these men to jail.

Copeland continued writing letters. A letter to Inspector Knox dated March 27, 1995 received no answer. A letter to Michael Bernstein, attorney general's office, on the same day also received no answer. An April 10 letter to Bernstein: no answer. April 10 to Knox: no answer. May 5 to Bernstein: no answer. May 5 to Knox: no answer.

Finally, on May 11, a letter from Bernstein on behalf of the attorney general: ``I have called the Metro Toronto police and I am waiting to hear back from them."

And then . . . No answer.

On Aug. 25, Copeland outlined the situation and wrote again personally to Harnick asking a charge be laid. He got no answer. He wrote again to the Attorney General on Oct. 25.

Again, no answer.

AUTHOR'S NOTE

This is a work of non-fiction. As is the case with any memoir, it is virtually impossible for an author to transcribe events and conversations from memory verbatim (unless otherwise indicated) and so I must write this disclaimer: the possibility always exists that there may be discrepancies between my memory and the sequencing or depiction of events, particularly as these events took place twenty years ago.

However, I am confident that I did my absolute best to recreate the past as authentically and accurately as I could. During the process of writing this memoir, I relied on every source I could access – memory as well as journal entries I kept at that time, newspaper clippings, sworn affidavits, public hearings and existing video recordings, wherever possible.

One of my affidavits, which includes Grant Bristow's handwritten target list of names and addresses belonging to anti-racists and community activists.

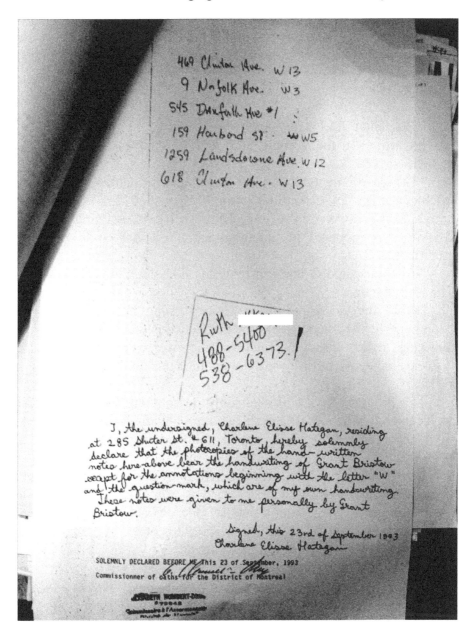

Please note that this is by no means a comprehensive list of resources.

VIDEOS

CBC, The Fifth Estate, October 4, 1994.

Excerpt from the Toronto Star, October 5, 1994, describing the content:

"The government-appointed CSIS watchdog, called the Security Intelligence Review Committee, wrote a top-secret 1992 report to Mr. Gray's Conservative predecessor, Douglas Lewis, warning that Mr. Bristow was involved in 'unlawful activities' that could 'generate controversy.'"

"CSIS is scared Grant will blow his lid," one police source tells The Fifth Estate.

"What they're scared of is Grant's going to say: 'Yeah, we desecrated Jewish synagogues. We threatened people's lives. We were throwing rocks through windows and we were manufacturing (violent) incidents and we were doing all of this on the instructions of CSIS'."

The program says CSIS not only did nothing to prevent these incidents but allowed Bristow's handler, whom it identified as Al Treddenick, to get Bristow out of trouble with police on several occasions.

It says Treddenick is a former officer of the discredited RCMP security service, disbanded in the early 1980s after it was found to have committed illegal acts against Quebec separatists and other domestic dissidents in the 1970s and 1980s. CSIS was created to replace the RCMP security service."

FIFTH ESTATE QUOTE: "When Elisse came out and said she was going to tell the truth, CSIS was saying they were going to get out and discredit her because at least Hategan was pointing the finger at Grant Bristow... we'll tear her to shreds".

White Pine Pictures, "Hearts Of Hate: The Battle For Young Minds". Peter Raymont, 1995.

It's About Time, VISION TV. "Racism, Sexism and Belonging." Sadia Zaman, 1994.

ARTICLES

Dunphy, Bill. " STIR IT UP. Spy Unmasked: CSIS Informant 'Founding Father' of white racist group," Toronto Sun, 14 Aug. 1994.

Dunphy, Bill. "Turncoat spied on racist group," Toronto Sun, 16 March 1994.

Dunphy, Bill. "Ex-racist's despair," Toronto Sun, 17 March 1994.

Platiel, Rudy. "Front played dirty, court told." Globe and Mail, 17 March 1994.

Platiel, Rudy. "Front tried to thwart agency, court told," Globe and Mail, 16 March 1994.

Oakes, Gary "Woman's hate-crime charges withdrawn," Toronto Star, 24 Jun 1994.

Salot, Jeff, Henry Hess. "Memo leaker questions CSIS conduct," Globe and Mail, 27 Aug. 1994.

Swainson, Gail. "Elite soldiers members of racist group, leader says," Toronto Star, 6 May 1993.

Speirs, Rosemary, David Vienneau, "Commons panel to probe CSIS," Toronto Star, 25 Aug. 1994.

Speirs, Rosemary. "CSIS told to 'clear its name' publicly," Toronto Star, 24 Aug. 1994.

Speirs, Rosemary, David Vienneau. "Who's watching whom?," Toronto Star, 27 Aug. 1994.

Vienneau, David. "Spy agency kept watch on CBC," Toronto Star, 19 Aug. 1994.

Vienneau, David, Rosemary Speirs, and Shawn McCarthy. Ex-aide admits leaking spy note," Toronto Star, 26 Aug. 1994.

Cal Millar and Dale Brazao, Parliament set to probe secret actions of CSIS spy Committee to see if Grant Bristow was a spy or racist. Toronto Star, September 12, 1994.

Derek Ferguson, "Report 'whitewash' of spy agency mole. Toronto Star, June 14, 1995

Toronto Sun, October 1995 MPs rip Bristow spying scandal: CSIS broke the law, leaked report says"

Clayton Ruby, Fighting racism going out of fashion. Toronto Star, December 13, 1995

Toronto Star, September 10, 1994. "Exclusive: CSIS spy snapped in Libya: Portrait of the vanishing spy: Grant Bristow was a man with great contacts and plenty of money to spend."

Dale Brazao, "Star finds Grant Bristow", Toronto Star, Apr 20, 1995.

BLOGS

Anti-Racist Canada Collective, A History of Violence, 1989-2011.
http://anti-racistcanada.blogspot.ca/2011/10/history-of-violence-1989-2011.html

Elisa Hategan, Incognito Press. Old Habits Die Hard
http://incognitopress.wordpress.com/2011/11/17/old-habits-die-hard-the-dubious-adventures-of-grant-bristow-or-how-csis-taught-me-everything-i-know-about-phone-hacking/